EDGAR CAYCE
AND THE
KABBALAH

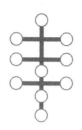

EDGAR CAYCE
AND THE
KABBALAH

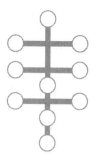

A Resource for Soulful Living

JOHN VAN AUKEN

A.R.E. Press • Virginia Beach • Virginia

A.R.E. Press
215 67th Street
Virginia Beach, VA 23451-2061

ISBN-13: 978-0-87604-569-5 (trade paper)

Original Illustrations by the Author

Cover design by Frame25 Productions

Contents

Part One: The Essentials

Part Two: The Details

Part Three: Occult Influences

Part Four: Spiritualization and Reunion

PART

1 The Essentials

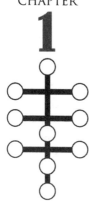

1

KABBALAH AND CAYCE HIGHLIGHTS

From a human perspective, the information you are about to read is perplexing. It does not fit with the evolution of matter. It does not fit with the visible universe. It does not even fit with much of what we know about ourselves. And yet it is a story that has been with humankind since the most ancient of times. It is a story of humanity that humans have treasured. They have guarded it for millennia, occasionally risking their lives to keep it alive. They have passed it along from generation to generation, as one would a most valuable family heirloom. Elements of this story can be found among people around the world. All people have their version of this story.

Now some will say that the ancient origin of these teachings causes them to be of no value, because everything old is primitive, that our generation is the pinnacle of evolution. They will say that the tales and lore of earlier humans are superstitions. They will say that the ancient ones did not understand the physical laws governing the material universe and the chemistry influencing their bodies and minds.

Some will say that the Kabbalistic version of this story of humanity appeared during a terrible time in human history: the "Dark Ages," the medieval period, the dreary Middle Ages—a time so filled with plague, inquisition, ignorance, and cultural decline that we may rightly ask how anything coming out of that period could be of value to us. This view overlooks the dating of Kabbalah's ancient sources and the geographical breadth of its recovered remnants of these teachings: from Spain to India, from Turkey to Egypt.

This story is about an invisible universe that exists just behind, closely around, but especially within the visible one we know. It is about a whisper, a whisper in the depths of human consciousness that says, We are more than we appear to be. It says, The origin of our life began long before the physical world. It whispers that there was an involution into matter from realms of energy and dimensions beyond the three-dimensional realm. It whispers angels, planes of existence, and reincarnation. It whispers that we are celestial soul minds, only temporarily incarnated in terrestrial bodies, and that we are destined to return to the heavens and nonphysical soul life. Of course, to the materially minded, these ideas are impossible; they don't fit with "reality." And yet this soul portion of our being is just on the other side of the thinnest, most subtle veil between human consciousness and soul consciousness. Fortunately, despite the opacity of this veil, the soul and its story slip through from time to time, and humans speak of these ideas again, as they have for ages.

Many feel that they have become better persons for having learned and practiced the wisdom of Kabbalah and that it has made their physical lives more meaningful and fulfilling.

Kabbalah, or Qabalah, comes from the Hebrew word *QBLH* (there are no vowels in the language), which is derived from the root *QBL*, meaning "to receive" but with the nuance "to correspond" in a manner that is "face to face"—as Moses received from God and communicated with God face to face, such that his face "shone" from the experience. (Exodus 34:29) The term is sometimes written "Qabalah" or "Cabala" but better reflects its origin and sounding when written in English as "Kabbalah"—pronounced variously as ka-*bal*-lah, *kab*-ba-lah, and ka-ba-*lah*, although most Westerners pronounce it ka-*bal*-lah, associated with the word *cabal* (of French origin), meaning a group of persons secretly involved in artifices and intrigue.

Legend holds that Kabbalah was first taught by God to a select group of angels. Then, after the fall of the angels (which is explained in chapter 8), Kabbalah was taught to humans—many of whom were fallen angels (more on this later). The wisdom was then progressively passed down from Adam, Enoch, Moses, Jacob, Joseph, Elijah, Ezekiel, and Daniel and traveled from Eden to Egypt, the ancient land of mysteries. Here the knowledge spread beyond the initial group to many others, even non-Jews, who made it their own, adding their perspectives and experiences to the wisdom. This may have been the origin of Hermeticism (based on the teachings of the Egyptian god Thoth; in Greek, Hermes), Gnosticism (from the Greek word *gnosis*, meaning "to know"), and Neo-Platonism (from a school founded by Plotinus and based on the teachings of Plato and earlier Platonists).

Some may say that Hermeticism, Gnosticism, and Neo-Platonism predate Kabbalah, but the stories, characters, mythology, and motifs in ancient Judaism reach back thousands of years before such similar teachings. Many date Adam and Eve of Genesis to about 4000 BCE; Abraham, 1800 BCE; and Moses, 1500 BCE. The Torah, "The Book of the Law," is dated to 1446 BCE. Even so, some separate ancient Mosaic Judaism from Rabbinic Judaism, and Rabbinic Judaism from Kabbalah, which they will only date to the works of medieval writers (from about the seventh century, reaching its peak in the twelfth and thirteenth centuries). Yet major portions of a most important book of the Kabbalah, the Zohar, are attributed to the writings of Rabbi Shimon Bar Yohai, who lived in the 100s! Also, the oldest book of the Kabbalah, *Sefer Yetzirah*, "The Book of Creation," is traditionally ascribed to Abraham! Its actual authorship is uncertain, yet scholars consider it to be at least 2,500 years old.

Another point of uncertainty argues that rabbis of the first and second centuries simply adopted Gnostic teachings to create Kabbalah. However, this is just too uncharacteristic of these men, their lives, and their writings to be the case. These men were raised and deeply studied in the particulars of their own faith and traditions. And even though they were open-minded seekers of truth, it is unlikely that they adopted an alien philosophy and its terminology. Rather, it is more likely that there was an enlightened realization that these philosophies and mythologies shared much in common, as did Neo-Platonism and Hermeticism. One of the most convincing arguments to counter the view that rabbis adopted Gnosticism can be found in the book *The Impact of the Kabbalah in the Seventeenth Century* by Allison P. Coudert (Brill, 1999). Professor Coudert writes:

> The frontispiece of the *Kabbala denudata* [*Kabbala Unveiled*] shows the high expectations Knorr [Christian Knorr von

Rosenroth, 1636-1689] and van Helmont [Francis Mercury van Helmont, 1614-1698] had of the Kabbalah in terms of religious peace and unity. It also reveals their conviction that the Kabbalah offered a key to understanding the natural world as well. Here the figure of a beautiful maiden [see illustration 17] with flowing hair and Grecian robes gazes skywards as she runs along a narrow ledge of earth separating the sea from a cave. Her destination is a doorway marked "Palatium Arcanorum" (Place of Secrets). "Intrat" (she enters) is written on the threshold of this palace, while the word "domat" (she calms, subdues) appears under her right foot and "alterat" (changes for the better, transmutes) under her left. The cave is designated "antrum materie" (the cave of matter) and within it appear the astrological and alchemical signs that stand for the planets and their comparable metals. In her right hand, which is stretched over the swelling waves, she holds a burning torch, under which is written "mare concupscientiarum" (the sea of concupiscence) [which, in this context, likely means ardent longing rather than sexual desire]. In her left she carries a scroll representing the Scriptures, on which is written "explicat" (she explains). A ship sails in the distance; while on the edge of the shore, almost submerged by waves, a tree grows. A great circle of light breaks through the clouds and darkness, and within this light are three circles, which in turn enclose three smaller circles. These stand for the ten kabbalistic sefirot [emanations], or the ten faces *(parzuphim)* of the hidden deity as he revealed himself in the act of creation. Where the sea meets the sky the words "Metaphysica gentiles" are written, suggesting that gentile wisdom has clear limits—it does not reach to, or come from, heaven the way the Kabbalah does. We have seen that Knorr attributed the divisions among Christians to their misplaced dependence on Greek wisdom, which far from being the source of true philosophy had simply muddied the pure water of divine Hebrew wisdom. The female figure in this complex landscape is, of course, the Kabbalah, and the keys hanging on a cord from her wrist indicate that the Kabbalah alone is able to unlock the secrets of both the Old and New Testaments. (p. 137)

Kabbalists considered their concepts to be the wiser and older teachings, not extensions of Grecian Gnosticism.

Finally, there has been a modern movement that presents Kabbalah as a social and moral teaching, ignoring the voluminous material on esoteric realms, angels, numerology, magical incantations, and much more. Because the Edgar Cayce volumes contain the esoterica found in classical Kabbalah, this book includes the whole of Kabbalah teachings. This is not to imply that Kabbalistic wisdom is not social or moral, it is, but there is so much more that should not be ignored, even though it adds much volume to the knowledge.

Though Kabbalah's mystical wisdom was always cast as secret knowledge to be kept from the mundane public and from the ruling authorities who opposed anything alien to the establishment, elements are found in the most popular and public of Scripture. For example, in 1 Chronicles (ca. 500 BCE) we find some of Kabbalah's secret *sefirot* (emanations). Chronicles is called "The Words of the Day" in the Hebrew "Bible" (Tanakh), and 1 and 2 Chronicles are combined in this Bible. Follow along with the Tree of Life illustrations (illustrations 1 through 6) to see the emanation numbers that correspond to this passage: "Thine, O Lord, is the greatness [emanation 10, which is also considered to be *majesty*], and the power [5, which is also *judgment*], and the glory [8, which is also *splendor*], and the victory [7], and the majesty [10]; for all that is in the heavens and in the earth is thine; thine is the kingdom [10], O Lord, and thou art exalted as head above all [1, the crown or the "I AM" of the "I am that I am"]." (1 Chronicles 29:11; Revised Standard Version, RSV)

A portion of these emanations is also found in the Lord's Prayer as recorded in select versions of Matthew 6:13 (King James Version, KJV, and World English Bible, WEB):

"For Thine is the kingdom [10], the power [5], and the glory [8] forever. Amen."

And we find this again in Revelation 5:12-13:

> "Worthy is the Lamb who has been killed to receive the
> power [5], wealth [10], wisdom [2], strength [9, also judgment],
> honor [7, also victory], glory [8, also splendor], and bless-
> ing [4, also loving kindness]!" I heard every created thing
> which is in heaven, on the earth, under the earth, on the sea,
> and everything in them, saying, "To him who sits on the
> throne, and to the Lamb be the blessing [4], the honor [7],
> the glory [8], and the dominion [10], forever and ever! Amen!"

Obviously, there is some correlation between these earlier biblical
writers (from Chronicles) and the later writers (Matthew, and John in
Revelation), and each would appear to have some knowledge of the
secret Kabbalah's emanations. Even the disciple John in his Revelation
sees and writes Kabbalah's number for the Beast: 666 (more on this in
chapters 10 and 13). You can also see this in illustration 26, with the
Gnostic serpent and chakras using Kabbalistic numbers and meanings.

Over the centuries, Kabbalah has moved into many of the various
Western mystical teachings, including non-Jewish ones. Among the
Jews, Kabbalists were and some continue to be the most open to their
teachings being inclusive to all souls, not just their own. Even so, as you
read this book, keep in mind that there are numerous Kabbalah groups,
past and present and both classical and modern, each with its own
variations of these concepts, stories, names, and terms. The writings that
comprise Kabbalah are voluminous and complex, even confusing at
times. What is presented here is a distillation of the various books, writers, and schools. There is no single book that is *the* Kabbalah. Rather,
Kabbalah is a collection of books supplemented by numerous treatises.

Even though Kabbalah has expanded beyond its original core, there
are those who still feel that only select initiates should receive knowledge of Kabbalah. The Scriptures and the words of the Lord provide a
counterpoint to this thinking: "No longer shall each man teach his
neighbor and each his brother, saying, 'Know the Lord,' for they shall all
know me, from the least of them to the greatest, says the Lord." (Jeremiah
31:34; italics mine)

Some believe that Kabbalah distracts people from fully investing in becoming better persons, which is the most important goal of each soul's incarnation. This is especially the case for young people, causing some teachers to believe that no one under forty years of age should begin to study Kabbalah, and even then, only after they have mastered the Talmud (a collection of discussions and commentaries by various rabbis) and the Tanakh (the Jewish Bible). *Tanakh*, or *TNK* (vowels were added to help us pronounce it) stands for *Torah* (T), *Nevi'im* (N), and *Ketuvim* (K). The Tanakh contains the Five Books of Moses (Chumashe Torah), the Prophets (Nevi'im), and the Writings (Ketuvim). The Tanakh composes much of what Christians and Muslems consider to be the Old Testament.

Some teachers also regard Kabbalah as too ethereal, too otherworldly, not practical enough to be useful in normal people's lives. This is certainly true of the complex cosmology of Kabbalah, but there are so many good, spiritual concepts that are valuable to life that a study of Kabbalah would benefit young and old. And since young people today are not finding meaning, purpose, and fulfillment in pursuing the typical, materially focused view of life, they want the vision of a greater life, no matter how otherworldly it may be. Many, young and old, seek to know more about the mysteries of life, more about higher levels of consciousness, more about how and why we were created and what our ultimate destiny may be, even if it is beyond this world and this incarnation. Mind, soul, and spirit are as important to many as two cars in the garage, a chicken in the pot, money in the bank, and a fantastic spouse. In fact, when people reach midlife, these material achievements are not as fulfilling as they anticipated. They want to know the ultimate destiny of their mind and soul. They want more from life than physical satisfaction and material gain. There is a spiritual hunger that needs nourishing. Kabbalah fills that hunger. It gives a vision of the greater life. Mundane physical pursuits and material successes are enlivened by the perspective found in Kabbalah. Once the soulful life becomes clear, it makes material life much more livable and meaningful. When others with whom we have relationships are viewed as souls rather than human personalities, relationships take on a whole new level of fulfullment and joy.

As one might expect, there are also those who are upset to see Kabbalah taught by non-Jews and by those who blend New Age enlightenment and Eastern teachings with Kabbalah. Their concern is that such teachings appear to transcend the law-structured Torah. But this has been the case with all religions. The establishment's dogma and traditions cannot stand against direct, personal spiritual guidance through revelation, dreams, visions, and communion with God and God's emanations in an individual's own life. Since these "knowings" occur between the individual soul and its Creator, instead of from the dictates of authorized codexes, it is difficult to maintain control over one's congregation. In Isaiah 1:11-13 the Lord overturns many of the earlier requirements in the Torah:

> "What to me is the multitude of your sacrifices?" says the Lord; "I have had enough of burnt offerings of rams and the fat of fed beasts; I do not delight in the blood of bulls, or of lambs, or of he-goats. When you come to appear before me, who requires of you this trampling of my courts? Bring no more vain offerings; incense is an abomination to me."

God seeks our hearts and minds, not our material offerings. Kabbalah provides the concepts and practices necessary to experience God in the temple of one's heart and mind. This is why it survives today, despite all of its esoterica and otherworldliness—it has touched too many people too deeply to be lost or ignored.

Kabbalah and Cayce's Universal Mysticism

This book contains the Christ-centered teachings of Edgar Cayce, and even though Cayce's Christ is universal, one may rightly ask how such a source can contribute to a traditionally Jewish wisdom. Let's read two Cayce statements that may help. These passages were a result of an ongoing study of the macrocosm and the microcosm, of how outer life is reflected in our inner life. Such perspectives go back to Hermes and his teaching: "As above, so below. As within, so without." Cayce gave these discourses from a meditative, trancelike state of consciousness.

They were stenographically recorded and published. His records are archived at the Edgar Cayce Center in Virginia Beach, Virginia, the Association for Research and Enlightenment (A.R.E.), and have been computerized for easy access on a CD-ROM and an Internet database at edgarcayce.org. Here are the two statements:

> Q: Would the history of the Jewish race from Abraham to Jesus parallel the development of the embryo from conception to birth?
>
> A: Rather would the history of man from Noah to Abraham; while that from Abraham to Christ would be the *mental* unfoldment of the body. For, that which leads to the Christ is the *mind*. And the mind's unfoldment may be that indicated from Abraham to the Christ.
>
> EC 281-63; italics mine

Clearly, Cayce acknowledges and honors the historical role of the Jewish tradition in the spiritual journey to reunion with God, our Creator, including the role of the Jew Jesus. He is affirming that the mental "unfoldment" (a term reminiscent of the Eastern unfolding of the lotus blossom, one petal at a time) was the journey of the Israelites.

In this next Q and A, Cayce expresses a Christian belief but takes it to a more universal level that includes all religions and all souls seeking reunion with God.

> Q: How may we regard the truth regarding Jesus in relation to the Jewish and Christian religions, and to all the other religions of the world?
>
> A: In that the man, Jesus, became the ensample of the flesh, manifest in the world, and the will one with the Father, he became the first to manifest same in the material world. Thus, from man's viewpoint, becoming the only, the first, the begotten of the Father, and the ensample to the world, whether Jew, Gentile, or of any other religious forces. In this we find the true advocate with the Father, in that He, as man, manifests in the flesh the ability of the flesh to make fleshly desires one with the will of the spirit. For God is spirit, and they who worship Him [God] must worship in spirit and in truth, just as Jesus manifested in the flesh, and able to partake of the divine, for making all laws susceptible to the mandates. For the will was one with the Father, and in this we find He takes

on all law, and a law unto Himself. For with the compliance, of even an earthly or material law, such a person *is* the law. And in that Jesus lived as man, and died as man, and in that became the ensample to all who *would* approach the Throne of God.

As we see in all the religions of the world, we find all approaching those conditions where man may become as the law in his connection with the divine, the supreme, the oneness, of the world's manifestation. In Jesus we find the answer.   EC 900-17

For a Christian mystic, Cayce's answer is so Jewish, expressing the law structure of the Torah as the foundation that aids all seekers to align their will with God's, making them one with the Divine Spirit while still in the flesh, while still in the world.

Historically, Christian Kabbalists have been known to exist since the twelfth century. Later, in 1694, Johannes Gottfried Seelig (later changed to Selig) arrived in America with his Christian mystical treatise, "Secrets of the Psalms," which was clearly based on the older Jewish text *Shimmush Tehillim* ("On the Use of Psalms"). Both contain magical phrasing of the Psalms as protective and healing spells. (More on this in chapter 9.)

The initial financier of the Edgar Cayce Center in Virginia Beach was Morton Blumenthal, a Jew and one of the brightest questioners of the famous "sleeping prophet," as one of the bestselling biographies of Edgar Cayce was also titled, an epithet given to Cayce because he mostly answered questions asked of him while in a deep meditation, appearing as if sleeping. Without Morton Blumenthal, we would not have some of the most profound discourses Cayce ever gave, because Morton's questioning garnered the deepest insights of all of Cayce's 14,000–plus readings. (They are called readings because Cayce felt that he was reading from the Book of Life, or the akashic records of Eastern teachings.) Morton received more than four hundred readings from Cayce, many of them dream interpretations. Here is an excerpt from one of Morton's dreams that reveals how universal he was—and a Kabbalist, whether he knew it or not:

Saw Rabbi Wise in pulpit and recalled his lectures on Christ—particularly those admitting Christ to be a perfect man—but not a God. I seemed to want to get up on that platform. Awakening then I found myself reasoning as though continuing right on from dream: Christ represents the Evolution of this Spirit Energy into Flesh Man—the Perfect Flesh Man, Wise concedes.   EC 900-147

Such terms as *Spirit Energy* and *Perfect Flesh Man* reveal that Morton had at least some knowledge of the mystical concepts found in Kabbalism and Gnosticism.

An example of Cayce's universal view is his natural comfort with the idea of souls incarnating multiple times in their journey toward enlightenment and soul growth—certainly not a standard Christian teaching; however, this concept fits with the Kabbalah, which also teaches that souls reincarnate. (More on this in chapter 2.)

Another exceptional concept found in Kabbalah and in Cayce's teachings is the curious concept of "the Word," "the Logos," "the Son," created by the heavenly Father and Mother, this Logos giving life to all souls. This is expressed in the first lines of the Gospel of John:

In the beginning was the Word [in Greek, Logos], and the Word was with God, and the Word was God. The same was in the beginning with God. All things were made through this One [the original Greek text does not use the masculine pronoun *him*, as most Bible translations do]. Without this One was not anything made that has been made. In this One was life, and the life was the light of humanity. The light shines in the darkness, and the darkness hasn't overcome it . . . The Word became flesh, and lived among us. We saw his glory, such glory as of the one and only Son of the Father, full of grace and truth.

Kabbalah teaches that there is a primordial being that is so one with the infinite, unseen God (Ein Sof) that it is the bridge between our souls and God. This first being is called Adam Kadmon. In Lurianic Kabbalah (a system that includes elements of Indian philosophy, Platonism, and Gnosticism) the original Adam soul is the Logos from which all souls have emanated.

Some schools teach that the great "I AM" emanated masculine wisdom (Chokhmah) and feminine understanding (Binah), and the two blended to conceive the Logos, the Soul-Consciousness, within which all souls were conceived (more on this in chapter 5 and throughout this book.)

With the Logos concept and that of reincarnation in mind, let's read another of Cayce's discourses:

Q: What part did Jesus play in any of His reincarnations in the development of the basic teachings of the following religions and philosophies? First, Buddhism:

A: This is just one.

Q: Mohammedanism, Confucianism, Shintoism, Brahmanism, Platonism, Judaism.

A: As has been indicated, the entity—as an entity—influenced either directly or indirectly all those forms of philosophy or religious thought that taught God was One.

In the first, as one that associated with—in the meditation or spirit of—that one guiding same, and those things that have been added to are much in the same manner that was added to in Judaism. Whether in Buddhism, Mohammedanism, Confucianism, Platonism, or what—these have been added to much from that as was given by Jesus in His walk in Galilee and Judea. In all of these, then, there is that same impelling spirit. What individuals have done, do do, *to* the principles or the spirit of same—in turning this aside to meet their *own* immediate needs in material planes, or places has made for that as becomes an outstanding thing, as a moralist or the head of any independent religious force or power; for, as has been given, "Know, O Israel, the Lord thy God is *one!*" whether this is directing one of the Confucius' thought, Brahman thought, Buddha thought, Mohammedan thought; these are as teachers or representatives, or to make more of the distinct change—as was in that as given by the apostle to the Gentiles: "I hear there are divisions among you. Some say I am Paul, another I am Apollos, another I am of Caiaphas. Paul may minister, Apollos may have watered, but it's God that gives the increase!" The Spirit of the Creative Force, and as such the Son represented in the spirit in that as was made manifest in the earth. Not as *only* one, but *the* only one; for, as He gave, "He that climbs up any other way is a thief and a robber." As the Spirit of the Master, the Spirit of the Son, was manifest—as was given—to each in their respective sphere. As it is today. As it was of yore. God calls on man everywhere to seek His [God's] face, through that channel that may be blessed by the Spirit of the Son—in whatever sphere this may take its form. Because there are contentions, because there is the lack of the giving and taking as to others' thought, does not change God's attitude one whit; neither does it make one above another; for, as has been given, there *is only* one—the others are as those acting in the capacity of the thought that was given to them through that same power, that "In the last days has He spoken unto us through the Son, as one born out of due season." We find the same contentions arising in that called in the present denominationalism, and each one crying, "Lo, here is Christ—Lo, this is the manner of approach—Lo, unless ye do this or that ye have no part in Him." "He that loves me will keep my commandments." What are the commandments? "Thou shalt have no other *God* before me," and "Love thy neighbor as thyself." In this is builded the whole *law* and gospel of every age that has said, "There is *one* God!"

EC 364-9; italics in the original

In this discourse Cayce reaches beyond religions and isms, capturing the essence of all spiritual pursuit: There is only one God, and that God is the God of all people. Love God and love one another (Deuteronomy 6:5 and Leviticus 19:18). Cayce often called God the "Universal Consciousness" and the "Life Force," further revealing his universal view.

Kabbalah Origins

From ancient times, Kabbalah was carried forward orally. Then, in the Middle Ages, its various elements, written and in lore, were finally codified in various texts and distributed as the mystical, esoteric books of an outgrowth of Judaism (it was never a part of traditional Judaism). Many Christians had copies of these texts or their own versions. The main books include The Mystery of the Chariot (Ma'aseh Merkabah), The Mystery of the Beginning (Ma'aseh Bereshit), The Book of Creation [or "Formation"] (Sefer Yetzirah), The Book of the Brightness (Sefer ha-Bahir), The Book of the Angel (Sefer Raziel), Life in the World to Come (Chayye Olam Ha Ba), and the most famous, The Book of Splendor [or "Radiance"] (Sefer ha-Zohar)—known today simply as the Zohar.

Many of these texts did not initially exist in one binding but were fragmented writings or pamphlets that were later compiled into various books. There is no single book titled The Kabbalah.

The Mystery of the Chariot was among the earliest writings in Jewish mysticism. It was based on a vision experienced by the prophet Ezekiel. While standing by a river in Babylon, Ezekiel saw a vision in the heavens of four winged creatures, spinning wheels, and a fiery throne. Seated on the throne was "the glory of the Lord." (Ezekiel 1) These earliest Kabbalists used this vision as a way of describing the realms of God, which are above the material reality that humans know.

The early mystics meditated on the image of the fiery chariot, using it as a visual mantra. They described the path through the upper world to the heavenly chariot as dangerous and terrifying. It led past seven palaces filled with armies of angels. Rivers of fire flowed out of the sky as angels drew the chariot through the air. The goal of meditating on the chariot was to overcome the obstacles en route to the chariot itself and to see the image of the Lord seated on the throne. Reaching the throne required extensive spiritual training, tremendous focus and concentration, and a deeply founded desire to know God.

This early book introduces the idea of the ecstasy that comes from direct communion with God on a physical and emotional level (more on this in chapter 12.) This notion of communication with God forms the core of all Kabbalistic thought. The Mystery of the Chariot also introduces the idea that close encounters with God can be dangerous to untrained minds. Though the Torah indicates that any faithful Jews could communicate directly with God without risk, Kabbalists believed that contact with a force as infinite and omnipotent as God could lead to madness. For this reason, Kabbalists initially limited study of Kabbalah to married persons over forty who had studied the Torah and the Talmud.

The Mystery of the Beginning developed from a mystical interpretation of the first chapters of Genesis, in which God created the universe and all the life within it. The Mystery of the Beginning explained that because God encompasses all of creation, humans are by default a part of God. Rather than merely accepting the biblical account of Creation, Kabbalists read meaning into every word of the Torah. They would ask questions like, What is implied by Eve coming from out of Adam? This penetrating, mystical interpretation of Genesis led Kabbalists to form their own account of Creation, and this became apparent with the publishing of The Mystery of the Beginning. Their account differed significantly from the traditional Jewish understanding of the origins of the universe, revealing a growing contrast between traditional Judaism and Kabbalism.

The Book of Creation is a short book that expands on the theories in The Mystery of the Beginning. The Book of Creation proposes that God created the world with thirty-two secret paths of wisdom. These paths of wisdom are composed of the ten emanations (sefirot) and the twenty-two letters of the Hebrew alphabet. The first chapter of The Book of Creation explains the emanations—and this is the first time this concept of divine emanations appears in Jewish literature. The emanations of The Book of Creation differ from the ten "aspects of God" that appear much later in Kabbalistic thought. Here they take the form of numbers with mystical qualities, each one representing a stage of Creation and a pathway from and back to God. The Torah tends to personify God as a humanlike being who can talk and interact with people on earth—the familiar image of an old bearded man in the sky. The Book of Creation presents God as an unknowable, genderless force entirely devoid of form or emotion. In the Torah, God creates simply by using the power of his word, his command. But in The Book of Creation, God creates through emanations, or projections of its being. God becomes a part of the universe, everywhere and nowhere at once, a spirit with infinite power. This initial mystical theory—that the world was created through emanations of the Divinity—forms the foundation of Kabbalistic thought and separates it further from traditional Judaism. This concept also created much controversy. Everything about the emanations, from where they came from to what they mean, has been debated for many hundreds of years.

The Book of Brightness begins with a discussion of The Book of Creation, and the second part is an attempt to clarify the order of the emanations, which The Book of Creation describes as ten numbers. In The Book of Brightness the emanations are described for the first time as attributes of God's being. In addition to representing a particular part of God, each emanation also corresponds to a stage in Creation and a character from the Bible.

Another concept that The Book of Brightness introduces for the first time is the Tree of Life, a visual representation of the ten emanations. The Book of Brightness describes the locations of each emanation on the Tree of Life. The Tree is intended to symbolize the body of "Adam Kadmon," also known as "primordial man," a prototype for the creation of human beings. Adam Kadmon is not the Adam of Adam and Eve in Genesis but a kind of mystical template for human beings that God made *before* creating them. He is proof that our being was created in God's image. Like the Word, or Logos, that Adam Kadmon represents, we are a part of God. The Tree of Life was considered to reflect the body of Adam and the spiritual form of God linked symbolically in visual diagrams of the ten emanations. Kabbalah is in many ways a spiritual movement that is both thorough and obscure. As Kabbalists tried to unravel the mysteries of the universe, such as Creation and the birth of humankind, they argued for centuries over passages in the Torah. The closer they looked at words, the more mysterious the universe became. Though exceptionally difficult, The Book of Brightness arranged and organized Kabbalah's sprawling ideas into a coherent form in one volume. Most importantly, it explained that the emanations are aspects of God's being, not just numbers. The emanations represent God's attributes, such as wisdom, mercy, and beauty, and Kabbalists believe they represent the core components to having a fulfilling life.

Today the Zohar is the most popular book of the Kabbalah. In 1280 CE, a Spanish mystic named Moses de Leon began circulating small booklets written in archaic Aramaic, an ancestral language to the Hebrew and Arabic alphabets. De Leon claimed that the booklets were taken from ancient texts written by the great second-century rabbi Simeon ben Yohai. Rabbi Yohai, fleeing persecution by the Romans in Palestine, hid in a cave for thirteen years with his son, Eliezar. Legend has it that Elijah actually visited Yohai and his son in the cave, after which God inspired Yohai to write down the wisdom he gathered from Elijah's teachings. De Leon claimed his pamphlets contained Yohai's writing. Kabbalists believed de Leon's story for hundreds of years. However, today some researchers believe de Leon wrote the pamphlets himself. The strongest argument against this is that de Leon was not a deeply spiritual man who was practicing deep meditative communion with God and was not a spiritually inspired poetic writer. The Zohar is poetic mystical wisdom, written in a style considered to be "automatic writing," or, as Cayce refers to it, "creative writing," with the Spirit inspiring the writer. This type of writing requires the writer to enter a mystical trance and write what comes to mind, no matter how scattered or unrelated. It is believed that this type of writing reaches through the veils of lower consciousness, allowing higher levels, even God's consciousness, to come through. Others contend that the bizarre style of the Zohar results not from the automatic writing but from the contributions of several writers over hundreds of years.

The Zohar describes the journey of Rabbi Simeon ben Yohai and ten companions through Galilee, the northern region of Palestine and formerly the kingdom of Israel. Along their journey, the travelers discuss their interpretations of the Torah and, specifically, the Torah's main characters. The characters become a part of the narrative of the Zohar, their lives weaving in and out of those of Yohai and his group. The companions come and go gracefully within their own group, turning from one character to another. The Zohar uses the term *Ein Sof* for God, meaning the "Infinite Eternal." Ein Sof is a departure from the traditional concept of divinity, which portrays God as a knowable presence, a being in the heavens that people can comprehend and feel. Ein Sof, on the contrary, is so vast that It is unknowable, beyond the boundaries of human comprehension. Kabbalists believe that, at most, they can know merely fragments of the Infinite Eternal, which they receive only through profound mystical experiences. The Zohar depicts God as a distant presence that sacrificed Its own being in order to create the universe.

Though the Zohar and its teachings spread quickly from Spain and Italy into other parts of Western Europe, it was slow to reach Eastern Europe—at least at first. After the expulsion of the Jews from Spain in 1492, study of the Zohar became more widespread as Jews fled eastward. The Zohar remains in print today and has been translated into English in a twenty-two-volume set.

In addition to these volumes, there are over a hundred texts elaborating on Kabbalistic concepts and practices. And even though we have these Kabbalah codices, wisdom is still sought and received directly from heaven through revelation, intuitive perception, prayful communion with the Divine, various forms of deep meditation, and even spontaneous enlightenment. The literature of the Hekhalot movement (Hekhalot meaning heavenly palaces or temples of God, containing stories of journeys to heaven) and the Merkabah movement (developed from Ezekiel's vision of the chariot of God, from the Hebrew RKB, "to ride" to heaven) describe in detail how seekers enter meditative-like trance states in order to commune with God—just as Edgar Cayce did. Many believe that God still speaks to the minds and hearts of those open to learning and following a more spiritual way of living. Yet intuitive "receiving" often comes after one has been studying and practicing the written knowledge in daily life. And often, in moments of quiet reflection, an inner awareness sparks a communion, even if only for a fleeting moment. But one can go with the energy and enlightenment of that moment for a very long time.

The Kabbalah story begins, as do so many ancient wisdoms, with God, and then it addresses the groupings of angels and the many spheres, or planes, of heaven. It covers the Creation and the journey of the souls. It contains the rituals, ceremonies, and magic words and names that evoke the powers of the unseen divine forces. It integrates the outer life with its inner source and the Creative Forces, from which the soul came into being. These concepts and experiences gradually enhance life, making it more meaningful, more bright, and more fulfilling than the materialistic, earthly approach.

Kabbalah also helps us become aware of the invisible forces of life and to discern the eternal from the temporary. We learn to feel the Infinite Eternal (Ein Sof) Mind and Spirit and Its oneness, which is often clouded by the dualities of this life: yin and yang, female and male, night and day, sleep and wakefulness, inside and outside, and so on. Kabbalah helps us perceive the oneness of infinite life that runs through the maze of multiplicity of the Creation and this temporary incarnation.

It does this by revealing the sources of creative energy, of consciousness, and of the oneness behind the multipicity.

Next, let's explore the invisible dimensions of Kabbalah, because the visible life comes from the invisible.

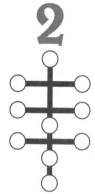

THE VISIBLE AND THE INVISIBLE

The Kabbalah teaches that behind the visible life is a vast, invisible reality from which the visible came into being and in which the visible exists. Cayce adds that these unseen forces are more powerful, more influential than the seen. (EC 262-8) He and the Kabbalah teach that the seen is actually an expression or emanation of the unseen, even a result of unseen dynamics. Life begins in the spirit, Cayce says, takes shape in the mind (thought form), and then manifests in the physical life—not the other way around. "As we have given, every force—in its manifestation—is from the One, or God. And that which is manifested in material things is a result, and not the motive force; for mind, mental (which may not be seen with the eye as termed in the material world, but with the spiritual eye) is the builder." (EC 347-2; parenthetical comments are Cayce's.)

Now you might quickly ask, If it is all from God, then why is the evening news so horrible? The answer is free-willed souls! They are allowed, for a time, to do as they choose. This is clearly expressed in Scripture: "I have set before you this day life and good, and death and evil" (Deuteronomy 30:15), the implication being that it is ours to choose which influence we will bring into this world, this life.

The conscious man Cayce was able to see and perceive beyond normal human ability. His psychic readings for himself explained that these sensitivities were a natural result of his level of spiritual development and that all humans would eventually become so sensitive as to see the invisible. Cayce could see discarnate souls among the incarnate. He could hear them and talk to them. He explained that it was like having a switch in his head, which he flipped on in order to see ghosts and communicate with them. He also saw auras around the bodies of incarnate people. These auras emanated colors and patterns that gave him insight into a person's mental, emotion, and spiritual condition, even as it changed during a conversation. Here are a few examples in his readings (notice his use of the Kabbalistic concept of "emanations").

[An] aura is the emanation, or the influence that is ever present with an animate body, that may change or alter as to that which is the impelling influence of or about same—or from within. Aura changes, to be sure, [according] to the *temperament*.   EC 282-4

The aura, then, is the emanation that arises from the very vibratory influences of an individual entity mentally, spiritually—especially of the spiritual forces.   EC 319-2

We find in the aura the physical and the mental and spiritual emanations, that show for developments and retardments as well as abilities for the studying, classifying and applying of same.   EC 1612-1

(Q) Am I beginning to see auras?
(A) Beginning to see auras. As life, light, and love—with understanding—is reflected in self, so may there be seen those of the *same* reflection from others.
(Q) What is the significance of the flashes and forms which I frequently see?
(A) Those of the higher vibrations of inter-between, as well as spiritual forces taking forms in or before the mental self.   EC 281-4

If Cayce came in proximity to a person, he psychically knew what he or she had been doing and thinking. His longtime secretary confided that she would sometimes avoid him because "it was just none of his business."

Cayce's wife, Gertrude, shared a story about the two of them asleep on the second floor of their home when someone tapped on their bedroom window! Edgar immediately knew who this spirit was and went downstairs to let the ghost in. He explained that she needed help finding her way to the next life because she had died recently and was lost as to what she should do and where she should be. She knew Mr. Cayce would know, but having arrived at his home after he and his wife had retired, she simply tapped on their bedroom window rather than enter into their private space.

Science tells us that there is much more reality than we physically see. Humans can see only within a very narrow range of the electromagnetic spectrum (EM spectrum), a range less than 5 percent of the entire EM spectrum. (See illustration 16.) The rods and cones on the inside of the human retina are nerve endings physically tuned to respond to a narrow range of energy wavelengths. When energy frequencies within the "visible light" spectrum strike the retina, electrochemical impulses are created that are transmitted to the area of the brain responsible for vision. A pattern in the visual cortex is created by these electrochemical impulses that mimics the visible light pattern striking the retina. Energy outside this narrow range of visible light produces no response from the retina's rods and cones, yet we know that many nonhuman species have rods and cones tuned to energy frequencies outside the visible light spectrum. Owls, hawks, and eagles, for example, can see infrared frequencies, that is, they can see the energy waves created by body heat. And even this is still a very narrow portion of the massive EM spectrum.

From the time he was a very little boy, Edgar Cayce could see fairies, sprites, angels, and invisible friends. As a child, he thought that everyone was seeing them, but as he grew, he learned that it wasn't so. He began to keep quiet about his abilities because they caused unpleasant reactions in others and ridicule of him and his family. When he became a more self-confident adult, he shared this recollection, which follows, and his stenographer recorded it:

I remember so distinctly the garden at my mother's old home place when I was a very small child. My mother's father was one of the first settlers in southwestern Kentucky; had a fine old place, and the old-fashioned garden, with all the old-fashioned flowers, was known throughout that part of the country. Your mentioning your mother destroying bleeding hearts [flowers] calls to my mind what beautiful bunches of these grew in that garden, with a large bunch of striped grass, some very old peonies, all kinds of buttercups, and the like; a gorgeous bed of sweet violets, and all those old flowers. It was here that often in my early childhood I met and played with those that others could never see. These are at least some of my experiences.

As to just what was the first experience, I don't know. The one that appears at present to be among the first, was when I was possibly eighteen or twenty months old. I had a playhouse in the back of an old garden, among the honeysuckle and other flowers. At that particular time much of this garden had grown up in tall reeds, as I remember. I had made a little shelter of the tops of the reeds, and had been assisted by an unseen playmate in weaving or fastening them together so they would form a shelter. On pretty days I played there. One afternoon my mother came down the garden walk calling me. My playmate (who appeared to me to be about the same size as myself) was with me. It had never occurred to me that he was not "real," or that he wasn't one of the neighbors' children, until my mother spoke and asked me my playmate's name. I turned to ask him but he disappeared. For a time this disturbed my mother somewhat, and she questioned me at length. I remember crying because she had spied upon me several times, and each time the playmate would disappear.

About a year or eighteen months later, this was changed considerably—as to the number of playmates. We had moved to another country home. Here I had two favorite places where I played with these unseen people. One very peculiarly was in an old graveyard where the cedar trees had grown up. Under a cedar tree, whose limbs had grown very close to the ground, I made another little retreat, where—with these playmates—I gathered bits of colored glass, beautifully colored leaves and things of that nature from time to time. But, what disturbed me was that I didn't know where they [the playmates] came from or why they left when some of my family approached. The other retreat was a favorite old straw stack that I used to slide down. This was on the opposite side of the road (main highway) from where we lived, and in front of the house. The most outstanding experience (and one that I am sure disturbed her much) was when my mother looked out a window and saw children sliding down this straw stack with me. Of course, I had a lovely little retreat dug out under the side of the straw ring, in which we often sat and discussed the mighty problems of a three or four year old child. As my mother looked out, she called to ask who were the children playing with me. I realized I didn't know their names. How were they dressed, you ask? There were boys and girls. It would be impossible (at this date) to describe their dress, figure or face, yet it didn't then—nor does it now—occur to me that they were any different from myself, except that they had the ability to appear or disappear as our moods changed. Just once I looked out the window from the house and saw the fairies there, beckoning me to come and play. That time also my mother saw them very plainly, but she didn't make any objection to my going out to play with them. This experience, as I remember now, lasted during a whole season—or summer.

A few years afterwards (when I had grown to be six or seven years old) our home was in a little wood. Here I learned to talk with the trees, or it appeared that they talked with me. I even yet hold that anyone may hear voices, apparently coming from a tree, if willing to choose a tree (a living tree, not a dead one) and sit against it for fifteen to twenty minutes each day (the same time each day) for twenty days. This was my experience. I chose a very lovely tree, and around it I played with my playmates that came (who then seemed very much smaller than I). We built a beautiful bower of hazelnut branches, redwood, dogwood and the like, with wild violets, Jack-in-the-Pulpit, and many of the wild mosses that seemed to be especially drawn to this particular little place where I met my friends to talk with—the little elves of the trees. How often these came, I don't know. We lived there for several years. It was there that I read the Bible through the first time, that I learned to pray, that I had many visions or experiences; not only of visioning the elves but what seemed to me to be the hosts [angels] that must have appeared to the people of old, as recorded in Genesis particularly. In this little bower there was never any intrusion from those outside. It was here that I read the first letter from a girlfriend. It was here that I went to pray when my grandmother died, whom I loved so dearly and who had meant so much to me. To describe these elves of the trees, the fairies of the woods, or—to me—the angels or hosts, with all their beautiful and glorious surroundings, would be almost a sacrilege. They have meant, and do yet, so very much to me that they are as rather the sacred experiences that we do not speak of—any more than we would of our first kiss, and the like. Why do I draw such comparisons? There are, no doubt, physical manifestations that are a counterpart or an expression of all the unseen forces about us, yet we have closed our eyes and our ears to the songs of the spheres, so that we are unable again to hear the voices or to see the forms take shape and minister—yea strengthen us—day by day!

Possibly there are many questions you would ask as to what games we played. Those I played with at the haystack were different from those in the graveyard, or in the garden. Those I played with in the wood were different. They seemed to fit more often to what would interest or develop me. To say they planted the flowers or selected the bower, or the little cove in which my retreat was built, I don't think would be stretching it at all, or that they tended these or showed me—or talked to me of—their beauty. It was here that I first learned to read. Possibly the hosts on high gave me my first interpretation of that we call the Good Book. I do not think I am stretching my imagination when I say such a thing. We played the games of children, we played being sweethearts, we played being man and wife, we played being sisters and brothers, and we played being visitors and preachers. We played being policemen and the culprits. We played being all the things that we knew about us.

No, I never have any of these visions now, or—if any—very rarely.

EC Report 464-12

When Cayce was fifty-four years old, he had a dream in which these same fairies and elves appeared to him again. The psychic reading on this dream (EC 294–128) explained that these were warnings that his soul would likely return to the spirit realms (to those on earth, that meant that he may die) if his mind did not become more active in this world and find more people requesting his unique services.

When asked during one of his psychic readings to explain brownies, he answered:

The manner in which those of the elementals—entities who have not entered into materiality—have manifested and do at times manifest themselves to the entity. Brownies, pixies, fairies, gnomes are not elementals, but elements that are as definite *entities* as man materialized.   EC 1265-3

In a past–life reading for another soul, he gave this account:

[B]efore this [incarnation] the entity was in the Scotch land. The entity began its activity as a prodigy, as one already versed in its associations with the unseen or the elemental forces; the fairies and those of every form that do not give expression in a material way and are only seen by those who are attuned to the infinite.   EC 2547-1

Seventy–two of Edgar Cayce's discourses mention the "the unseen forces," defined in the readings as "a consciousness of that divine force that *emanates* in Life itself in this material plane." (EC 281–7; italics mine) Notice how beautifully this description fits with the Kabbalistic concepts of the Unseen Infinite Eternal (Ein Sof) and the knowable emanations (sefirot).

All projected life in this world comes from unseen influences within, not without. Even human weaknesses and evil are a result of the misuse of free will, a misuse that began in the spirit and mind, long before material life began to express it. The implication here is that all outer influences, whether they are good or evil, emanate from the unseen realms of spirit and mind through the use and misuse of free will.

Consider the worst criminal acts by humans. These are due more to unseen forces within the spirit and mind of the perpetrator than his or her upbringing or genes (not to exclude the effects of both of these). Many souls have been raised by bad parents or nonexistent ones and in terrible environments; some of these children become good people and make much of their lives, while others grow up to virtually destroy everything and everyone they touch. The key element is the influence of the *spirit within* them and the *dark thoughts* that make them so dangerous and coldhearted versus the disposition of those that keep on keeping on in ways that are constructive rather than destructive, despite the surrounding circumstances.

Cayce's readings acknowledge the "warring" that often occurs within humans, between the unseen realms and the seen. (EC 281-7) His readings even call this war the true Armageddon (EC 3976-15, from Revelation 16:16), a battle within each soul between the energies and thoughts of dark, destructive influences and the energies and thoughts of illuminating, constructive influences.

Even the Light-bearing souls have to struggle to maintain their hold on the Light. It is difficult to be pure channels of the Light in this life, in our families and workplaces and in our own hearts and minds. It is a terrible battle between selfishness, contention, and faultfinding versus loving care for others and for self, and valuing the light of truth, hope, and love.

Cayce's readings warn the Children of God, the Children of the Law of One (as he often referred to them), to seek and maintain their awareness of the Divine Forces, for these will protect them from dark motivations within themselves and dark intentions in others.

As experienced by many, in opening self to the unseen forces about us, yet warred ever by those influences save when in the presence of His [God's] influence, then as the forces are raised in self *know*—without doubt—there *are* His protecting influences, able, willing, capable, and *will* aid in that direction in which such vibrations, such influences, are raised to those individuals to whom they be directed, even by the spoken word; for, as is seen, as is understood by many, by most, the *unseen* forces are the *active* forces, the *active* principles." EC 281-7

To avoid the influence of evil and selfishness, even the best among us must seek the protection and assistance of the Divine's influence, that consciousness of the Divine with us in our daily lives. "The spirit is indeed willing, but the flesh is weak," taught the masterful Jewish teacher Jesus, who faced Satan's temptations and walked away, free from the temptations. (Matthew 26:41 and Mark 1:3) And when we fail to maintain our mindfulness of the Divine and the higher bodily vibrations of the Divine awakened within us, we must get up and try again, never condemning ourselves or limiting the Divine's ability to redeem us, to cleanse us, and to make us stronger. Cayce taught:

Be not faint hearted because failure *seems* to be in thy way, or that self falters—but "how many times shall I forgive, or ask forgiveness—seven times?" "Yea, seventy *times* seven!" or, "not how I faltered, but did I seek His face again?" "Could ye not watch with me one hour?" The *man* crying out! "Sleep on, now, and take thy rest, for the hour cometh when I shall be even alone." So we find the changes, the weaknesses in the flesh— yet he that seeks shall find, and as oft as ye knock will the answer come. Seek to be one with Him [God], in body, in mind, in soul!   EC 281-7

Life is a challenge. It is a dance between the loneliness of self-consciousness and the cooperative consciousness that is aware of and seeking the guidance of the Creative, the Good Forces, and the higher vibrations.

Consider the challenges Jesus, a Jewish-trained master, faced—as described in this Cayce discourse.

In sending such forces out, then, be mindful that there is no doubt that these will bring that as He [God] sees fit, "Not my will, Of Father, but Thine be done!" What did *this* bring to Him [Jesus]? The cross, the burdens, the crown of thorns—yet in its essence it brought those abilities to overcome death, hell and the grave. So, as in our raising ourselves to that understanding that His [God's] presence is guiding and directing those influences about those to whom we would direct His cause (for they have called on us), then *know* His will *is being* done in the manner as *thou* hast sent same to that individual!"   EC 281-7

Why the struggle? Why the confusions and misgivings? Because we are godlings in the making, lost angels with the potential to become God's companions forever. We are not simply newly born humans trying to live our lives so that our deaths will lead us to a good afterlife. We are celestial entities that have been alive from the moment our Creator said, "Let there be Light" (Genesis 1:3), "Let us make them in our image, after our likeness," (Genesis 1:26) and "You are gods, sons and daughters of the Most High." (Psalm 82:6). We come into this incarnation with many, many karmic influences from preincarnation activity. We need to become aware of our lives as celestial souls, not just our lives as physical personalities.

Our present reality is too terrestrial and too physical. Deep within us is a celestial soul that has existed before, exists now, and will exist after our physical death. The transition from terrestrial, self-conscious beings to celestial souls and minds consciously one with the forces of Life and Light requires some adjustments, some breakthroughs. Holding us back are deep, karmic habit patterns that we have built over many incarnations and even in sojourns in nonphysical dimensions of life. These transitions can be compared to a woman pregnant who is attempting to adjust her body to deliver a new life. We have conceived in the wombs of our consciousness our true selves, our divine nature, yet we have to dilate our minds and hearts sufficiently to deliver this soul self, this resurrected, wiser self, which is destined to be an eternal companion to the Creator of the entire Cosmos.

Reincarnation

It may not be widely known, but the reincarnation of souls is not only an Edgar Cayce concept, it is also a Kabbalistic teaching (*gilgul neshamot*, meaning "cycles of the soul"). Much of the unseen influences in life are from our souls' many experiences before this life.

Kabbalah teaches that the destiny of every soul is to return to the source whence it came. Those who have not developed the purity and perfection necessary for gaining access to their heavenly source must undergo incarnation in a subsequent body and even repeat that experience more than once before they are permitted to return to the celestial region in a purified form.

This idea of correcting one's condition by trying again is expressed in Plotinus's often quoted lines in *The Enneads*, I.6.9:

Withdraw into yourself and look. And if you do not find yourself beautiful yet, act as does the creator of a statue that is to be made beautiful: he cuts away here, he smoothes there, he makes this line lighter, this other purer, until a lovely face has grown his work. So do you also: cut away all that is excessive, straighten all that is crooked, bring light to all that is overcast, labor to make all one glow or beauty and never cease chiseling your statue, until there shall shine out on you from it the godlike splendor of virtue, until you see the perfect goodness surely established in the stainless shrine.

Kabbalah uses the term *cycle* (*gilgul*) for reincarnation. However, there is another type of reincarnation. It involves receiving a new (higher) soul during one's lifetime, that is, a new soul comes into a person's heart while he or she is still incarnate. This is called *ibbur* (pregnancy or incubation), because it is like gestation or pregnancy. The incarnate person becomes "pregnant" with this new soul while he or she is still alive. This is an explanation of how some people go through dynamic changes in their perception and character. They undergo a change of mind, a change of lifestyle, and thereby ascend to the next spiritual level. They are now hosting a "new" soul—or, more accurately, a higher part of their own soul. This is what occurs when a person is ready to advance in soul evolution. This is why the soul has five parts, each higher than the other. This is not possession by a different soul, not a "walk-in," in the sense that some write about today, though some may confuse *ibbur* to be such. It is more aligned with being "born anew," as Jesus explained to Nicodemus (much more on this in chapter 3.)

Soul Growth

Each day, each situation, each relationship, each conversation, each thought in our heads is an opportunity to move closer to the Divine or away from it. As Cayce's readings often point out to us, it is our free will that must be engaged, engaged with the help of the unseen forces that emanate from the Divine. The greatest gift given us for resurrection and enlightenment is the will to choose and the help of the unseen forces of the Divinity, our Creator, who loves us and seeks our conscious companionship.

It is not, as so many have portrayed it to be, a life of denial and joylessness. There is a deep, comforting joy that accompanies the daily dance between the dark and the light, between misgivings and Light-filled faith, between low energy and high vibrations. Love flows. Light comforts, guides, and strengthens us. Peace and contentment subdue the ups and downs, creating a stable sanctuary within us. Even so, life is not without its challenges and changes; that is the nature of this journey. There is no growth without change and no enlightenment without challenges to the present perspective. The unseen forces have three major channels to our outer lives: *intuition, dreams,* and *meditation.* The first, intuition, is a knowing which comes from nowhere, yet we sense its rightness. Our dreams bring many impressions and images from within our mind and heart, occasionally from very deep levels within us. Our meditations raise the body's vibrations and expand the mind to higher levels. Unseen forces may manifest in many ways, some spectacular and some so subtle that we often miss them, but all are vital to our spiritual development.

Here's an example of how powerful the unseen forces can be. A mother asked Cayce to help her with her eleven–year–old boy. He was suffering from a debilitating pathological and emotional disorder that caused him to wet the bed every night for eleven years straight! This is Cayce's response:

> It is in the practice of peace within self, of love made manifest in self, that you make same manifest in your relationships to others. Not as a goody-goody individual, but as one good *for* something; bringing peace, joy, gladness, hope. When all about you seems disturbed, when all seems lost, know that He in His love, and in His patience, can turn such conditions into victorious joy, into gladness that makes the heart, the mind, the eyes, the body, the voice, joyous in living for the Christ's [Messiah's] sake."   EC 3165-1

Cayce went on to explain to her that, in a past incarnation, the boy had been a dunker of witches in Massachusetts and that his soul carried much regret over this. The karmic effect was that he awoke each morning soaked by his own water—urine. Cayce suggested that the mother carry these forgiving and loving thoughts into her sleep state, meditating on them in her heart and mind as she fell asleep, for she had suffered this boy's wrath in that same lifetime and needed to forgive him for it if she were to heal him.

Cayce also directed her to give her son a positive suggestion as he fell asleep. Interestingly, Cayce instructed her not to make any suggestion about his bladder control but about the opportunities of the life that now lay before him and that his hopes and aspirations be guided by God and God's love for him.

She did apply Cayce's guidance as she searched her heart, and meditated as she fell asleep, and the very first night that she gave a loving, positive suggestion to her son as he fell asleep, the boy did not wet the bed. After eleven years of consistent bedwetting, he never wet the bed again! The healing within each of them was complete. Joyous victory had been achieved through the deep, inner processes of the unseen forces emanating from the Divine influence within each of them. Cayce told this mother that her boy was her body, and as she healed and forgave herself (for whatever mistakes she had done with free will in past incarnations), so would that forgiveness heal him. Add to this that her voice—which Cayce instructed her to use with no doubt or fear in it—gave vibrations of forgiveness and hope to him. His body responded to his mother's body, and both were healed.

Of the many teachings that came through Cayce's attunement to the Universal Consciousness, those on understanding, seeking, and applying the unseen forces in our lives and relationships have to be among the most important, especially in these days of preparation for a new era of enlightenment and soul growth. The new era will be one in which evil cannot have its way freely. The book of Revelation expresses this by stating that it will be a thousand-year period when Satan is bound. There will be no evil, no temptation for the incarnate souls of that era. It is a golden age of enlightenment and soul growth. But this means that no souls can incarnate during this period unless they have subdued their darker inclinations and resolved the past-life memories that hold them down. All must be cleansed and released. Forgiveness and lovingkindness are the keys to preparing oneself for this coming age.

The Beginning

The Kabbalah ties the invisible influences to the Creation story. It goes something like this. Before anything existed, there was nothing—absolutely nothing. Only infinite emptiness and stillness existed. This was the condition of the Creator before the Creation. How, then, could the Creation occur? How could something come from out of nothing? This is the mystery and the difficulty with our seeking to know God, to know the almost unknowable. However, if we think of this pre-Creation condition as a consciousness, an infinite, universal consciousness that was perfectly still, with no thoughts, then we can see how it could be empty and yet possess the power to conceive. The unseen gave birth to the seen. In this process, the initial expressions or emanations reflect the nature of the Unseen God, allowing us to know the God of pre-Creation to some degree, even though we are among the created, the seen. It also helps us to appreciate that the seen universe is within the unseen and was given life from the unseen, original essence that is pre-Creation God. We may think of it as the womb of our Mother's mind.

What were some of the initial expressions of the infinite, universal mind of pre-Creation God? Well, at one moment there arose the will to create. This is the Divine Will motivated to create. Therefore, two of Unseen God's qualities are Will and the Creative Forces.

The Kabbalah teaches that God had to make room for the Creation, so a portion of the pre-Creation Creator retreated into an unknowable, unreachable "place." After this, the Creation exploded! The big bang of Life burst forth. And Kabbalah helps us understand the initial energies and original patterns through the ten emanations that reflect the nature of the invisible, infinite Creator into the visible reality. The emanations are in both the macrocosm and the microcosm. They are within us and flow through us. They are seen in the outer reality in a reflective manner, allowing us to intuit their unseen nature. And, best of all, we can awaken to them and use them to illuminate and energize our bodies, minds, and souls.

Living out here in the seen creation, we would be wiser and stronger if we opened our hearts and minds to the unseen Creative Forces and harmonized our free will with the flow of the Creator's will.

Creation, in Kabbalah, is explained in this mystical manner: within the unbounded womb of "Infinite Nothingness," that which is the essence of "Infinite Something" moved, expressing itself in a burst of "Light Without Limit." This light is both consciousness and luminescence.

"Infinite Nothingness" is Ein (also spelled En and Ayn) and is comparable to Gnosticism's "the Depth" and "Non-Being God" (*ouk on theos*) as well as "Unknown God" (*hagnostos theos*). "Infinite Something" is *Ein Sof* (also spelled Ein Soph, En Soph, and Ayn Sof) and is comparable to Gnosticism's "Fullness of Being" (*bythos pleroma*). "Light Without Limit" is *Ein Sof Aur*, possibly comparable to Gnosticism's "First Father" (*propator*). The Infinite Something emanated ten aspects of itself and twenty-two channels of energy and consciousness. The Infinite's expression flowed outward to four concentric planes of consciousness: (1) The first is concealed God, the Creator, the Infinite. It is a point in "the deep" (Genesis 1:2) that is everywhere and nowhere. It is unknowable but has emanated ten orbs of its nature, so it may be known by its emanations. These first ten emanations are known as the "Names of God," each revealing a characteristic of the Ineffable One. This is the Plane of Emanations (Olam Azilut). (2) Around this infinite point is the second plane of consciousness and life, and in it are ten more emanations. These second ten emanations are "The Intelligences," and are identified with the names of archangels. This is the Plane of Creation (Olam Briah). (3) Next comes the plane of consciousness and life called "The Hierarchies," of which there are also ten emanations. It is the Plane of Formation (Olam Yetzirah). (4) Finally, we have the fourth plane of consciousness and life, the realms of matter and the material cosmos. It is the Plane of Activity (Olam Asiyah) This last plane is the visible one; all the others are invisible. (See illustration 12. We'll cover more on these in chapter 4.)

There is a variation on this brief description, which teaches that the Infinite conceived of the Primordial Being first, and subsequently, the Primordial Being (or prototype) conceived all the beings. (See illustration 13.) This is comparable to Gnosticism's idea that First Father conceived the central Monad (*monas*), an indivisible oneness that pervades all life, seen and unseen. This Monad is comparable to the Logos, the Word—as the disciple John wrote: "In the beginning was the Word, and the Word was with God, and the Word was God. All things were made through this One." There is a First Source (*proarche*), which may be compared to Edgar Cayce's "First Cause." Humankind (*anthropos*) came out of the indivisible oneness of the Monad. In Kabbalah, humankind came out of the first being, Adam Kadmon.

We will learn much more about these as we continue our study.

PART

2 The Details

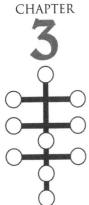

3

DIVISIONS OF OUR WHOLE BEING

As physical and earthly as we may feel, Kabbalah teaches that our true nature is not physical. We are beings of mind, soul, and spirit that are only temporarily using a physical body and living in a physical realm. And even while we are here, we live a good portion of our incarnate life beyond the body, as on average we sleep one-third of our incarnation. During sleep the nonphysical portion of our being may reach far beyond this plane of existence. Add to this that the death of the body is not the death of our nonphysical self. A major portion of our being survives death. We live on and may even return to incarnate in a new body—or not. According to Kabbalah and many other schools of thought, there is much activity on planes beyond this physical universe that we are so fully invested in.

Not only is a major portion of our being alive beyond sleep and death, it is amazingly active! We will cover more on this in chapter four.

Over the past many years, books have been published recounting hospital near-death testimonials that have contributed to our understanding of life while the body is dead. Of course, the testimonials come from those whose bodies were resuscitated, but the accounts are amazingly similar to one another. The patients each experienced existence outside their dead bodies and saw imagery of loved ones who had died previously as well as realms of light and activity. Then, when the chemistry, electricity, and physical manipulation were sufficient to revive their bodies, they felt themselves drawn back into their bodies and this world, as if traveling rapidly through a long tunnel. Bang! They awoke on the operating or emergency room table with bright lights glaring at them.

Can we imagine this nonphysical aspect of our being? Can we feel our being without a body? If so, then we are aware of our higher nature, and this is much of what Kabbalah is about.

Ancient and modern philosophies and religions acknowledge various components of our whole being; most common is the simple body, mind, and spirit or soul arrangement. The ancient Egyptians identified five distinguishable parts to us, as does Kabbalah, although most teachers focus on the three aspects that are most present with us now.

These divisions are delineations of a oneness for the benefit of understanding and awareness, not a fixed condition. Oneness is the true, eternal condition; division is a temporary measure for the purpose of assisting us. We are whole, but consciousness and energy may be more focused in certain areas at any given time. Certainly, in this realm, the physical is dominant for most people.

The ancient Bereishit Rabbah ("Great Genesis," a *midrash*, or homiletic study, section 14:9, on Genesis) speaks of five levels, or qualities, of our being. A problem occurs in that the five Hebrew words for these divisions are all translated in English as the same word: soul. And it does not help that three of the Hebrew terms are similar in their meaning: breath, wind, and breathing. We simply must understand that the distinctions are subtle, because we are talking about a wholeness of being. Even so, the distinctions are helpful to our understanding.

In a wonderful metaphor and using some of the imagery in the Zohar, Kabbalists Shim'on Lavi (1492–1585, an old guy for those times, ninety-three, although Shim'on Lavi may have actually been a father–and–son team by the same name) and Moshe Cordovero (1522–1570) compared these parts of our being to a glassblower, one who creates a beautiful, projected object by blowing through a pipe with molten glass on the end until the glass object is formed and then cuts the object from the pipe so that it sits on its own. In this metaphor, the glassblower's essence is our highest level of being, the glassblower is the next level, the *breath* of the glassblower is the third level, next is the expressed breath of the glassblower through the pipe that forms the glass and, finally, the breath inside the glass object is the last level of our being—it is as the breath inside our physical body, the glass object our physical body.

Let's begin at the physical level which we know so well and then move to the highest level of our being. The first three parts are the only ones involved with the physical body. These are (1) the Living Being (Nefesh), (2) the Soul Mind (Ruach), and (3) the Soul Being (Neshamah). The higher two levels, (4) the Spirit Mind (Chayah) and (5) the Spirit Being (Yechidah) do not reside in the body. Yes, there is a portion of each of us that has not touched this world or our physical body.

The Living Being (Nefesh)

Translating the Kabbalah term Nefesh is easy, but understanding its meaning in this context is tricky. It means "breath," but as the glass-blower metaphor indicates, it is the breath *inside* form, inside the glass object, which is the body. Kabbalah considers this portion to be the "Living Being," in the sense of a "breathing creature" encased in form. Notice that the form is not the creature; rather, the creature is inside the form. This portion was the *second* Creation, which occurred in Genesis 2, not the first one, which occurred in Genesis 1, in the image of God. Here is the passage related to this Creation: "And the Lord God made man from the dust of the earth, breathing into him the breath of life, and man became a living soul." (Genesis 2:7) The word *man* in this passage is actually the Hebrew word *adam*, with a lowercased a̱, not the name Adam that is later used but the Hebrew word that means "beings" or "persons." The word *adam* has the connotation of being reddish in color, resulting from the reddish flush of life-giving blood in this being. What is most disappointing is that in the biblical book of Numbers (considered to be the fourth book of Moses), the term *adam* is always translated as "persons" (Numbers 31:28, 30, 35, 40, 46), while the Hebrew word *ish* is used to mean "male" or "man" (Numbers 1:4 and throughout). But, in Genesis, *adam* is translated as "man" instead of "persons," leaving us with a misconception that the first being was masculine.

These beings were formed from the dust of the earth, and the breath of life was breathed into them. Here the translators use the masculine pronoun "him," despite the fact that, at this point in the Creation (Genesis 2:7), the being contained both feminine and masculine qualities—it was androgynous! The separation of the gender qualities did not occur until later, in 2:21. The reason for the separation of the genders was that, in this new realm of duality (life and death, good and evil, night and day, yin and yang), where the heavenly oneness is now separated into individual bodies (one soul to a body), the beings were alone inside separate bodies, and they were lonely: "Then the Lord God said, 'It is not good that the man [adam=beings] should be alone; I will make him a helper fit for him.'" (Genesis 2:18; RSV) But no helper that was fit for this level of being was found among all the creatures in this new dimension, so God took a portion from within the beings and made the companion.

> The man [beings] gave names to all cattle and to the birds of the air and to every beast of the field; but the man [beings] had no one like himself as a help. And the Lord God cast a deep sleep upon the man [beings], and took a rib [*tsela* means a "side" of its whole nature, not just a rib] from him while he was sleeping, joining up the flesh again in its place. And from the rib [side] which the Lord God had taken from the man [beings] he made a woman [*ishshah*=female], and took her to the man [*ish*=male].   Genesis 2:20-22

Another important detail of this Creation is that there were actually two creations of the feminine. The first was Lilith and the second was Eve. Curiously, Edgar Cayce's readings state that there were also two Edens. The first one was in Poseidia, Atlantis, the birthplace of Lilith, and the second was the biblical Eden between the Tigris and Euphrates rivers, in what is today modern Iraq, the birthplace of Eve. This idea of an initial companion that preceded Eve is found in the writings of many early Jewish writers. There are also ancient depictions of Lilith. See illustration 18. In Cayce's chronology, the first Eden, with Lilith, occurred roughly a hundred thousand years before Eve's Eden.

We should note that when we properly translate the term *adam* as "persons," even "humankind" as a whole, we find the answer to the age-old question of how Cain could have found a wife, when the previous passages give the impression that the earth only had Adam, Eve, and Abel for Cain to choose from! The term *adam* indicates that the Creator used the dust of the earth and the breath of life to create *humankind*, not just one person, and certainly not one male, from which a little rib was taken to create his companion.

It is also important that we realize that humankind was created twice, once in the image of God (Genesis 1:26) and once from the dust of the earth (Genesis 2:7). This is the origin of the idea that we have a dual nature: divine and human, godly and earthly, spirit and flesh, essence and form, energy and matter. Next, we must realize that we, as godlings, have been diminished further through the separation of the gender qualities that were originally combined, naturally one, in every soul. A male is projecting only half of his whole soul being, and a female, only half of hers.

As we are now on the ascent of our soul journey through matter, it is natural that, for many years now, men have been struggling to get in touch with their feminine side and women have been struggling to get in touch with their masculine. It is only natural, because the soul self is both feminine and masculine.

Let's move on to the animal nature of this portion of our being. This fifth and lowest part of our being influences and is influenced by the bodily instincts, our animal nature, which contains all the base urges, cravings, and desires of bodily existence. But here also is our human nature, with its three-dimensional mind and personality, so shaped by our cultural and socioeconomic upbringing and genetic makeup. The animal and human nature compose our earthly Living Being. It is a thing apart from the heavenly, divine portions of our being.

Even when not incarnate, the cravings and habit patterns of this portion possess us, like a ghost that still desires physical sensation. Remember, the creature is inside the body, not the body itself, so even after the death of the body, this aspect of our being continues to influence us.

This "Living Being" is a dynamic that needs to be subdued, trained, and directed. Hinduism depicts this portion as a charioteer with the reins of the five stallions of the physical senses, which want to run wide and free! If the charioteer restrains self-seeking, self-gratifying impulses, then he or she opens the door to higher consciousness.

This lowest portion of our being is symbolized in the biblical character of Cain, whose name in Hebrew means "acquired" (from the Hebrew verb *qana* and explained by Eve herself in Genesis 4:1, "I have acquired one with the help of the Lord."). This is an acquired aspect of our total being. It is willful, self-centered, self-seeking, and not perfected, as reflected in Cain's character. God says to this aspect of our being, as to Cain: "Sin is crouching at the door [of your heart and mind]; its desire is for you, but *you must master it*." (Genesis 4:7, italics mine) Sin, in Kabbalah, is imbalance and disharmony, most often caused by rebelliousness among the free-willed forces of life. When Cain rules, Abel (meaning "breath" in Hebrew but with the connotation of *vapor*, implying something transitory) is killed!

Abel is replaced with Seth (in Hebrew, Sheth), this name implying a new appointment. Again, Eve explains her choice of the name: "God has appointed [*shath*, meaning "replaced"] me another offspring . . . " (Genesis 4:25) Seth is the ancestor of Noah, whose generations repeople this part of the world after all the evil ones are cleansed by the Great Flood. Cain's progeny has moved far from Eden to the Land of Nod, east of Eden, which is modern-day Afghanistan. Cain is buried south of Kabul, Afghanistan. Isn't it interesting that we find ourselves back in the lands of Nod (Afghanistan) and Eden (Iraq), and struggling over the Holy City of Jerusalem? Yet these involvements indicate that we are on our return path whence we came.

This acquired outer self has become so dominant that we assume it to be our whole being—who we feel we are—the rest of our being having fallen into our unconsciousness.

Edgar Cayce often addressed the issue of our outer, earthly self. In the following record, a young man asked Cayce how he might receive guidance from higher forces while in the body.

> Q: How can [this] body become aware of the higher forces in himself as a guidance?
> A: *Seeing* it, close self—mind, eyes, ears—to the outside world; recognizing as a fact that, "If I would know, if I would be, if I would comprehend, I must *open* my inner self—not the *outer* self—to those influences." And then the awareness flows in.   EC 257-170

Here is another of Cayce's comments on this aspect of our being:

Let the light that shines without be lighted by that *light which is created from within*, making the activities of the inner self and the outer self in accord.   EC 262-40; italics mine

Since this is such a physical level of our being, the incarnate portion, it is also important to consider the body's effect on our being. Cayce was very much aware of this, and as a holistic health resource, he (named "the father of holistic medicine" by the American Holistic Medical Association) often associated bodily conditions with feelings of separation between the outer self and the inner self. Here's one example:

The sympathetic system has been under such strains that all along those centers where there are particular centralization between the cerebrospinal and sympathetic system, makes for those of heaviness to the body, depressions in the feelings, as of far away feelings, as separations at times between the outer self and the inner self . . . as if the heart and lungs were too full for the body, heaviness in the lower portion of the torso, the feet feel as if they would drag, stretchy feelings through the lower portion of the limbs themselves. These are rather indications than causes. These are reflexes from an overtaxed mental and physical being, with improper nourishment or sustenance coming from the blood supply to bring buoyancy to the whole physical being; the brain feeling at times dull, as if unable to think farther on, as if it would stop. This all from the sympathetic system, and needs rather that of the resuscitation of elements in the physical being as would bring to the body those of renewed energies that would supply the whole system."   EC 4393-1

Our outer being, this Living Being, is very much affected by the body's condition and its physical surroundings. The mental portion inside the body needs the body to be properly assimilating nutrients and eliminating toxins that build up. Our outer being also needs to turn within to find the true light, love, and life. However, the inner path is often perplexing to the outer self. The inner path does not fit within the three-dimensional model of life. Let's consider this further.

To help us grasp the odd, inner way to enlightenment and spiritual breakthrough, Cayce recommended reading *Tertium Organum* by Ouspensky. Among other things in this text, Ouspensky explains that a dimensional breakthrough requires an altered state of consciousness, because the next dimension does not exist in the present dimension. For example, imagine a one-dimensional being searching for the second dimension. This being may run back and forth on its single plane of existence and not find the second plane. The second dimension is perpendicular to its entire reality. It is totally alien to its current plane of existence. To clarify, imagine the first dimension as a single line ——. The second dimension would be a perpendicular line to that line⏌. Note that the second dimension does exist in the first. It is another reality, at a 90° angle to the first. And the third dimension does not exist within these first two dimensions. A two-dimensional being may run up and down and back and forth in its reality, but it will not find the third dimension without having a breakthrough from normal consciousness, because the third dimension runs in a plane that is perpendicular to the first and second dimensions, creating the corner of a cube.

This brings us to our three-dimensional selves and our search for higher dimensions beyond our reality. We now understand that the higher dimensions are not in the third dimension. We must experience an altered state of perception. Nothing in the projected, three-dimensional reality will lead us to the fourth dimension. What is more perpendicular to an object-oriented being than venturing within itself? We must move from objects to thoughts and mental images within our minds. These are the "things" of the next dimension. Consider that they have no physical form, no projected shape, yet they have substance. Their form is not matter but the energetics of thoughts, imagery, and feelings are very real to us. It is not a physical cube but the thought form and feeling of it that is fourth-dimensional.

Grandmother's body may have died, but her deeper mind and core energetics live on; thus we can feel her, even see her with our deeper, dreaming mind's eye.

Cayce could not always distinguish thoughts from actions in the astral accounts of persons he was giving readings for. That is, he was not always able to determine whether the person had actually done something or just thought about doing it, because thoughts are as real as actions in the higher dimensions he was attuned to!

> Thoughts are things, and may be miracles or crimes in action.
>
> EC 105-2

> Each thought, as things, has its seed, and if planted, or when sown in one or another ground, brings its own fruit; for thoughts *are* things, and as their currents run must bring their own seed.   EC 288-29

We find these same teachings in Scripture:

> For as he thinks in his heart, so is he.   Proverbs 23:7

The inner dimensions are as real and potent as the outer. The outer self must seek within to know these higher dimensions. This naturally leads us to the next level of our being: the soul mind.

Soul Mind (Ruach)

Our Soul Mind—Ruach (from *ruah*, for wind or air)—is the moral consciousness that may subdue the urges and patterns of the Living Being. Here we have the ability to distinguish between good and evil, to subdue the most powerful instinctual urges for reasons higher than the gratification of these urges. This is the discerning mind and conscience. It is the involved mind that analyzes and correlates desires and measures them against the entity's deepest ideals. It is the expressed breath or "wind" of the glassblower. It is with us inside this projected experience (the glass).

This is also the portion of us that is the dreamer. When we are in this portion, we feel perfectly comfortable. We are ourselves. However, there is a subtle yet opaque veil separating this deeper mind from the outer consciousness. We know these two aspects of ourselves well. For example, each of us has had the experience of waking from an attention-getting dream, only to notice that the bladder is full, so we get up to empty the bladder, then return to the bed to review the dream—but it's gone! We have none of the content of the dream that so captured our attention just moments ago. How is this possible? It is possible because we have just experienced these two parts of ourselves: the Soul Mind, which dreamed the dream, and the Living Being, which accommodated the full bladder but did not dream the dream. So subtle is the veil between these two that we don't even notice when we move through it, yet it is so opaque that we cannot see back through the veil. That is, unless we learn to. Then the veil becomes much more transparent, and we become more sensitive to subtle shifts in states of consciousness.

The Soul Mind is the subconscious, but with a much greater expanse than we normally give to the subconscious.

In Cayce's discourses this aspect of our being is tightly integrated with our outer mind (the conscious mind) and our body. One of the common communication channels between these two parts is dreaming.

> We have the body, the enquiring mind, [Ms. 288], with dreams as come to the body from time to time. These, as we see, are applicable to the body, in the study of forces as are manifested in the physical world, and are correlations of mental mind, body-mind, soul, and the subconscious forces, or mind of the soul.   EC 288-14

> These dreams as come to these individuals are lessons to be applied in their daily lives and are the correlating of the developments of the mind, the body, the soul forces of same, acted upon by the soul forces of subconscious mind in inductive forces and emblematically given to the mind as instructions, see?   EC 294-36

Inner life goes on in a manner reflective of how it does in the physical, material plane. Let's consider an example of love living beyond the physical in this following communication between two souls who knew each other while incarnate and are continuing to commune after one has passed on from the physical world. They were mother and daughter. The mother's nickname for the daughter was "Sister." It begins with a simple dream interpretation requested by the daughter, who had dreamt about her mother, who had died. After the reading's initial comments, it quickly becomes a direct communication with the mother, who now lives in another plane, using Cayce's attunement as a medium for this conversation.

MHB: You will have before you the body and enquiring mind of |Ms. 243|, present in this room, and the dream this body had of recent date, in which her mother, |Mrs. 3776|, came to her and put her arms around her, and told her that she loved her. The body |Ms. 243| asked her if she knew how much she had always loved her, and the mother replied, "Yes, you've proven it always."

EC: Yes, we have the body and the enquiring mind of this body, |Ms. 243|, present in this room. "The dreams, as we see, come to individuals through the subjugation of the conscious mind, and the subconscious being of the soul—when loosed—is able to communicate with the subconscious minds of those whether in the material or the cosmic plane. In this as is seen the body-mind takes that concept of the subconscious that is closest to the soul forces of the body, and the mother in the living being as it is, then, gives that assurance to the body through this means of its full life existence:

"Sister—Sister—as is seen by you, Mother sees, Mother knows, Mother feels those same feelings of that love which is in the earth that makes of the heavenly home. And while I am in the spirit planes I am yet present in the minds and hearts of those who express to me the love as builded in the being—the love the Master shows to all when He gave that He would prepare the home for those who would come after Him.

"Love those about you in the way that Mother gave, and be that as Mother would have you be—for Mother does not leave you, Sister— and Mother knows! For the life is the whole life, even as the Master gave that He was the life and the light of the world, in that same concept as shown in that felt as Mother gathers Sister in her arms—and Mother knows! Mother Knows!"

Q: The mother guides, guards, as the living angel, though unseen to sensuous eyes?

A: In this there is seen that as has oft been given, that through the subjugation of physical forces the subconscious—which is the mind of the soul—communicates those same feelings, those same expressions, which are that which really builds in the material plane—for as is experienced by this body-conscious mind, [Ms. 243], there is seen the love that is expressed through the mother love. *Not* as that which is passed, or gone, or not present, or not among the living! For GOD is God of the living, the Savior is the Savior of the living. Let him that is dead bury the dead. Let him that is alive be alive to that which may be gained by those closer manifestations of the guards that keep those who seek to know His way.   EC 243-5

Soul life and consciousness are not far from physical life, and relationships extend beyond the separation that occurs when a body dies. This requires that we awaken to our Soul Mind, develop an awareness of the veil that separates us, and learn how to transform the veil's opacity to transparency. As we do this, we become aware of our next higher Self! This self is beyond the personality that we know in the projected life in physicality.

Soul Being (Neshamah)

Our Soul Being—Neshamah (from *nasham,* meaning "to breathe")—is our soul self, the ghost self of our whole being. It is the bridge between the physical incarnation and the heavenly tiers of our being. It is both in the body and beyond it. This is the portion of our being that is *striving to save* the Living Being from the wheel of desire and karma, to free it from its servitude to self–seeking entanglements. Edgar Cayce called this our individuality, in contrast to our outer self's personality. It is our higher nature, in contrast to our human or animalistic nature. He referred to the Soul Being as our "better self." (EC 1662–2 and many others)

This is the breath of the glassblower.

These first three divisions are often considered to be the human being. As such, it is developing, changing, and ever moving toward earthliness or toward heavenliness, often somewhere in between. The body is its temple and is either filled with the fires of self–seeking and gratification or the incense of love, kindness, and helpfulness toward others, and a sense of the godly connection and destiny. In many cases, there is a battle waging between these two opposing interests. Living Being (Nefesh) is often pulling in one direction and Soul Being (Neshamah) in the other. The Soul Mind (Ruach) is analyzing and correlating the activities and thoughts, giving its conscientious insights to help minimize the struggle—leading the two toward a cooperative effort to make the most of the immediate incarnation.

Cayce illustrates and explains this, as well:

The entity finds self a body, a mind, a soul; in a three-dimensional world. In the physical or material we see, the more often, the manifestations of the mental and the material successes, failures, or confusions in the experience of individuals. Life—as manifested in this three-dimensional plane—is a combination not only of the present experiences, the present problems, the present urges (as has been indicated for the entity), but of *all* the experiences; and the awareness of same is only manifested through that phase or portion of the mental self as it seeks to know its source of activity—or the spiritual or soul self.

The spiritual or soul self is the eternal. Hence the mental is both of material and of spiritual, or divine origin.

Hence, the individual who aided man in setting forth laws, rules or regulations—or who is known as the lawgiver [Moses]—gave expression to that which, if it is wholly understood in the consciousness of an individual, puts before him all the problems and yet the answers to same, day by day.

Then, as he gave, it is not who will descend from heaven to bring you a message, or who will come from over the seas or from without to make you aware; but lo, the whole answer is within thy own consciousness. For, as ye become aware of this, in thy relationships, there is the realization within self of that spiritual awareness which may enable self to *do* that which is ever the constructive exercising of the will in materiality; for: "Today there is set before thee good and evil, life and death; choose thou."

That factor of the spiritual self, or of the soul (the will), then enables the individual to cooperate with that spirit, that truth, that fact which has ever been set before man—"If ye will be my son, I will be thy God—

If ye call, I will hear—Behold, I stand at the door and knock; I will enter, if ye ask."
Then, these are not mere sayings! They are *facts*, truths, life itself! but the individual is not made aware of same through the material things nor material-mindedness; rather through spiritual-mindedness, as to purposes and activities of the soul in its lessons, its tenets that it has carried through its expressions in the earth.   EC 1797-3

Body, mind, and soul are commonly understood to be parts of our being and are comparable to Living Being, Soul Mind, and Soul Being. Let's now move beyond these and consider two portions of our being that are not common: Spirit Mind and Spirit Being. These are significant concepts in Kabbalah and Cayce.

Spirit Mind (Chayah)

Our Spirit Mind—Chayah (the "living one")—is beyond anything earthly. It relates to the first flash of consciousness and the Giver of the gift of consciousness. Here is our spiritual mind, the womb of individual creativity, from which we use our very own free will to conceive. This level of our being can give life, can return life after illness or even death, and can "quicken" us, as is often said of the Spirit.

This is the glassblower. This is our divine consciousness. The glassblower's breath (Soul Being), its expressed breath (Soul Mind), and its encased breath (Living Being) journey out to experience the universe and the freedom of individual life.

This Spirit Mind maintains contact with the perfection of the Creator and the Creator's consciousness. It is the same yesterday, today, and tomorrow.

We can lift up lower portions of ourselves (soul mind and soul being) into this portion, but Spirit Mind does not normally descend to our level. And when it does, it is profoundly overwhelming to our soul mind and barely perceivable by our conscious mind.

Though it rarely descends, we can lift up our soul and Soul Mind to it. Once the connection is made, we gain access to and help from the powerful Spirit Mind. But it is important to remember that the Spirit

Mind has nothing earthly or worldly in it. Soul Mind is the savior, understanding the weaknesses of the Living Being. Spirit Mind is absolute truth with no room for vagaries. When in the Spirit Mind, we would not perceive activity as we do in a dream of the Soul Mind. In the Spirit Mind, the imagery is more like a vision. It would be images like those the prophets described when seeing heavenly things, wondrous features, and dynamic energies. Cayce identifies this level of consciousness as the "superconscious," as does Hinduism. Here's an example:

> Q: Explain and illustrate the difference in the faculties of Mind, Subconscious and Superconscious.
>
> A: The superconscious mind being that of the spiritual entity, and in action only when the subconscious is become the conscious mind [meaning deep sleep, deep meditation, or death]. The subconscious being the superconscious of the physical entity, partaking then of the soul forces and of the material plane."   EC 900-31

Notice that our subconscious mind is as the superconsciousness to our outer, conscious mind. But when the outer, conscious mind is subdued or absorbed into the higher mind, the subconscious becomes the active consciousness and the superconscious is as the subconscious is to us today in our present condition.

This may seem unnecessarily confusing, but it is really helpful when one is attempting to make passage through dimensions of consciousness. For example, when meditating, we must still the conscious mind and personality and all the concerns of the earthly portion of our being. As we do this, our soul mind and soul being become our natural condition of beingness—we are a soul. If we stay with the meditation, then we may move even deeper by subduing our soul self and awakening to our spirit mind, which is connected to God's mind. Now we are entering the deepest levels of meditation. This process also occurs in deepest sleep when visions rather than dreams come.

When asked to illustrate this level of consciousness, Cayce gave two examples. The first is the biblical scene in which Saul is on the road to Damascus, is suddenly surrounded by a brilliant light, and hears a voice speaking to him from the light. (Acts 9) In this instance, Cayce says that Jesus' superconscious mind was attempting to communicate with Saul's subconscious and, to a degree, his conscious mind. But the presence of such a high level of consciousness overwhelmed Saul, who fell to the ground and struggled to comprehend the experience and capture the message in the voice. His traveling companions could not comprehend the experience, only seeing the light but not hearing the voice.

The second example is in Revelation 19, when John, deep into his ecstasy, sees an angel in heaven. The angel gives him information, after which John falls down to worship the angel, believing it to be God's projection. The angel balks at this, saying, "You must not do that! I am your fellow servant and your brother . . . Worship God." (Revelation 19:10) Cayce explains that, when Peter and John were arrested, Peter was to be executed and John exiled to the Isle of Patmos. As they parted, Peter told John that he would endeavor to come to him after his death. Cayce says that this angel was Peter in the higher, superconscious quality of being, and as such, he appeared to John as an angelic expression of the Lord (remember, a portion of us was made in the image of God). The angelic aspect of his former colleague and brother in the cause corrects his mistake and directs him to the God of all the godlings.

Spirit Being (Yechidah)

Our highest level of being is Spirit Being—Yechidah (meaning the "single one"). Here is the ultimate unity of the individual in God, as an individual spirit within and one with the Great Spirit. The Spirit Being is the highest of the five levels of being. It is the one made in the image of God. (Genesis 1:26) Here we also find that the superconscious mind is one with the Universal Consciousness of the Creator.

Cayce viewed the spirit entity as a thing apart from anything earthly. Here's one example:

Q: Does the spirit entity have a separate consciousness apart from the physical, and is it as the consciousness of [Mr. 900] when he dreams, or has visions, while asleep?
A: The spirit entity is a thing apart from any earthly connection in sleep,

yet connected. For the earthly or material consciousness is ever tempered with material conditions . . . [the spirit entity] partakes of the spiritual forces principally. In consciousness we find only projections of subconscious and superconscious, which conditions project themselves in dreams, visions, unless entered into the superconscious forces. In the consciousness of earthly or material forces there enters all the attributes of the physical, fleshly body. In the subconscious there enters the attributes of soul forces, and of the conscious forces. In the superconscious there enters the subconscious forces, and spiritual discernment and development.   EC 900-16

We have three basic levels of mind: physical consciousness, soul subconsciousness, and spirit superconsciousness. The physical is far from the spiritual, but the soul bridges this gap, connecting all of our parts—from the highest to the lowest and back again. There are also three distinct qualities of being: our outer projected self, our inner soul self, and our infinite spiritual self.

Levels of Being and the Chakras

The Cayce readings and other sources would associate the four lower chakras—root, navel, solar plexus, and heart—with the Living Being (Nefesh). These chakras are also associated with the four children of Horus in Egyptian mysticism, as well as the four beasts in Ezekiel, in Daniel, and in Revelation. (Much more on these will be covered in chapter 13.) The three higher chakras—throat, third eye, and crown—would be associated with the Soul Mind (Ruach) and the Soul Being (Neshamah). See illustrations 27 and 28.

In Cayce's teachings the throat chakra is associated with the will and is thus the first step to reconnecting with heavenly awareness and oneness with God. As one subdues his or her personal will and seeks God's will, one turns from this outer, lower reality to the inner, higher ones. The crown and third eye are luminaries of higher consciousness and renew energy in the body. This energy flows from heavenly realms through the crown (the soft spot in the head of our body as infants). When flowing, it opens the closed third eye, the mind's eye. This is also the region of the large frontal lobe of our brain, which so distinguishes us from animals. This area contains most of the dopamine–sensitive neurons associated with reward, attention, long–term memory, planning, and drive. In the frontal lobe resides the ability to conceive of future consequences resulting from current actions, to choose between good and bad actions, to recognize the best choice from among several options, to override and suppress unacceptable social responses, and discern similarities and differences between things or events.

Cayce recommended meditation for improving one's bodily condition and raising one's level of consciousness. He spoke of drawing up the energy and consciousness from the lower chakras to the higher ones. In his meditative method, the energy and consciousness rise up from the base of the spine to the base of the brain; then to the center of the brain, where the crown chakra awakens (the soft spot); and then flows over to the great frontal lobe, where the hypothalamus and pituitary glands (the master glands of the body) are located. Interestingly, Cayce associated the seven chakras with the body's seven endocrine glands, which secrete their hormones directly into the blood system. The root chakra corresponds with the gonads (testes in males, and ovaries in females), the navel with the Leydig cells, the solar plexus with the adrenal glands and pancreas, the heart with the thymus, the throat with the thyroid, the crown with the pineal, and the third eye with the pituitary gland.

The Origin of Evil

Cayce also teaches that the three lower aspects of being—Soul Being, Soul Mind, and Living Being—existed long before we ever contacted the third dimension and physical life, clarifying that original sin was not a sin of the flesh, as is so often taught, but occurred in the spirit, in the soul, *before* it entered physical life. Souls brought their lower urges with them; flesh did not cause these urges, but it certainly facilitated a heightened expression of them. (EC 262–52)

Kabbalah teaches the same idea. When there is sin, darkness, or a defect in the creation, it is caused by a separation of what should be united. Souls may become, by misuse of their free wills, so completely focused on themselves that they become separated from the Whole. Of course, there really is no way that we can be outside of the Whole, but we can become unconscious of our oneness with the Whole. When this occurs, the mediating flow between the Creator and the created is broken, disrupting the creative flow and bringing darkness, evil, illness, and a sense of separation and aloneness. Even angels fall when this occurs.

The Counter to Evil

However, there is a countering influence to this separation. Both Cayce and Kabbalah teach that the higher aspects of our being, Spirit Mind and Spirit Being, are as pure and perfect as the moment they were conceived by God in God's image. These higher portions have never left the presence and "throne of the Most High." Even the least among us has his or her pure being in God's presence.

The Zohar teaches that only the Nefesh is capable of sin. But that sin occurred *before* carnal life. This is why so many spiritual teachers purport that sin occurs in the heart and mind before it is manifested in the life of the body.

Changing the Name of God

Let's conclude by reviewing stages of our Creation as expressed by changes in the name for God.

The Scriptures begin, *breshit bara elohim* [there is no distinction between lowercased and uppercased letters in Hebrew], "In the beginning God . . . " The first name for God, as seen is this first line of Genesis, is Elohim. It is a plural Hebrew word that may be interpreted as "the Deities," and the verse about creating us is translated in the plural as well : "Let *us* make man in *our* image, after *our* likeness." (Genesis 1:26; emphasis mine) By using the plural form, the authors were likely attempting to convey the collective nature of the Creator, to keep us from thinking that God is a divine individual, projecting individuals in its image, and that God is in some way a separate Being from us. Rather, it is a collective consciousness within which all the Creation was conceived and in which all exists. Elohim may be likened to the great as-

sembly spoken of in Psalm 82:1, indicating all exists within this collective: "God is in the assembly of God; he is judging among the gods."
Curiously, though, when this plural name is used, it is commonly con-
strued with singular verbs and adjectives, adding to the belief that this
is not polytheism but the collective nature of God. Before we leave this
psalm, consider verse 6: "I said, 'You are gods, all of you are sons [and
daughters] of the Most High.'" This is clearly a reference to our highest
level of being, the Spirit Being with the Spirit Mind.

Kabbalah uses another name for the highest of God's qualities, a
name that does not appear in any Scripture. It is Ein Sof, which relates
more to God beyond the Creation. This is God transcendent (ad le-ein
sof). Gershom Scholem (December 5, 1897 to February 21, 1982), widely
regarded as the founder of the modern, academic study of Kabbalah
and the first professor of Jewish Mysticism at the Hebrew University of
Jerusalem, taught that Ein Sof is the emanator of the emanations (sefirot).
Sefirot are God's energy and consciousness emanating throughout creation and found in the Kabbalah Tree of Life, which we will study in a
later chapter.

Let's continue with God, ourselves, and the evolving changes in the
name of God.

As the Creation progresses, the name of God is changed. Changing the
name of the God reflects changes in our relationship to God, not God's
changing condition. God is unchanged. Originally, we were created in God's
image, in Elohim's image. (Genesis 1:26) Then, in chapter two, Yahweh
Elohim (often interpreted as "Lord God") creates us out of the dust of the
earth and breathes life into us. (Genesis 2:7) In chapter four, Yahweh
(Lord) is used during and after the birth of Cain and Abel. As the Bible
story continues, God is called Adonai (Master), El (Mighty One), El 'Elyon
(Most High God), El Shaddai (God Almighty), El 'Olam (Everlasting God),
El Hai (Living God), and Avinu ("Our Father," as found in Isaiah 63:16;
Jeremiah 31:9; Psalms 103:13; and 1 Chronicles 29:10). In the New Testa-
ment, Jesus continues the Jewish concept of God as Father, using Abba
("Father" in Aramaic and in colloquial Hebrew at the time of Jesus).

All of these names reveal our shifting relationship with God as we
grow away or toward oneness with our Creator. Consider how God identified Him–Herself to Moses on the mount when answering Moses's

question about His name: "I am that I am."

> And Moses said unto God, "Behold, when I come unto the
> children of Israel, and shall say unto them, the God of your
> fathers hath sent me unto you; and they shall say to me,
> What is his name? What shall I say unto them?" And God
> said unto Moses, "I AM THAT I AM"; and he said, "Thus shalt
> thou say unto the children of Israel, I AM hath sent me unto
> you."   Exodus 3:13-14

We may read this as indicating that the collective cannot possibly be
separate from the Creation; therefore, the sense of self that we feel in
our expression "I am" is a portion of the Great I AM in whose image all
of the little "I am's" were created and exist. Edgar Cayce expressed it this
way: "This is that portion of the lesson as is to be grounded into the
inmost Self until all come to know that not only God is God but the self
is a portion of that Oneness." (EC 900-181)

Why the Lower Levels of Being?

In the Garden, after eating from the Tree of the Knowledge of Good
and Evil, Adam and Eve hid from God because they felt naked in God's
all-knowing presence. Now there was no way they could be outside of
the Whole or beyond God's all-knowing consciousness, but out of love
for them, God developed the illusion of time and space and privacy. In
this way they would feel that they had time to become comfortable in
God's presence; they would have a sense of their private realm of im-
perfection until they could become cleansed and perfect again. The projected, lower, outer mind and being was this opportunity. It was
symbolized by God making clothes for Adam and Eve and by their
leaving the Garden of God's immediate presence. The lower divisions of
our being gave us the time and space to use our wills to choose life over
death, good over evil, and eventually feel comfortable in the All-
Knowing's presence. The separation that we sought eventually becomes
a thing of the past as we resolve our discomfort in the presence of the
All-knowing. That which had become separated is thus united again.

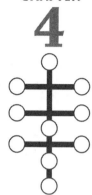

CHAPTER

4

PLANES OF EXISTENCE

The universe we know is not the first one to have been created, but it is the longest lasting, according to Kabbalistic tradition—and for a good reason. The Creator desired to create companions, companions that chose to be so, thus they had to have free will. These potential companions would also need to grow into their role, gradually becoming fully aware of the life forces flowing through all of creation as well as all that is concealed in the depths of the Infinite Womb. None of this growth and learning would be possible if God's perfect nature permeated the entire universe, so God withdrew a portion of Itself to allow for the imperfections of Its developing companions, using freedom and choice to grow into their potential. Fortunately, the all-wise Creator established a very effective law to control the possibility for chaos; that law is what we know today as karma: As we sow with our free will, we experience; and as we measure out to others, so it is measured back to us. This law was not established to mete out punishment or retribution, as so many teach, but to provide our souls with the enlightenment and education of experiencing the effects of our free-will actions and thoughts. The Creator's intent was to help each soul make better choices and become eternal companions to the Creator—consciously and interactively, even co-creators with the Great Creator.

Our wondrous potential is expressed in the Kabbalistic text Hekhalot Zutarti:

> What is the man that he is able to ascend upwards, to ride wheels, to descend downwards, to explore the world, to walk on dry land, to behold his radiance, . . . [missing text

61

here], his crown, to be transformed through his honor, to
say praise, to combine signs, to say names, to peer upwards
and to peer downwards, to know exactly the living and to
behold the vision of the dead, to walk in rivers of fire and to
know the lightning.   Hekhalot Zutarti, Section 349

The Zohar provides a map of four different planes of consciousness,
as do other treatises, old and new. We traverse these planes in our soul-
growth journeys. Soul-life experiences occur on these planes, and we
may actually have flashes of awareness of these four planes.

In Lurianic Kabbalah (a system containing Indian philosophy,
Platonism, and Gnosticism), there are five planes of existence, because
they add to the four basic planes the Primordial Being (Adam Kadmon)
as a plane of consciousness all its own. See illustration 13. This means
that the archetype of the Primordial Being is another plane of experience in our soul growth. The Logos plane becomes a conduit into the
Infinite, Ineffable God.

Before we learn about the planes, let's briefly discuss the Hebrew
word *olam*. Most agree that the word relates to both distance and time,
in the sense of "a far distance" and "a long time." It is so very hard to
take our three-dimensional framework and stretch it to grasp fourth,
fifth, and higher dimensional realities. Most writers have translated *olam*
as "world" but agree that it could also mean "a plane of unimaginable
distance and time." Even this definition is inadequate, because space
and time only exist in our present reality—the third dimension. Fortunately, many of us have come to understand states of consciousness,
degrees of awareness, and realms of perception. For example, we recognize the difference between a materialistic person, who mostly lives in
the physical reality, as opposed to a person who has a mind that reaches
far beyond physicality. We know people who perceive elements of musical experience far beyond normal people—thus possessing a level of
perception beyond the norm. We know minds that comprehend the
laws governing the universe, while others just live in it, not aware of
what is involved. Today we grasp the concept of paradigms, archetypes,
and mental constructs; theoretical frameworks of unseen influences
upon reality are within our appreciation. All these ideas help us to grasp

planes of soul existence and to interpret the word *olam* in broader understanding.

Now we might quickly use the term *states of consciousness*, except that the Cayce readings warn that even in higher dimensions, where the physical body is not manifested, there are magnetic-like forces that create vessel-like orbs of being for individual soul-mind entities—a type of "body." We might think of them as energy fields that form multidimensional bodies. Even so, these are not like the degree of encasement we experience in a physical body on earth, because the energy fields of our individual consciousness can expand into infinity and back again.

With all of this in mind, let's interpret *olam* as a plane of existence in which a personal consciousnesses with a bodylike concentration of beingness experiences life.

Here are the four planes that are common to most Kabbalistic texts and teachings. They are concentric circles of existence surrounding a point. As you read, see illustrations 12, 13, 14, and illustrations 3 and 30 for the planes and the triads.

1. Plane of Emanation (Olam Atzilut)

The first realm of existence is the Plane of Emanations. On this plane the Expression of Life (of which we are a part) unites with the unseen Source of Life. Here we may know oneness with the Infinite Eternal (Ein Sof). This is the Celestial Triad of the emanations: I AM, Wisdom, and Understanding—from which all of the emanations are expressed. We will study the emanations in detail in the next chapter.

This is the plane of the powers of God, the Divine Visages (*partzufim*), and the Brilliant Light. Here is the realm of the Infinite God, the Omnipotent, All-knowing, Universal Mind and Spirit. This plane is also known as the "Boundless World of Divine Names" and "Rings of Sacred Names." All of creation is in this plane but in its uncontaminated state, pure as the moment it was divinely conceived. The perfection of this realm is not affected by what goes on in the lower realms; however, the ideal of this perfection is in all the realms below it.

Here the ten emanations of God are maintained as the Lights—pure and brilliant—eternal and untouched by the lower realms. To touch this realm or live in it is to be in ecstasy, bliss, nirvana, samadhi, and all the other terms humans have used to describe this peace that passes understanding and yields complete contentment. One is what one was meant to be.

2. Plane of Creation (Olam Briah)

The second realm is the Plane of Creation, also known as the plane of conception. That which came out of "the deep" expresses its quintessence. Here are the Creative Forces. This is the dimension of the Moral Triad of the emanations: Mercy, Judgment, and Beauty. This is the plane of the archangels and divine souls (neshamot mekoriyyah). Here is the Lord of Hosts. The life essence of the Creator permeates this realm, giving goodness to all.

This plane is also known as the "Archangelic World of Creations," revealing that it is the dimension of the archangels who play a major role in the whole of creation.

In the first plane, the ten emanations of God are called Lights; in this plane they are called Spirits—divine beings who serve in the establishing of orders and intelligences throughout the seen and unseen universes.

3. Plane of Formation (Olam Yetzirah)

The third plane is the Plane of Formation. Here the unseen essences take form, in the sense of energies and consciousnesses, not bodies. This is the Mundane Triad of the emanations: Persistence (Victory), Surrender (Splendor), and Remembrance (Foundation). This is the plane of angels and the Orphanim (Never–sleeping Watchers/Guardians). Here we find the laws that shape the patterns of creation and form the sevens: seven heavens, seven planets, seven chakras, seven ages, and so on. Here we find the higher element of ether, or akasha in Sanskrit; this is the most subtle and expansive of the five elements. Every thought, word, and action of every soul makes an impression upon the akasha and may be "read." This is the Book of Life of each soul.

Here the ten emanations of God are called the "Hierarchies of Celestial Beings," sometimes referred to as Choirs.

4. Plane of Actions (Olam Asiyah)

The fourth plane is the Plane of Actions. It is the physical realm where the created engage their wills to do as they desire and experience the result, experience the reaction—which we know to be karma. This is the plane of inferior and fallen angels and the broken vessels (Kellipot) that were not perfect enough to contain and pass along the Light of the I AM as it flowed out of the Infinite Eternal (Ein Sof). Here we find the four elements of the lower plane: solid/matter (earth), liquid/fluid (water), plasma (fire), and gas/vapor (air). In this realm we find the physical universe, particularly our galaxy, and the forces of the zodiac, the seven planets, the two great lights of the sun and moon, and the realm of testing: earth, the causal world.

This plane is also called the "Elemental Plane of Substance."

In this plane the ten emanations of God are called "Shells" (Kellipot). This is also the realm of demons, tempters, and distortions. The shells and demons are listed as the dark, or shadow, side and consist of the "Twins of God" (Thaumiel), the "Two-Headed" (doubled-mindedness, wanting God and mammon), Satan, Moloch (the impious god of fire sacrifices), Adam Belial ("Wicked Being"), "Confusion of God's Power" (Chaigidel), "Those Who Go Forth into the Place Empty of God" (Ghogiel), Beelzebub ("Lord of Flies"), Lucifuge (opposite of Lucifer the Light Bearer, this name means "Flees the Light"), Devourers or Wasters (Gamchicoth), Destroyers (Golachab, Golab, and Usiel), "Builders of Ugliness" (Thagirion), Lord of Darkness (Baal), desolation (Samael), pollution (Gamaliel), and frightening sounds and strange desires (Nehemoth). These are the shells and demons that plague this realm. However, there are Light Forces battling these dark influences all the time—each struggling for the souls and minds of the incarnate.

This brings us to the forces of "Repairing and Perfecting the Plane" (Tikkun Olam). In Lurianic Kabbalah, the vessels that shattered because they could not contain and distribute the original Light of God, and their shards became sparks of light; but these are trapped within the material of creation. Contemplative prayer releases these sparks and allows them to reunite with God's essence, thus repairing this plane and restoring God's essence throughout it. This is a promised time when Satan is bound and the earth goes through a golden age of no evil, no temptation, and God's essence is manifest in the material plane.

Cayce and the Planes

Cayce's discourses often address planes. In one reading he confirms the Kabbalah's four (five, if using Lurianic Kabbalah) planes but adds that much has developed since those original times, indicating that there are now more planes!

> In most every group that has approached such subjects, *planes* are rarely understood. They are accounted as to the first, second, third, fourth, fifth plane; yet we find *these* only in the beginnings of the activities of those influences of the souls of men.   EC 507-2

He explains:

> In flesh must the entity manifest, and make the will one with the God, or Creative Force, in the Universe, and as such development reaches that plane, wherein the development may pass into other spheres and systems, of which our solar system is only a small part; in this, then, is meant the entity must develop in that sphere until it (the entity) has reached that stage wherein it may manifest through the *spiritual planes*, as would be called from the relation to physical or fleshly plane.
> EC 900-25; italics mine

Cayce teaches that a soul must progress through all the planes to become completely companionable to its Creator:

> In the soul's development to reach that plane wherein the whole entity may become one with that creative forces, that creative energy, that Oneness with the God, this we find needs then that development through all the planes in the Universal Forces, or throughout the Universe; hence the necessity of developing in that plane. All bearing, then, the relative condition, position, action, state of being, to that creative force, and that created.   EC 900-24

In one reading (900–355) Cayce correlates "planes of conditions" with "phases of consciousness," giving us that most modern of concepts: growth and transformation occur within the mind and progress through various phases of awareness and understanding. Other planes are not reached by traveling to them but by developing *awareness* of them. Such awareness may not be fully in the conscious mind except by an intuitive knowing. But Cayce would say that it is certainly a reality in the deeper subconscious and superconscious level of a person's mind.

As man passes into the spiritual plane from earthly existence, the development in the spiritual plane becoming the same evolution in spiritual planes as is acquired in the physical plane, and until man becomes in the spiritual sense the oneness with the Creator's forces, as is set by example of the Son of Man coming in the flesh to the earth plane to manifest in the flesh the will made one with the Father, passing through the physical plane, passing through the spiritual planes, making *all* one with the Father. This we find then is evolution. Man's development through man's acquiring man's understanding of spiritual laws, of earthly laws, of God's laws, and applying same in the earth. Then truly is it given, "The righteous shall inherit the earth."   EC 900-70

One of the most fascinating aspects of Cayce's views on planes of consciousness is his concept that this entire solar system, which we see as a star with nine planets, is actually a university for the soul with nine colleges that focus on individual disciplines of learning, disciplines that match the classical teachings of ancient astrology! In other words, Mercury is the college of mental development; Venus of art, music, and personal love, and so on. Thus, souls do not just incarnate in the physical realm of earth alone to learn and apply themselves to soul growth; during time between earthly incarnations, the souls actually dwell in spheres of activity associated with the nine planets and their special focus. To follow is one of the most fascinating of Cayce's readings. It divulges how a soul passes from incarnation to planetary sojourn and back to incarnation again and again until it is sufficiently developed to be free of these lessons. This reading was requested by Cayce himself.

Note: The initials GC refer to Gertrude Cayce, Edgar's wife and frequent conductor of his sessions. Cayce's readings, because of their King James Bible language and odd syntax, are difficult to read; nevertheless, they are quite packed with insights. Reading slowly may be helpful. Bracketed comments are the stenographer's comments or references. Those in parentheses are Cayce's asides or additions. Italicized comments in brackets are my added details to help you understand the whole story.

GC: In all Life Readings given through this channel there are references to sojourns of the soul-entity between incarnations on the earth plane, in various planes of consciousness represented by the other planets in our solar system. You will give at this time a discourse which will explain what takes place in soul development in each of these states of consciousness in their order relative to the evolution of the soul; explaining what laws govern this movement from plane to plane, their influence on life in this earth plane and what if any relationship these planes have to astrology.

EC: Yes, we have the information and sources from which same may be obtained as to individual experiences, sojourns and their influence.

As we find, in attempting to give a coherent explanation of that as may be sought, or as may be made applicable in the experience of individuals who seek to apply such information, it is well that an individual soul-entity, the record of whose astrological and earthly sojourns you have, be used as an example.

Then a comparison may be drawn for those who would judge same from the astrological aspects, as well as from the astrological or planetary sojourns of such individuals. What better example may be used, then, than this entity with whom you are dealing [Edgar Cayce? Case 294].

Rather than the aspects of the material sojourn, then, we would give them from the astrological:

From an astrological aspect, then, the greater influence at the entrance of this entity that ye call Cayce was from Uranus. Here we find the extremes. The sojourn in Uranus was arrived at from what type of experience or activity of the entity? [*Another Cayce reading identifies Uranus, with Venus as a second influence, as the dimensional sojourn of Cayce's soul prior to this incarnation as Edgar Cayce.*] As Bainbridge [*one of Cayce's two prior incar-*

nations in early America using this same name], the entity in the material sojourn was a wastrel, one who considered only self; having to know the extremes in the own experience as well as others. Hence the entity was drawn to that environ. Or, how did the Master put it? "As the tree falls, so does it lie." [Ecclesiastes 11:3 by Solomon.] Then in the Uranian sojourn there are the influences from the astrological aspects of *extremes*; and counted in thy own days from the very position of that attunement, that tone, that color. For it is not strange that music, color, vibration are all a part of the planets, just as the planets are a part— and a pattern—of the whole universe. Hence to that attunement which it had merited, which it had meted in itself, was the entity drawn for the experience. What form, what shape?

The birth of the entity into Uranus was not from the earth into Uranus, but from those stages of consciousness through which each entity or soul passes. It passes into oblivion as it were, save for its consciousness that there is a way, there is a light, there is an understanding, there have been failures and there are needs for help. Then help *consciously* is sought!

Hence the entity passes along those stages that some have seen as planes, some have seen as steps, some have seen as cycles, and some have experienced as places.

How far? How far is tomorrow to any soul? How far is yesterday from thy consciousness?

You are *in* same (that is, all time as one time), yet become gradually aware of it; passing through, then, as it were, God's record or book of consciousness or of remembrance; for meeting, being measured out as it were to that to which thou hast attained.

Who hath sought? Who hath understood?

Only they that seek shall find!

Then, born in what body? That as befits that plane of consciousness; the *extremes*, as ye would term same.

As to what body—what has thou abused? What hast thou used? What hast thou applied? What has thou neglected in thy extremes, thy extremities?

These are consciousnesses, these are bodies.

To give them form or shape—you have no word, you have no form in a three-dimensional world or plane of consciousness to give it to one in the seventh—have you?

Hence that's the form—we might say—"Have You?"

What is the form of this in thy consciousness? It rather indicates that everyone is questioned, "Have you? Have You?"

That might be called the form. It is that which is thy concept of that being asked thyself—not that ye have formed of another.

With that sojourn then the entity finds need for, as it were, the giving expression of same again (the answering of "Have You?") in that sphere of consciousness in which there is a way in and through which one may become aware of the experience, the expression and the manifesting of same in a three-dimensional plane.

Hence the entity was born into the earth under what signs? Pisces, ye say. Yet astrologically from the records, these are some two signs off in thy reckoning. [Cayce noted in other readings that the tropical zodiacal eph-emerides used today have not accounted for the gradual precession of the equinox over the years; thus the signs are currently 30° off, or different from, their physical loca-tion, or actual constellations (signs).]

Then from what is the influence drawn? Not merely because Pisces is accredited with an influence of such a nature, but because it is! And the "Have You" becomes then "There Is" or "I Am" in materiality or flesh, or material forces—even as He who has passed this way!

The entity as Bainbridge was born in the English land under the sign, as ye would term, of Scorpio; or from Venus as the second influence.

We find that the activity of the same entity in the earthly experience before that, in a French sojourn, followed the entrance into Venus. [Cayce's soul incarnated for only nine years in France, passing on at this young age with a "broken heart" to the plane of Venus.]

What was the life there? How the application?

A child of love! A child of love—the most hopeful of all experiences of any that may come into a material existence; and to some in the earth that most dreaded, that most feared!

(These side remarks become more overburdening than what you are trying to obtain! but you've opened a big subject, haven't you?)

In Venus the body-form is near to that in the three dimensional plane. For it is what may be said to be rather all-inclusive! For it is that ye would call love—which, to be sure, may be licentious, selfish; which also may be so large, so inclusive as to take on the less of self and more of the ideal, more of that which is *giving*.

What is love? Then what is Venus? It is beauty, love, hope, charity—yet all of these have their extremes. But these extremes are not in the expressive nature or manner as may be found in that tone or attunement of Uranus; for they (in Venus) are more in the order that they blend as one with another. [*Cayce's readings often noted that Uranus brings the extremes, not the blending, as Venus.*]

So the entity passed through that experience, and on entering into materiality abused same; as the wastrel who sought those expressions of same in the loveliness for self alone, without giving—giving of self in return for same. [*Here speaking of the incarnation as Bainbridge, first in precolonial America and then again in Ohio during the French and Indian period.*]

Hence we find the influences wielded in the sojourn of the entity from the astrological aspects or emotions of the mental nature are the ruling, yet must be governed by a standard.

And when self is the standard, it becomes very distorted in materiality.

Before that we find the influence was drawn for a universality of activity from Jupiter; in those experiences of the entity's sojourn or activity as the minister or teacher in Lucius. [*Bishop of the early* Jewish/Christian *congregation at Laodicea in Asia Minor.*] For the entity gave for the gospel's sake, a love, an activity and a hope through things that had become as of a universal nature.

Yet coming into the Roman influence from the earthly sojourn in Troy, we find that the entity through the Jupiterian environment was trained—as we understand—by being tempered to give self from the very universality, the very bigness of those activities in Jupiter.

For the sojourn in Troy was as the soldier, the carrying out of the order given, with a claim for activities pertaining to world affairs—a spreading. [*This was one of Cayce's most difficult incarnations, so much so that he committed suicide after Troy was lost to the Greeks.*]

What form, ye ask, did he take? That which may be described as in the circle with the dot, in which there is the turning within ever if ye will know the answer to thy problems; no matter in what stage of thy consciousness ye may be. For "Lo, I meet thee *within* thy holy temple," is the promise. [*The circle and the dot compose the symbol for the Egyptian god Ra, one of Cayce's best incarnations. But the next incarnation is in ancient Persia; then comes Troy. As you can see, the reading is taking him back through his major incarnations toward the first ones.*]

And the pattern is ever, "have you?" In other words, have you love? or the circle within, and not for self? but that He that giveth power, that meeteth within, may be magnified? Have you rather abased self that the glory may be magnified that thou didst have with Him before the worlds were, before a division of consciousness came?

These become as it were a part of thy experiences, then, through the astrological sojourns or environs from which all take their turn, their attunement.

And we find that the experience of the entity before that, as Uhjltd, was from even without the sphere of thine own orb; for the entity came from those centers about which thine own solar system moves—in Arcturus. [*Cayce's readings identify the star Arcturus as the star gate in and out of this solar system. Having come from Arcturus means that his soul was in a more universal condition before this incarnation, thus bringing great wisdom and understanding with him.*]

For there had come from those activities, in Uhjltd, the knowledge of the oneness, and of those forces and powers that would set as it were the universality of its relationships, through its unity of purpose in all spheres of human experience; by the entity becoming how? Not aliens, then—not bastards before the Lord—but sons—co-heirs with Him in the Father's kingdom.

Yet the quick return to the earthly sojourn in Troy, and the abuse of these, the turning of these for self—in the activities attempted—brought about the changes that were wrought.

But the entrance into the Ra-Ta experience, when there was the journeying from materiality—or the being translated in materiality as Ra-Ta—was from the infinity forces, or from the Sun; with those influences that draw upon the planet itself, the earth and all those about same. [*Ra-Ta was the name of Cayce's soul incarnate in ancient Egypt. Ra-Ta became High Priest during a very early and exciting time in Egypt.*]

Is it any wonder that in the ignorance of the earth the activities of that entity were turned into that influence called the sun worshippers?

This was because of the abilities of its influences in the experiences of each individual, and the effect upon those things of the earth in nature itself; because of the atmosphere, the forces as they take form from the vapors created even by same; and the very natures or influences upon vegetation!

The very natures or influences from the elemental forces themselves were drawn in those activities of the elements within the earth, that could give off their vibrations because of the influences that attracted or draw away from one another.

This was produced by that which had come into the experiences in materiality, or into being, as the very nature of water with the sun's rays; or the ruler of thy own little solar system, thy own little nature in the form ye may see in the earth!

Hence we find how, as ye draw your patterns from these, that they become a part of the whole. For ye are *relatively* related to all that ye have contacted in materiality, mentality, spirituality! All of these are a portion of thyself in the material plane.

In taking form they become a mental body with its longings for its home, with right and righteousness.

Then that ye know as thy mental self is the form taken, with all of its variations as combined from the things it has been within, without, and in relationship to the activities in materiality as well as in the spheres or various consciousness of "Have you—love, the circle, the Son?"

These become then as the signs of the entity, and ye may draw these from the pattern which has been set. Just as the desert experience, the lines drawn in the temple as represented by the pyramid, the sun, the water, the well, the sea and the ships upon same—because of the very nature of expression—become the *pattern* of the entity in this material plane.   EC 5755-1

Each soul has a story similar to this one, of sojourns in nonphysical realms or planes and incarnations into the physical dimensions of this world, all for the purpose of soul growth. Each of us eventually becomes companionable to the Creator of the entire cosmos, our celestial, infinite Father and Mother, who love us and long for our conscious companionship and co-creative sharing of the creation.

5

EMANATIONS OF GOD

The Infinite Eternal (Ein Sof) reveals its nature through ten emanations (sefirot). These emanations reflect attributes of the Infinite Eternal that reveal the Divinity's energy, consciousness, and qualities.

The life force of the Infinite Eternal flows from the hidden Creator throughout the observable creation in a specific pattern depicted in the Tree of Life. See illustrations 1 through 7. The emanations and the Tree are the mystical "image of God" (*tzelem Elokim;* also *tselem Elohim*). Since we were created in the image of God (Genesis 1:26), the emanations and the Tree reveal how we are constructed and how the Life Energy flows through us.

The Tree is like a map of the macrocosm of the universe and the microcosm within us. Our spiritual journey into existence and to re-union with the Creator follows according to the Tree and its emanating orbs. Think of these emanations as metaphysical orbs of the Divinity's energy, consciousness, and qualities.

The origin of the term *sefirot* (plural of *sefirah,* sometimes written *sephiroth* or *shephirah*) remains a mystery of antiquity. The Hebrew word SPHR (remember, there are no vowels in the language) means "to form," especially to form in a sphere or orb. Some writers point out that this term is akin to the Egyptian term *khefer,* also meaning "to form," but in the context of the sacred Egyptian beetle, Khephra or Khefra, which rolls its dung into a ball and toward the rising sun in the morning. It plants a seed in the dung ball, and by high noon, new life awakens—symbolizing resurrection from the dung of material life by cooperating with the sun or Ra, the sun god, seen as the source of light and life.

Some writers believe sefirah refers to numbering rather than form-

ing spheres. Thus, the emanations reflect the sequence of their formation and rank. Whatever the case, each sefirah is an orb and a number
representing an energy, a consciousness, a vibration, and a disposition
(or arrangement).

The word *sefirah* may also mean, in some contexts, "to write" and "to
speak," associated with the word *lesaper*, "to express," "to communicate."
Thus the emanations are an expression, a communication from the Infinite Eternal to the created.

These emanations are comparable to Gnosticism's aions, syzygies,
sonships, and light kings. In Gnosticism, all emanations are paired; in
Kabbalah, only six of the ten emanations are paired: Wisdom with Understanding, Mercy with Judgment, and Victory with Splendor. See illustration 1.

Kabbalah teaches that when the Creation burst forth from the darkness of the deep, it did so with such intense brilliance, awesome power,
and extreme velocity that it broke wide open all the orbs (*shevirat ha-
keilim*: "breaking of the vessels"). The orbs were unable to contain the
Light (*netzotzot*)—that is, all except the *tenth* orb: Kingdom and the little "I
am" of those created in the image of the Great I AM. Wonderfully the
contained Light then flowed backward to its Creator, gathering all the
shards (*kelipot*) of the broken orbs and repairing them! Miraculously the
image of God as expressed in the Tree of Life was whole again for all of
creation to comprehend.

Before the repair, chaos reigned. As the Light flowed backward, order
was reestablished. The Infinite was now revealed in a balanced manner.
According to Kabbalah, this balance was achieved by "hinging" energies
and perspectives that appeared to be opposing forces, but in the balance, they complemented one another in specific triads, or trinities.

Three primary, triangular balances were created. In the first triad, the
Godhead of the great "I AM" (emanation 1: Crown) held in balance the
"Father of Fathers" (emanation 2: Wisdom) and the "Mother of Mothers"
(emanation 3: Understanding). In the second triad, Beauty (emanation
6) held in balance Mercy (emanation 4) and Judgment (emanation 5).
And, in the third triad, Foundation (emanation 9) held in balance Splendor (emanation 8) and Victory (emanation 7). These triads are depicted
in illustration 3.

With all of these repaired, in balance, fully illuminated, energized, and conscious, the Light and Life flowed evenly throughout the creation—from the Creator to the created and back again. All was in balance and in harmonic motion.

From a Kabbalistic perspective, "sin" is a separation of a portion of the Tree of Life from the whole. When this happens, the flow is broken, the balance lost. To restore health and well-being, reunion must be achieved. This reunion includes the rebalancing of the energy, consciousness, and qualities of the orb that has been separated.

Knowledge of these ten emanations provides us with ten precepts (rules), ten energies, and ten paths that lead us closer to our true nature and our ultimate destiny. By understanding these and applying them in our lives, we gradually become more heavenly, more eternal—less temporary, less materialistic, and less bound and constrained by the limitations of our physical reality. As our consciousness expands, our heavenly heart grows, and the forces of eternal life flow through us with strength and vigor, illuminating our minds and souls. Life, love, and relationships are enlivened. The purpose and meaning of life and relationships are more apparent, even if only intuitively understood. When these are applied properly in our daily lives, we naturally become better people—better friends, neighbors, spouses, and parents. We gain a patience that is rare in this world, a patience that changes the very dynamics of a physical life and awakens the spiritual life.

When we view the Tree of Life's structure (illustrations 1 through 7), we see ten orbs, three triads, three pillars, and twenty-two pathways. This structure is purposeful and reveals important details for us to use in our soul growth and journey. As we continue our study, we will examine these.

Here is a quotation (the first several paragraphs) from one of the seminal works of Kabbalah: The Book of Creation (Sefer Yetzirah):

Ten and not nine, ten and not eleven. Understand with wisdom, and be wise with understanding. Test them and investigate them; know and ponder, and form (a mental image). Explain the matter clearly, and restore the Creator to his place. And their measure is ten, for they have no end.

Restrain your heart from thinking; restrain your mouth from speaking. And if your heart races, return to the place from whence you came. Their measure is ten, for they have no end. Their end is fixed in their beginning as the flame is bound to the burning coal (Ezekiel 1:13). Know and ponder, and form (a mental image) that the Lord is unique and the Creator one, and he has none second to him; and before one, what can you count? Their measure is ten, for they have no end—dimension of beginning and dimension of end, dimension of good and dimension of evil, dimension of above and dimension of below, dimension of east and dimension of west, dimension of north and dimension of south. And the unique Lord, a trustworthy divine king, rules over them all from his holy abode forever and ever. Looking at them is like looking at lightning, and their end? They have no limit. His word is in them as though running (Ezekiel 1:14), and they pursue his command like the storm wind, and before his throne they bow down. Ten sefirot and twenty-two fundamental letters, three matrices, seven double letters, and twelve simple ones; and the Spirit is one of them [or *one in them all*]. One—the Spirit of the Living God; His throne is established from of old (Psalms 93:2). Twice blessed is the name of him who lives forever. Voice, and breath, and speech—this is the Holy Spirit (also, Sacred Breath).

Let's examine each of the ten emanations, from those closer to heaven to those closer to earth, remembering that the Divine is in all of them in a balanced manner.

Emanation 1
The Crown and the "I AM"

The first emanation is the Crown, the "I AM" of the "I am that I am." (Exodus 3:14) It is the emanation of the unseen Creator *as* the Godhead, the biblical "Most High" God. The Creator's Essence emerged from "the deep" (Genesis 1:2) as a light piercing the endless darkness—the first brilliant, shining orb, out of which the remaining emanations emerged. The plan of the entire universe is contained in this first emanation. The concept of unity amid diversity was born and is maintained here.

Some Kabbalists believe the first emanation "shields" the physical universe and the creation from the blinding Light of the original Creative Spirit. In this mission it is considered to be the Concealed Consciousness, veiled from manifested life. Some believe it is unknowable. Others teach that it is indeed knowable but only after one has ascended to a much higher level of vibration and consciousness than most humans possess. This sphere of being is the highest state of consciousness and the most sublime vibration, second only to the united harmony of the whole Tree. The Crown is both our origin and our destiny. We came from it and are destined to unite with it again. One may think of it as God-consciousness.

When the Great I AM conceived us, it put a bit of itself in each of us, the little "I am" of the Great I AM. This explains God's answer to Moses when he asked what name he should use with the people waiting for his return: "I am that I am." Our sense of "I am" is a reflection of the Supreme Being, the Great I AM, who conceived us and is always within us.

Here are Cayce's comments on this:

When ye say Creative Force, God, Jehovah, Yahweh, Abba, what meanest thou? . . . In the various phases of thine own consciousness; or of those who in their activities seek, as thou (if thou seekest aright), [seek] to be one with Him yet to *know* self to *be* self, I *am*, in and with the *Great I AM*.   EC 262-86

Life—or the motivative force of a soul—is eternal; and that portion of same that is motivated by the mental and spiritual attributes of an entity has experienced, does experience the influences that have guided or prompted same through its sojourns.

For each soul seeks expression. And as it moves through the mental associations and attributes in the surrounding environs, it gives out that which becomes either for selfish reactions of [its] own ego—to express—or for the I AM to be at-one with the Great I AM THAT I AM.

What then are the purposes for the activities of an entity in a material plane, surrounded with those environs that make for self-expressions or self-activities in the various ways and manners?

What meaneth these? That self is growing to that which it, the entity, the soul, is to present, as it were, to the Great I AM in those experiences when it is absent from materiality.

These become hard at times for the individual to visualize; that the mental and soul may manifest without a physical vehicle. Yet in the deeper meditations, in those experiences when those influences may arise when the spirit of the Creative Force, the universality of soul, of mind—not as material, not as judgments, not *in* time and space but *of* time and space—may become lost in the Whole, instead of the entity being lost in the maze of confusing influences—then the soul visions arise in the meditations.   EC 987-4

Notice that the first emanation on the Tree of Life has a direct connection with the tenth emanation, exactly as the Great I AM has with the little "I am."

The crown also symbolizes rulership, and the Scriptures teach that we are heirs to the kingdom of our Father.

> Hearken, my beloved brethren; did not God choose them that are poor as to the world to be rich in faith, and heirs of the kingdom which he promised to them that love him?
>
> James 2:5

As difficult as it may be to accept, we are sons and daughters of the Creator:

> God has taken his place in the divine council; in the midst of the gods he holds judgment. I said, "You are gods, sons [and daughters] of the Most High, all of you."
>
> Psalm 82:2, 6; RSV

How do we, who are so far from this awareness and level of being, reach our godly potential? From Cayce's readings we find that the crown is gained by bearing the cross of subduing our earthly, selfish tendencies. Consider these two Bible passages:

God created man in his own image. In God's image he created him; male and female he created them. God blessed them. God said to them, "Be fruitful, multiply, fill the earth, and *subdue* it." Genesis 1:27-28, RSV; italics mine

God said to Cain, "Sin is crouching at the door [of your mind and heart]; its desire is for you, but you must *master* it." Genesis 4:7, RSV; italics mine

Cayce's readings say:

Each in their respective lives, their own experiences, find their cross overcoming the world, overcoming those things, those conditions, those experiences, that would not only enable them to meet the issues of life but to become heirs with Him of the Crown of Glory. EC 262-36

Think about this. How could a three-dimensional, physical being, with a materialistic mind and a heart full of earthly desires, reach into the consciousness and presence of the Creator of the entire universe and all that is in it? It would require a significant transformation and transcendence. Fortunately, there is powerful help. Also, the transition is accomplished one step at a time—here a little, there a little—until the whole journey is complete and the crown is received.

The writers of Kabbalah consider this first state of consciousness to be "Concealed Consciousness."

Emanation 2
Wisdom

The God-consciousness of the first emanation naturally leads to the second emanation: Wisdom. Such wisdom comes not from knowledge, experience, or study but from receptiveness to God and God's responding blessing. The Scriptures have this to say:

> Where shall wisdom be found? And where is the place of
> understanding? Man knoweth not the price thereof; neither
> is it found in the land of the living. The deep saith, "It is not
> in me"; and the sea saith, "It is not with me." It cannot be
> gotten for gold, neither shall silver be weighed for the price
> thereof. Whence then cometh wisdom? And where is the
> place of understanding? Seeing it is hid from the eyes of all
> living, and kept close from the birds of the heavens, De-
> struction and Death say, "We have heard a rumor thereof
> with our ears. God understands the way thereof, and he
> knows the place thereof."
>
> Job 28: 12-28; American Standard Version, ASV

God knows the place where wisdom hides, and contact with God
brings this wisdom. As we lift our minds up to God, expanding our
consciousness into the infinite mind of God, we gain this wisdom. It is
an inner knowing that comes to us as from out of nowhere, seemingly
from everywhere. The more we lift ourselves into God–consciousness,
the more we become godlike.

This wisdom is like intuition. It is humble, not self-exalting. It even
surprises us at times because we know we did not conceive it; it simply
came upon us, a natural consequence of our increasing proximity to
God's all-knowing mind.

Surprisingly, throughout the Scriptures, a criterion for wisdom is "fear
of the Lord." In this passage from the book of Job, we find this same idea
expressed by God:

> And unto man He [God] said, "Behold, the fear of the Lord,
> that is wisdom; and to depart from evil is understanding."
>
> Job 28:28

And Cayce offered this insight:

Wisdom, then, is fear to misapply knowledge in thy dealings with thyself [and] thy fellow man. For as ye are honest, as ye are patient, as ye are sincere with thyself in thy meeting with thy God, thy Savior, thy Christ, in thy meditation, ye will be in thy dealings with thy fellow man.

EC 281-28

Fear of the Lord may be understood as the fear to misapply knowledge we gain from our growing relationship with the All-Knowing. Imagine how disciplined we would have to be if we gained all-knowingness. If we knew the hearts and minds of everyone we met, we'd have to have control of our human tendency to judge, even condemn. If we gained precognitive knowing, imagine how tempted we would be to abuse this advantage. Thus, to avoid shattering the vessel of our own consciousness, the orb of our being must first hold to an alert concern for misapplication of the knowledge God's presence bestows upon us. This is the beginning of wisdom.

Throughout this book, as we read Cayce's comments in reference to Kabbalistic teachings, many will contain references to Christ; so for those of you who are not of a Christian persuasion or who are former Christians, understand that Cayce's view of Christ goes beyond the dogma of the church or evangelistic persuasion. In reading 281-13, Cayce equates Christ with "love of the God-consciousness," and in discourse 991-1, he explains, "*Christ* is not a man! *Jesus* was the man; Christ the messenger; Christ in all ages, Jesus in one, Joshua in another, Melchizedek in another; *these* be those that led Judaism!" And in the next reading, he gives more insight:

Jesus is the man—the activity, the mind, the relationships that He bore to others. Yea, He was mindful of friends, He was sociable, He was loving, He was kind, He was gentle. He grew faint, He grew weak—and yet gained that strength that He has promised, in becoming the Christ, by fulfilling and overcoming the world! Ye are made strong—in body, in mind, in soul and purpose—by that power in Christ. The *power*, then, is in the Christ. The *pattern* is in Jesus.   2533-7

Returning to the emanation of Wisdom, a key to "receiving" (as the term Kabbalah means "to receive") the emanation of wisdom is selflessness. As the individual empties itself of its own interests, desires, and willfulness, it makes room for God to flow in.

The consciousness Kabbalists associate with this emanation is the Illuminating Consciousness. This consciousness generates action. It is a light that seeks to reach out. We have the creative plan in the Crown; now we have the impetus, the enlightened and inspired desire to bring forward the creation according to the plan. Action is a quality of wisdom.

Cayce agrees with this Kabbalistic view of wisdom, saying that for knowledge or understanding to become wisdom, it must be applied in life. Wisdom results from action. Wisdom is the creative plan in action. It is not a static state of being or knowing. God gives the gift and we apply it in life.

This emanation is considered to be masculine, and as such, it is known as the Father of Fathers. It is also considered to be Eden, in the sense that the Garden was the prototype, or pattern, for companionship with our Creator. In the midst of this Garden is the Water of Life. Writers of Kabbalah have called it the "Wisdom–Gushing Fountain," the "Water of the Wise," that bathes and nourishes those who enjoy the counsel of God, enabling them to share their lives and consciousness with their Creator's in communion through prayer, meditation, inner listening, and being conduits of God's love and grace to others.

Emanation 3
Understanding and Insight

The Crown of God–consciousness and the subsequent Wisdom that follow lead to the third emanation: Understanding. Here the individual soul's mind gains perception, comprehension, and appreciation.

These first three emanations are beautifully expressed in the following passages of Scripture:

> Get wisdom; get understanding. Forget it not; neither decline from the words of my mouth. Forsake her not, and she shall preserve thee. Love her, and she shall keep thee. Wisdom is the principal thing; therefore get wisdom. And with

all thy getting get understanding. Exalt her, and she shall promote thee. She shall bring thee to honor, when thou dost embrace her. She shall give to your head an ornament of grace, a *crown* of glory shall she deliver to thee.

Proverbs 4:5-9, KJV; italics mine

Cayce combines virtue with understanding in his discourses, explaining:

> Well that this be understood, that virtue and understanding deals primarily with self and self's relationship to the Creative Forces, or God, and that virtue and understanding in self is *reflected* in self, rather than a *judgment* upon another. Judge self by thine understanding and thine own virtue, *not* another—for these are of the spirit and must be judged by the spirit.
>
> EC 262-19

He continues this line of thought by stating that virtue and understanding are attributes we develop as we seek to develop a relationship with the Creative Forces, and part of this process includes our relationships with others. (EC 262–20) How we interact with others directly affects our personal relationship with God, because God reaches out to us, to all God's children, even those who are far from God–consciousness.

This discussion of the interrelatedness of our relationship with God and our relationship with others is reminiscent of a biblical teaching about the greatest commandment:

> A lawyer asked him a question, to test him. "Teacher, which is the great commandment in the law?" And he said to him, "You shall love the Lord your God with all your heart, and with all your soul, and with all your mind. This is the great and first commandment. And a second is like it, you shall love your neighbor as yourself. On these two commandments depend all the law and the prophets."
>
> Matthew 22:36-40; WEB

In this answer, Jesus is quoting from Deuteronomy 6:5 for the first commandment, and from Leviticus 19:18 for the second. But the point we
need to catch here is that loving others is "like" loving God, as the
second commandment is like the first. How can this be, when we may
more easily develop a good relationship with God than we can with
others? We may see others as so difficult to live with—so muddled, so
willful, so diverse in their ways. The answer lies in a realization that the
God we love, though very personal, is in fact infinite, and all beings
exist within God; and God cares about them all. In fact, the piece of God
placed in us is also in each of them—as imperfect as they (and we) may
be. This is the understanding required of us, and in order to fulfill the
second commandment, we must change our focus to minimize their
weaknesses and vices, and maximize their strengths and virtues. This
then reflects again upon us as a natural effect of the law of karma, of
action and reaction. If we understand and minimize others' weaknesses
and vices, our weaknesses and vices will be understood and minimized.

The emanation of Understanding is considered to be female, and as
such, it is the Mother of Mothers. The Mother (Understanding) blends
with the Father (Wisdom) to produce the Logos, the central monad of all
consciousness.

Here we come to a complexity of these teachings that we need to
consider. The vast, infinite, unseen essence of God, interacting with the
spirit of the emanated Father and Mother, created the Logos—what
Kabbalah calls Adam Kadmon, meaning "Primal Being." This is very
similar to the Hindu teaching of the Cosmic Beingness—Purusha—the
original self-awareness that pervades the entire creation and is the state
of God's being made knowable. The Logos allows our conscious communion with God.

The Primal Being, or the Logos, is not an intermediary keeping us
from direct contact with our Creator, as some write, but a conduit from
where we are to where God's pure, pre-Creation presence abides. The
Logos is one with Concealed God; it is a comprehendible expression of
Concealed God. Remember, the brilliance and awesome energy of the
Infinite Eternal One had to retreat into the deep for the Creation to
occur. Through the expression of Father (wisdom) and Mother (understanding), and their blending, we have an access to the Creator, whose

presence will not destroy us; this is the Logos. The Logos is the Avatar of all avatars, the Collective Consciousness of all consciousnesses. It is the Messiah prophesied by the archangel Gabriel to the prophet Daniel. Each individual may unite its consciousness with this Universal Consciousness, and in its role as Messiah, it redeems and enlightens everyone who opens and receives it.

Jesus, filled with the Spirit of the Logos, explained it this way:

> In that day you will know that I am in my Father, and you in me, and I in you.   John 14:20

> In that day you will ask in my name; and I do not say to you that I shall pray the Father for you; for the Father himself loves you.   John 16: 26

Here are the first lines of John's Gospel:

> In the beginning was the Word (Logos), and the Word was with God, and the Word was God. This One was in the beginning with God; all things were made through this One, and without this One was not anything made that was made. In this One was life, and the life was the light of men. The light shines in the darkness, and the darkness has not overcome it.   John 1:1-5

Note: There is no masculine pronoun in the original text; the term is "this One," not "he," as in so many Bible translations of this passage.

As you can see from this passage, we are speaking about the Primal Being, its consciousness and its role.

It was the Primal Being (Adam Kadmon) who communed with God in the Garden of Eden. The Primal Being is the Father of Fathers, the Mother of Mothers, and all the children live within its Universal Consciousness. This means that a deep aspect of ourselves communed with God in the Garden.

This consciousness touches the pre–Creation God's Concealed Consciousness, and it is through this Logos that we come to know the Infinite Eternal One—albeit intuitively, in a manner that is a knowing unlike normal human knowing. More on this as we continue.

Writers of Kabbalah consider the consciousness of this emanation to be the "Sanctifying Mind." We can see how this fits well with the effect of the Messiah consciousness on our minds.

The triad of the first three emanations—I AM, the Father of Fathers, and the Mother of Mothers—creates the center essence of all consciousness, all life. From out of this triad, at the top of the Tree of Life, comes all the following emanations.

Emanation 4
Loving Kindness and Mercy

Now we move into the heart (not the pump). Here we have the sphere of the fourth emanation: Loving Kindness and Mercy. If we are to know God, to companion with our Creator, then we must become loving and merciful, for these are attributes of God.

When God directed the building of that most mysterious device for communicating directly with Him—the Ark of the Covenant—one of the last features to be added was a mercy seat, protected by two angels. God instructed Moses:

> You shall make a mercy seat of pure gold; two cubits and a half (45") shall be its length, and a cubit and a half (27") its breadth. And you shall make two cherubim of gold; of hammered work shall you make them, on the two ends of the mercy seat. Make one cherub on the one end, and one cherub on the other end; of one piece with the mercy seat shall you make the cherubim on its two ends. The cherubim shall spread out their wings above, overshadowing the mercy seat with their wings, their faces one to another; toward the mercy seat shall the faces of the cherubim be. And you shall put the mercy seat on the top of the ark [of the Covenant]; and in the ark you shall put the testimony that I shall give you. There I will meet with you, from above the

mercy seat, from between the two cherubim that are upon the ark of the testimony . . .   Exodus 25:17-22; RSV

Mercy is a required energy, consciousness, and disposition for direct communication with God. God seeks to commune with us and has arranged for us to make contact with that knowledge that He is all-merciful so that, even with our many weaknesses, we may come to Him.

Today this Ark, its angels, and its mercy seat have moved into our hearts and minds. They are no longer external devices. It is here within us that the Divine wishes to meet and commune with us.

The disciple Paul wrote about this communion, using the model of the Ark of the Covenant and the mercy seat:

The first covenant had regulations for worship and an earthly sanctuary. For a tent was prepared, the outer one, in which were the lamp stand [seven-candled menorah] and the table and the bread of the Presence; it is called the Holy Place. Behind the second curtain stood a tent called the Holy of Holies, having the golden altar of incense and the ark of the covenant covered on all sides with gold, which contained a golden urn holding the manna, and Aaron's rod that budded, and the tables of the covenant; above it were the cherubim of glory overshadowing the mercy seat. Of these things we cannot now speak in detail. . . . When Christ [i.e., Adam Kadmon, Primal Being, the Word, the Logos] appeared as a high priest of the good things that have come, then through the greater and more perfect tent (not made with hands, that is, not of this creation) he entered once for all into the Holy Place, taking not the blood of goats and calves but his own blood, thus securing an eternal redemption. For if the sprinkling of defiled persons with the blood of goats and bulls and with the ashes of a heifer sanctifies for the purification of the flesh, how much more shall the blood of Christ [the Logos], who through the eternal Spirit offered himself without blemish to God, purify your conscience from dead works to serve the living God. Therefore he is the mediator of a new covenant, so that those who are called may receive the promised eternal inheritance . . . Christ [the Logos] has entered, not into a sanctuary made with hands, a copy of the true one, but into heaven itself, now to appear in the presence of God on our behalf.

Hebrews 9:1-24; RSV

When Cayce spoke of the mercy seat, it was in the context of the angel carrying incense in the book of Revelation. Cayce explained that this angel symbolizes that our good thoughts and actions are like a sweet incense that rises up to the All-Knowing, to the Creative Forces, to God. Our kindness, gentleness, patience, mercy, and longsuffering rise "before the throne of the mercy seat *within* self to that of an incense of satisfaction." (Italics mine) This dispels our sense of unworthiness, which often blocks us from seeking communion with the all-knowing God. (EC 281-30; italics mine) God knew us too well to build a contact point without a mercy seat and cherubs.

Cayce's discourses teach again and again that love and lovingkindness are key to one's full enlightenment. Here are a few examples:

Know the laws—or the love; for the law of God is *love* of God, and is not a hardship. For the law as man's law kills, but the love of the law as of God makes alive—every one. And thy Lord, thy God, is God of the living. Make thy life and thy love of thy fellow man a living thing in thine experience day by day. Smile oft. Speak gently. Be kind.   EC 262-109

Keep thy paths straight. Know in whom ye have believed, as well as in what ye believe. For the love as passes understanding *can*, does and will make thy pathway brighter. Keep in that way. . . .

The beauty of thy life rises as a sweet incense before the altar of mercy. Yet it is not sacrifice but peace, grace and mercy that we would manifest among the children of men. For God is love.   EC 262-116

As He has given from the beginning, "If ye will be my children, I will be your God." So, as individuals, in the application of that known in their experience as to what the will of the Father is, go about *thinking*—and *thinking* it in such a manner that the words of the mouth and the activity of the hand bespeak the will of the Father; then this activity, this thought, makes the individual the channel through which the manifestations are in the earth.

For, who may know in the earth the heart of the mother save a mother? Who may know the will of the Father, God, save those that put into the acts of their hands, in the thoughts of their minds, those things that He has given and as He shows forth in the experience of all men from day to day?

So simple, then, is it to know the Father that all stumble in that they *think* of themselves more highly than they ought to think. Be rather as a channel through which the Father may make His love, His glory, manifest in the earth. *Listen* to the voice from within. For, He is very nigh unto each of you, if ye will but look *within*.   EC 262-58

Writers of Kabbalah consider the consciousness of this emanation to be "Mindful of Others," quite naturally a condition of mercy and lovingkindness.

Emanation 5
Judgment and Might

Here's a paradox: how can the disposition of lovingkindness and mercy naturally flow into the fifth emanation of Might and Judgment? If real power is love and good judgment is mercy, what is the role of this fifth emanation?

The secret is that might and power, as they emanate from God, are more the nature of faith and patience. This is the secret of the mystical quality of longsuffering, so misunderstood by many. Why is longsuffering a virtue and listed among the various fruits of the Spirit? First, it is a quality of God: "But thou, O Lord, art a God full of compassion, and gracious, longsuffering, and plenteous in mercy and truth." (Psalm 86:15) "The Lord passed by before him [Moses] and proclaimed, 'The Lord, The Lord God, [is] merciful and gracious, longsuffering, and abundant in goodness and truth.'" (Exodus 34:6) And second, the path that a human must walk, in an attempt to awaken to his or her godly nature and godly role with the Creator, requires many profound changes in the heart and mind, changes that bring painful adjustments. One must live through these with faith, patience, and longsuffering in order to get to the goal. This is the might of the fifth emanation.

This human–to–godling passage of the soul has been compared to a woman pregnant, in this respect: we have conceived in the womb of our consciousness that our truer nature is godly, or divine; we have gestated this to full term; now the process requires that we dilate our hearts and minds to deliver this eternal part of ourselves! (See illustration 27.) It is as painful an adjustment as a woman's birth canal dilating to deliver a new baby. There are many cycles of labor pains and various stages in the process of birth, as there are in the journey of our spiritual birth. Much suffering occurs as the earthly desires, habits, and beliefs are moved out of the way for the passage of the divine self and its perspectives. The shift from self–driven will to cooperative will with God's will is challenging. It is a breakthrough physically, mentally, emotionally, and spiritually. Anyone who has been on the so–called spiritual path for any length of time knows this.

Cayce addressed the pain of transformation, using Scripture:

> Know "Whom the Lord loves He chastens and purges every one"; for corruption may *not* inherit eternal life, and must be burned up. Know that thy God is a consuming fire, and must purge every one, that ye may enter in. In patience does one overcome.   EC 262-26

This is real power, real might, and is the quality abiding in the fifth orb. Cayce addressed this issue again in this next discourse:

> Might and power are of the Lord. For no man, no entity, no purpose in the experience of any soul is existent save by the grace of God that the earth might become His footstool, and the dwelling place of *who*? Those that are righteous within their own selves? No; they that have *humbled themselves* and are *faithful to the trust and purposes* that have been put into their ways, into their opportunities for being that channel of blessings to someone day by day. *These* shall indeed inherit the earth. For they

that love the Lord shall inherit the earth. That ye love, that ye bow to.
For where the treasure is, there the purpose and desires of the heart are
also.   EC 1440-2; emphasis mine

Let's now consider the aspect of judgment in this emanation. Here
too we find a paradox. We are told not to judge less we be judged, but
we are also told to discern the spirit of truth from that of darkness.

(Q) What is judgment?
(A) With what judgment shall *you* be judged? Law is love; Love is law.
Judgment is weighing love, law, according to the *intent*, the *purpose* of the
activity in its relationships to you and to the force that impelled such. A
weighing of evidence in an activity; as Law is that through which, by
which, in which all are judged.   EC 262-81

But, then, Cayce's readings also say:

The law of the Lord is perfect. Love of the law, love of the Lord is perfect. For, love is perfect if it is selfless in its reactions to associations
one with another. The first and the last commandments are the whole
law: *Thou shalt love the Lord thy God with all thy heart, thy mind, thy soul, thy*
body; and thy neighbor as thyself. The rest only explains, only interprets,
only manifests for the individual the tenets of the law. For the law is
love, and love is law. And the Lord is one in same.   EC 2905-3

Let mercy and justice be thy watchword rather than judgment upon
others. For "Judge not that ye be not judged" is the same as saying show
mercy to those that are wayward, to those that are awkward, to those
that are unkind, to those that are rude—if you would have God show
these to you. For in thy awkwardness, in thy stumbling, ye oft find fault
in yourself. Do not judge yourself. Let God's mercy and love rule thee.
                                                                  EC 262-109

Finally, our discernment is addressed and distinguished from our
judgment in this reading:

Study to show thyself approved unto Him, the giver of all good and
perfect gifts; rightly discerning, rightly dividing the words of truth, keeping self in such an attitude, in such an activity as to bring to self's own
conscience no condemnation; nor the condemning of any other.

EC 1151-25

These are the qualities of might and judgment in the fifth emanation,
and Kabbalists consider the consciousness of this emanation to be
"Truth Minded." In this we again have the paradoxical balancing of Love
with Truth. Might and judgment are not blind to truth while maintain-
ing love and mercy. Many call this "tough love." It is a love that does not
ignore the truth of the situation, the relationship, or the pattern of actions and thoughts yet maintains a loving, merciful manner. These con-
tending forces lead us to the next emanation.

Emanation 6
Beauty and Balance

We have seen how lovingkindness and mercy lead to an unusual
form of might and judgment, and these now lead to the sixth emanation: Beauty and Balance.

The quality of beauty in this emanation was well stated by the poet
John Keats (1795–1821) in his *Ode on a Grecian Urn:* "Beauty is truth, truth
beauty—that is all ye know on earth, and all ye need to know." The Truth
Mindedness of the previous emanation naturally leads to Beauty and
Balance.

In Proverbs 20:29, "The *beauty* of old men is the grey head," and, in
Proverbs 16:31, the grey head is a "crown of glory." In plain words, God
finds beauty in one's having lived rightly and gaining the truth that is
found in old age.

The greater balance comes when truth is balanced with love. To
achieve balance, one must maintain the presence of truth.

Cayce addressed this, as well:

Being made in the flesh, heir to the weaknesses of same, one becomes
more *spiritual* by the even balance that is obtained by making *personal*

application, doing that . . . that will aid another; *not* that self is to be crucified that another may have *ease* in the material sense. When the desire and the purpose, the application, is one—then it becomes easy; but when they are at variance one to another, hard *is* the way, and the call of the flesh becomes strong.   EC 538-30

In this respect, we must balance our personal needs and duty to God with our role as channels of God's love and light to others—our inner nourishment and our outer service must find a balance. When there is imbalance, Cayce warned, the physical (the flesh) will win out, for it is the weaker part of us.

This leads to another consideration related to our paradoxical nature of being both human and divine. To retain sanity, we have to balance our physical and our spiritual development. Given this challenge, balance is one of the most important orbs on the Tree of Life.

Among all the key teachings in the Edgar Cayce volumes, balance holds a special place. Here's an example:

[Keep] an equal balance in the physical, mental and spiritual aspects of the body-functioning. To be sure, it is necessary for normal physical functioning. It is necessary for normal physical reactions, or the exercise as well as relaxation. The same should apply also to the mental, and also to the spiritual aspects. For, they are one. But keep a normal balance, not being an extremist in any direction—whether in diet, exercise, spirituality or morality—but in all let there be a coordinant influence. For, every phase of the physical, mental and spiritual life is dependent upon the other. They are one, as the Father-God is one.
                                                                                 EC 2533-3

In many respects, incarnate life is a balance of opposites. It requires amazing tranquility, the patience of Job, and the mindfulness of a tightrope walker. Kabbalists consider this emanation's consciousness to be the "Mediating Mind." One who strives for the beauty of truth and balance will be victorious, which leads us to the next emanation.

Emanation 7

Victory and Fortitude

When the mind and the heart are enlivened by the first six emanations, the seventh naturally emerges: Victory and Fortitude. This emanation and the next two are said to depict God's activity in manifested life on earth.

The seventh orb expresses the Divine's eternal quality of being. If one is eternal, then one innately has the fortitude to endure through all the challenges of animated life and will realize victory. The saying "this too shall pass" is a reminder that we should not get so upset about situations that appear to block or detour us from our ideal life, relationships, and health, because challenges will not endure and will not last forever. Yet God and our godly nature are eternal—forever. Therefore, good ultimately overcomes evil; hardship ultimately yields to harmony, joy, and contentment. This is our destiny; it ends in victory. As the Jewish teacher Jesus taught, "He who endures unto the end shall be saved." (Matthew 10:22; RSV) The very vibration of fortitude, endurance, and keeping on, generates a disposition that reflects that eternal, immortal portion of God's nature that is in each of us.

Cayce's discourses state this concept in various ways:

Keep on keeping on as you are, but grow in grace and in the knowledge and understanding that comes with the closer walk with Him. EC 281-8

Keep on keeping on. Be cheerful, knowing that as He sees fit, so will He give. Keep on working with, for, toward, the more perfect understanding—each and every one.   EC 281-9

Meet all characters of situations with *fortitude*, if the activities of such are not rushed upon the body of a sudden but given the opportunity to ponder, to meditate, to pray, most any experience physical, mental or of the spiritual influences may be met with *fortitude*.

EC 513-1; italics mine

Speaking of our ultimate destiny as godlings within the Most High God, the disciple Paul wrote:

> Behold, I tell you a mystery: We all shall not sleep, but we
> shall all be changed, in a moment, in the twinkling of an
> eye, at the last trump; for the trumpet shall sound, and the
> dead shall be raised incorruptible, and we shall be changed.
> For this corruptible must put on incorruption, and this mor-
> tal must put on immortality. But when this corruptible shall
> have put on incorruption, and this mortal shall have put on
> immortality, then shall come to pass the saying that is writ-
> ten, "Death is swallowed up in victory' [Isaiah 25:8]."
>
>   1 Corinthians 15:51-54

We all will eventually put on immortality. It is our deeper nature. We all will eventually be raised up to perfection and put on incorruption—forever. Holding this in our hearts and minds as we walk this strange journey will ensure our victory over all that besets us—whether it be within us or around us or both. There is an ember of immortality and perfection within us. And though it is a mystery today, we will all be changed in the twinkling of an eye, as the Scripture states, and our eternal, divine self will emerge. Fortitude is required now. Victory will be ours.

The Kabbalists consider this consciousness to be "Focused Mind," and rightly so, for such a journey as ours requires just that.

Emanation 8

Splendor and Glory

The realization of the earlier emanations brings us more in harmony and compatibility with our Creator's nature, allowing us to draw even closer. Such proximity to the Divine expresses the eighth emanation: Splendor and Glory. With this vibration and awareness, one is filled with light and patient peace. Why worry when God is so near? This is the presence of the Divine with us on our journey—and much easier is our journey with God's companionship.

Let's consider what this may be like in both the macrocosm and our microcosm. We begin with Scripture's description of the descent of God upon Mt. Sinai to bring the new Temple, the Ten Commandments, the

Ark of the Covenant, and most importantly, His very Presence into the physical world.

> The Lord said to Moses, "Come up to me on the mountain, and wait there; and I will give you the tables of stone, with the law and the commandment, which I have written for their instruction." So Moses rose with his servant Joshua, and Moses went up into the mountain of God. And he said to the elders, "Tarry here for us, until we come to you again; and, behold, Aaron and Hur are with you; whoever has a cause, let him go to them." Then Moses went up on the mountain, and the cloud covered the mountain. The glory of the Lord settled on Mount Sinai, and the cloud covered it six days; and on the seventh day he called to Moses out of the midst of the cloud. Now the appearance of the glory of the Lord was like a devouring fire on the top of the mountain in the sight of the people of Israel. And Moses entered the cloud, and went up on the mountain. And Moses was on the mountain forty days and forty nights.
>
> Exodus 24:12-18

This biblical passage is a key to understanding this emanation: It appears that the Infinite and we little, finite, heartfelt seekers cannot meet—as indicated in Job: "And now men cannot look on the light when it is bright in the skies, when the wind has passed and cleared them [clouds]. Out of the north comes golden splendor; God is clothed with terrible majesty." (Job 37:21–22) Who can look upon the Omnipotent? Ah, but we underestimate the Omnipotent's love for us. God cloaked His terrifying majesty in a form that allows us to approach, as did Moses and Joshua.

Here is how Edgar Cayce described this wondrous meeting of the Infinite and the finite:

> They had seen the Lord Jehovah descend onto the Mount, they had seen the Mount so electrified by the presence of the od of the people and ohm of the Omnipotent to such an extent that no living thing could

remain on the Mount, save those two [Moses and Joshua] who had been cleansed by their pouring out of themselves to God, in the cleansing of their bodies, in the cleansing of their minds.   EC 440-16

Cayce's mention in this reading to the "od of the people" refers to a phrase coined by Reichenbach (1788–1869) to explain an unseen force in nature that manifests itself in magnetism, hypnotism, and light: the "odic force." The word *od*, most likely derives from the Greek *hodos*, meaning "path" or "way," and is used in such modern electrical words as *anode* and *cathode*, indicating poles of an electromagnetic field or ray (as seen in a cathode ray tube). Cayce's use of the word *ohm* is most likely referring to the term coined by one of Reichenbach's contemporaries, Georg Simon Ohm (1789–1854), and used today to define a measurement of electrical resistance. However, Cayce seems to be equating *ohm* directly with electricity. Therefore, we could translate this Mount experience metaphorically as the magnetism of the people's hearts and minds seeking God so long and so hard that it draws the Omnipotent upon the Mount. The nature of the Omnipotent is best equated with the powers of electricity, powers that may destroy or enlighten, depending on how pure the conductors (Moses and Joshua).

Cayce also correlated the macrocosmic Mount with the microcosmic crown chakra of the human body, located at the top of the head, the newborn's soft spot. This idea is also found in Hopi legend, in which "Great Uncle" guided his people to the new world by communicating to them via the soft spot on top of their heads. The crown chakra is the sacred mount in us. If we raise our energy and consciousness to this area and wait quietly upon the Spirit, as God instructed Moses to do, guidance will come to us. "Be still, and know that I am God." (Psalm 46:10)

The splendor and glory of the Lord may be known. The Omnipotent will respond to our desire to commune. A cleansing, a preparation, and a transition may be required, but God so loves us that a way may be prepared for us to unite. We have to do our part: seek and prepare ourselves to be in the presence of the Almighty. One element of this preparation is implied in the Hebrew word for this emanation: Hod. It has a connotation of "submission." By subduing our will to God's will, God may descend upon the "mount" of our consciousness in a form that will not kill us or do irreparable harm. This begins the covenant between us and our Creator, and continues as an eternal relationship. The Splendor and Glory may be ours to experience and enjoy.

According to the Kabbalists, the consciousness associated with this emanation is "Perfecting Mind." Sharing our consciousness with God leads to the perfecting of our minds.

Emanation 9
Foundation and Bonding

Experiencing the glory and splendor of the Presence of God builds Foundation and Bonding: the ninth emanation. From this place, this condition, all things take on a new order, and goodness abides with us. As the biblical injunction states this truth, "Seek ye first the kingdom of God, and His righteousness; and all these things shall be added unto you." (Matthew 6:33; KJV) With this established, a foundation has been laid and a bonding with the Divine has begun.

Some of the qualities of Foundation may be found in the Psalms and Proverbs:

> Righteousness and justice are the foundation of thy throne. Loving kindness and truth go before thy face. Blessed is the people that know the joyful sound. They walk, O Lord, in the light of thy countenance.   Psalms 89:14-15

> Righteousness and justice are the foundation of his throne.
>   Psalm 97:2

> When the whirlwind passes, the wicked is no more; but the righteous is an everlasting foundation.   Proverbs 10:25

In the Toledano Kabbalah teachings (Toledo, Spain, ca. 900s to 1300s), this orb is also associated with remembering. In the Old Testament book of Malachi, we have this little insight:

> Then they that feared the Lord spoke often one to another:

and the Lord listened, and heard it, and a *Book of Remembrance* was written before Him for them that feared the Lord, and that thought on His name. And they shall be mine, said the Lord of hosts, in that day when I act they will be my precious possessions; and I will spare them, as a man spares his own son that serves him. Then shall you return, and discern between the righteous and the wicked, between him that serves God and him that serves him not.

Malachi 3:16-18; italics mine

The Revelation speaks of the "Book of Life from the foundation of the world," in which are written the names of the souls who have earned a passport to heavenly realms. (Rev. 13:8 and 17:8) In the Psalms, we find:

You keep track of my wanderings. You put my tears in your flask, in your record.   Psalm 56:8-9

I come in the volume of the book that is written of me.

Psalm 40:7

Thy eyes beheld my unformed substance; in thy book were written, every one of them, the days that were formed for me, when as yet there was none of them. How precious to me are Thy thoughts, O God! How vast is the sum of them! If I would count them, they are more than the sand. When I awake, I am still with Thee.   Psalm 139:17-19

For Cayce, the Book of Remembrance, or the Book of Life, was a very real dynamic, because in his deep, meditative state of consciousness, he felt that he was reading from the Book of Life of each soul that sought his help. When asked to explain the Book of Life, he replied, "The record that the individual entity itself writes upon the skein of time and space, through patience—and is opened when self has attuned to the infinite, and may be read by those attuning to that consciousness." Cayce was also asked about "The Rolls of Graphael," and responded: "The records of an individual, *as an archangel.* The records of those activities with the

Announcer, the Way, in association with the Christ–Consciousness." (EC 2533-8; italics mine) We rarely think of ourselves as having an angelic level to our whole being, but we do (more on this in the chapter 8).

Cayce could thus read these records. In one reading, he began by saying, "In interpreting the records as we find them here, the seal of life of the entity is most unique as well as interesting, and is upon the book, the record of the entity." (EC 2448-2)

In the following reading, Cayce gives insights into the righteous aspect of the foundation, and he does so in the same manner as Kabbalah:

> Then there may be a lesson here gained by each—that sin versus righteousness is that sin . . . is separation from God; and righteousness is adhering to, making at-onement with God's purposes—even as indicated in the prayer of the publican, "God be merciful to me, a sinner." Or, as He gave in the prayer, "As I ask forgiveness, so I forgive others," or, "With what measure I ask for mercy, for care, for love, for thought, that love and care and consideration I seek to give to others."
>
> Thus may we draw a lesson in our daily experience from this attitude, this condition, this experience through which each soul finds itself passing in a material world. The flesh is weak; the spirit is willing.
>
> Will you each as individuals be led by the spirit of truth? or will self, thy own ego, thy own material desire, so outweigh that purpose, that hope, that mission for which each soul is given the opportunity in material expression, that it may be said of you, "except your righteousness exceed the life of the self-righteous, ye shall indeed perish"?
>
> EC 262-125

The true foundation lies with the Spirit of God, the Spirit of Life that is Eternal Life.

> Know that the ideal must ever be founded upon something that is continuous; and only the Spirit is continuous! For, all that is of a material or of an earthy nature must pass away. Only purpose that is creative, that is prompted by truth as founded in spiritual things, spiritual activities, spiritual relations, continues.
>
> To be sure, man in a material world needs to have that activity which

will bring things of a material nature into his experience; but, let these be as a result of the expression or manifestation founded in spiritual things and purposes, and not as the primary purpose alone. For, if there will be the success that will live on, the material results must be founded upon creative influences and forces.   EC 2172-1

This emanation is also associated with "bonding," a bonding that comes from sharing one's life with God, by inviting God into one's life and one's relationships and living the life together. It also requires our seeking to know God's presence and God's will and allowing God to share these with us. This builds the bond in our hearts and minds. This occurs not only through prayer but by inner listening to that still, small voice that Elijah heard in the cave and knew to be the true voice of God, the voice that he could not find in the lightning, thunder, earthquake, or fire. (1 Kings 19:12) It was within him. It was still. How does one hear a still voice? One *feels* it. This is the mystical experience that builds the bond: prayer and deep, inner listening—not with our carnal ears but with the ear of our souls. Further, it comes more as a feeling of the Presence of God and God's guidance than the hearing of a voice. Elijah expressed it well: "a still, small voice within"—one feels a still voice.

Upon these aspects of the ninth emanation, we build an enduring foundation and bond with our Father–Mother Creator and eternal Companion.

Kabbalists identify the consciousness associated with this emanation as the "Purifying Mind."

Emanation 10
Kingdom

This is the vessel (*kli*, in Hebrew; singular of *keilim*) that received the original burst of God's power and light at the moment of the big bang of Creation and did not break! When all other orbs shattered, this amazing little orb absorbed the Light of God and allowed it to flow back, repairing each of the broken orbs, until all was as it was intended to be. Out of the chaos came the repair that established the Kingdom of God and the Tree of Life.

Here is the true Holy of Holies, the zone where God has promised to meet us face to face. And though it is strange to us in our three-dimensional, projected life, this Kingdom is within us. Our being, the little "I am," is the temple of the living God, the Great I AM. And in this temple does the communion occur.

The disciple Paul, asked: "Don't you know that you are a temple of God, and that the Spirit of God dwells in you?" and "Don't you know that your body is a temple of the Holy Spirit which is in you, which you have from God?" (1 Corinthians 6:19)

The disciple John alludes to this when he recounts in his gospel an event in which Jesus was asked, in the great temple in Jerusalem, to show the people a sign:

> Jesus answered them, "Destroy this temple, and in three days I will raise it up." The people at the temple said, "Forty-six years was this temple in building, and will you raise it up in three days?" But he spoke of *the temple of his body.*
>
> John 2:19, RSV; italics mine

Cayce often addressed the importance of the body temple, as in these selected discourses:

Know that your body is the temple of the living God; there you may seek communion. There you may seek counsel as to the choices to be made, the directions to be taken.   EC 622-6

He has promised. "If you will but open the door of your consciousness, of your heart, I will enter and abide with you." This is not a fancy; this is not hearsay. You may experience such. For it is the law, it is the way, it is *life* itself!   EC 1632-2

Seek and you shall find. Not without but from within. For in thine own temple He has promised to meet you.   EC 2677-1

All that you may learn of the Father God is already within self. For your body is indeed the temple of the living God, and as you meet Him there you may gain in your own consciousness the satisfaction of walking and talking with Him. When these consciousnesses are yours and you are one with Him, then indeed may you see that the kingdom of heaven dwells within.   EC 5155-1

This is a promise to you, to each soul; yet each soul must of itself find that answer within self. For indeed the body is the temple of the living God. There He has promised to meet you; there He does. And as your body, your mind, your soul is attuned to that divine that answers within, so may you indeed be quickened to know His purpose; and you may fill that purpose for which you entered this experience.   EC 622-6

This orb, or emanation, is also known as Shekhinah, meaning the Divine Presence, and is the feminine aspect of God. In the womb of our consciousness we have conceived our godling nature and destiny. Here, in the tenth emanation, the "I am" is born anew and seeks to unite with the Great I AM of the first emanation, after which oneness, harmony, contentment, and life reign forever. Again, see illustration 26.

Adam's Secret Sin and the 10th Emanation

In the Zohar, the sin was that "Adam drove out Et!" What is Et? It is found in this little passage: "Yahweh Elohim expelled him from the Garden of Eden . . . He drove out *et* Adam." (Genesis 3:23–24) Actually, there is no interpretation for the Hebrew term *et* because it is not really a word; it is simply an accusative particle of the sentence with Adam as the determinate objective. It does not have a meaning, simply a role in grammar. However, its odd placement in this passage caused Kabbalists, who studied these passages ad infinitum, to suspect that there was a secret message here. They came to believe that *et* was a code term for the tenth emanation of God. (Here aspects of the story of Lilith and Eve get involved, but it can become so complicated as to be of little use to us, so I am deferring this to a later part of the book and a better context in which to address it.)

Kabbalists believed that the Shekhinah is symbolized by the Tree of the Knowledge of Good and Evil that was in the Garden of Eden. Adam's sin was that he worshiped and partook of Her [Shekhinah] *alone*, not in harmony with the other nine emanations. This split Her off from the Tree of Life, the other Emanations of God, and "divorced" Her from Her "husband," Tiferet, the sixth emanation of Balance. This disrupted the unity of the Cosmos and the harmony and balance that God established.

Here is the passage from the Zohar (I have retained its original, poetic form):

> Rabbi El'azar said:
> "We do not know who divorced whom,
> if the Blessed Holy One divorced Adam
> or not.
> But the word is transposed:
> 'He drove out et.'
> Et, precisely!
> And who drove out Et?
> Adam.
> Adam drove out Et!
> Therefore it is written:
> 'YHWH Elohim expelled him from the Garden of Eden.'
> Why did He expel him?
> Because Adam drove out Et,
> as we have said."

Traditionally, Adam's principal sin was believed to have been disobedience by eating the fruit of the Tree of the Knowledge of Good and Evil. However, it was the experience of knowing right from wrong—having gained the knowledge of good and evil —which caused him to hide from God, because his actions and desires were now obviously out of harmony with God's. In the Bible, the expulsion from the Garden comes right after this passage spoken by Yahweh Elohim: "Behold, the man has become like one of us, knowing good and evil; and now, lest he put forth his hand and take also of the tree of life, and eat, and live forever..."—here the passage abruptly shifts to the expulsion from the

Garden. But, for the Kabbalists, the sin was that Adam so desired the feminine presence of God in matter, in the earth, that he possessed Her for his own. This strange idea is reinforced in Genesis 6:2: "The sons of God saw the daughters of men that they were fair; and they took for wives all of them that they chose." The separation of the Divine Feminine essence into an individualized, physical expression was so appealing that the spiritual godlings divorced their marriage to the Spirit and sought only the physical bonding with the Shekhinah, causing Her to be separated and, in a manner of speaking, divorced from Her marriage to the heavenly Tree of Life. This could not be allowed to continue, so God brought the cycle of death and rebirth upon them until this could be resolved—keeping them from making this a permanent condition. Interestingly, in the last chapters of Revelation, the redemption of this situation has been realized: the Bride is presented to the heavenly Groom, and the sons and daughters of God are again allowed to eat from the Tree of Life and live forever.

The tenth emanation is the home of the awakening of the little "I am" and its relationship with the Great I AM. It is the place of meeting, in the bodily temple of the individual heart, mind, and soul, the universal Mind and Collective Soul. Separation is not an eternal option; union and oneness are the ultimate conditions for true happiness and eternal life.

Kabbalists consider this emanation's consciousness to be the "Oneness Mind," expressing the need to stop the separation and reunite in oneness.

Let's recap the ten emanations:

1. The "I AM," Crown, Concealed Consciousness—Keter or Kether
2. Wisdom, Illuminating Mind—Chokhmah or Hokhmah
3. Understanding, Sanctifying Mind—Binah
4. Mercy and Loving Kindness, Mindful of Others—Chesed or Hesed
5. Judgment and Might, Truth Minded—Gevurah (sometimes Din)
6. Balance and Beauty, Mediating Mind—Tiferet or Tifereth
7. Victory and Fortitude, Focused Mind—Netzach or Netsah
8. Splendor and Glory, Perfecting Mind—Hod
9. Foundation and Bonding, Purifying Mind—Yesod
10. The "I am," Kingdom, Oneness Minded—Malkuth or Shekhinah

This is the classic listing of the sefirot of the Tree of Life, the emanations of God in manifested life.

Da'at–Knowledge

Some schools of Kabbalah add an emanation called Knowledge, or Da'at, in Hebrew, often written Daat. There are various interpretations surrounding this sphere. Often those promoting this sefirah omit the Crown sefirah and begin the Tree of Life with Wisdom, Understanding, and Knowledge as the first triad, calling this the Triad of Intelligence. See illustration 6 for this alternate form of the Tree.

There are good reasons for omitting Da'at (Daat) and staying with the classical arrangement of the Sefirot. One is built around the location of the sefirah Da'at. These schools place Da'at in the so-called "empty place" in the Tree, but this empty place is classically considered to be the Abyss or "the deep," which is in the second sentence of the Bible: "darkness was upon the face of the deep." (Genesis 1:2) The Deep is a very special place in the Tree of Life.

The Abyss–"The Deep"

Notice the "empty place" in the classic layout of the Tree of the Life (see illustrations 1 and 2), considered to be the Abyss, the Deep, or the Void of Eastern teachings. This empty space is believed to be a portal, an opening from the visible universe to the invisible. As such, the Deep is a mystically significant region in the Tree of Life. Blocking this passageway—especially with something as cluttering as knowledge (Da'at)—does not seem wise. The stillness, quiet, and silence that abides in this empty space are also characteristics required to pass through this portal to the Infinite Eternal One. "Be still, and know that I am God." (Psalm 46:10)

To clarify, this abyss is not the pit into which Satan is cast. It is not the pit of evil darkness. It is the fathomless "deep" of God's mind and being. It is the womb of pre-Creation. In here is a stillness, a silence, that rejuvenates and rebirths the soul. It is the original home, with which our souls long to reconnect. The primal sacred sound OM reminds us of this place of our origin, of our heavenly "hOMe."

Emanations and the Cayce Lesson Plan

It may be a bit surprising to find that some of the ten emanations of God correlate well with Edgar Cayce's "Search for God" teachings, the 262 series of his voluminous readings. This should not surprise us, given that Cayce's own readings state:

> As the preacher gave, "There is nothing new under the sun." [Ecclesiastes 1:9] For, in the beginning all was made that was made, and as it unfolds from what man terms time to time, period to period, there is only the renewing of the First Cause. Isn't the last apple also that portion of the first one created? Isn't the first friend the same purpose and principle that has been held, or that has grown to be a part of the consciousness?   2946-2

As we can see, from Cayce's perspective, truth was known in the most ancient of times, and if it is truly true, it is so whenever it is taught.

Let's briefly compare the two sources of wisdom. In the Tree of Life, we have "Crown." Cayce's *Search for God (SFG)* material has the "Crown" (Book I, Lesson X), to which he adds the "Cross," explaining that one cannot properly wear the Crown unless one has also carried the Cross: "crucify desire in self that ye may be awakened to the real abilities of helpfulness that lie within thy grasp." (EC 2475-1)

In the Tree, we have "Wisdom." In Cayce's *SFG* material we have "Wisdom" (Book II, Lesson X), referring to the biblical teaching, "The fear of the Lord is the start of wisdom, and the knowledge of the Holy One gives a wise mind." (Proverbs 9:10) Cayce states it this way:

> If in any of the approaches to Wisdom it is then an exaltation of self, as an aggrandizement of self's own motives, this is a lack rather than an application of Wisdom of the Lord. But rather that in the application self is not abased but used in selflessness, in the ideals of the glorifying, the exalting of the Prince of Peace, the glory of the Father and not of self, [then] this is the approach, this is the beginning. For as has been indicated, in the knowledge or in the fear is knowledge and wisdom of God. Then the willingness to be abased that the Name that is above *every* name may be exalted.   EC 262-104

In the Tree, we have "Understanding," as does Cayce in the *SFG* (Book I, Lesson V), to which he adds "Virtue," explaining that one cannot have true understanding until that understanding abides in a virtuous heart.

In the Tree we find "Glory," as we do in Cayce's teachings (Book 11, Lesson VIII). Cayce expressed it this way:

> Glory is that which is sought in the experience of each and every individual. It, Glory, is the natural expression also of every thing, condition, circumstance that gives to man and his mind a concept of Creative Forces as they manifest in materiality. Hence this, then, is the natural seeking of man. Yet, as with *every* phase of man's experience with conditions that deal with the fellow man, this may be turned into that which may become a stumbling block to self or to others. *Glory*, then, in all its phases in man's experience, and as related to the Creative Forces in the manifestations in the earth, is to be studied. Then, we may find Glory in those activities, those expressions that may bring joy, peace, happiness, understanding, knowledge, wisdom, in the experience of all. These be the expressions of man in glorifying not self but that purpose, that ideal, for which the Season, the period stands in the experience of each that seeks to know the Glory of the Father. For, as was given of old, the Glory of God shall be manifested among men; for He, God, hath spoken it, hath promised it to the sons of men. Yet this Glory must become aware in the experience of each in the same order, the same manner, as every law of the Lord. They that would know God or His Glory must believe that He *is*, and a rewarder of those that diligently seek Him. If ye would know God, if ye would know His Glory, *do good* unto thy fellow man!   EC 262-91

These are the direct correlates between Cayce's discourses and the Kabbalah. But there are also implied correlations, such as the emanation of God's Kingdom in this world, which correlates to Cayce's "God, the Father, and His Manifestations in the Earth" (Book II, Lesson III), as explained in the following:

> God, the Father, the first cause, seeking—in the manifestations of self— brought the world, as we (as individuals) observe it about us, into be-

ing—*through* love; giving to man, His creation, His creatures, that ability to become one with Him.

In the beginning was the word, and the word was God. He said, "Let there be *light*"—and there was light. Like begets like. It *is* both cause and effect, and they that choose some other way become the children of darkness; and they are these: Envying, strife, hate; and the children of these are sedition, rebellion, and the like. The children of light first love . . .   EC 262-46

The emanation Foundation compares well with Cayce's lesson on the ideal (Book I, Lesson III). With Foundation, the Tree adds Bonding, which may be compared to Cayce's "Oneness" (Book I, Lesson XI). In Cayce's transcendant consciousness, the foundation of all human good is found in the ideal held as one seeks and uses free will:

[T]hat which gives more understanding of the relationships of self with the creative forces of a universal experience, rather than individual, makes for a closer walk with God, that from which the essence of life itself has its *emanation* [italics mine; note Cayce's use of the Kabbalistic term *emanation*]. . . .

One fed upon the purely material will become a Frankenstein that is without a concept of any influence other than material or mental.

                                                                     EC 262-20

Let's go beyond Cayce's 262 series and include more of his readings. By doing so, we will see how well Cayce's teachings correspond to the Kabbalah's Tree of Life.

The emanation Mercy and Loving Kindness compares well to Cayce's many discourses on the "fruit of the spirit," which include love, kindness, and mercy. Here's an example:

First begin by sowing, then, the seeds of the fruit of the spirit; as in patience and longsuffering, the lack of hate; showing brotherly love, the lack of animosity and the lack of intolerance. Rather show tolerance and loving kindness, and patience above all.

And in these we will find there may be given thee more and more that which is necessary. It is as one uses and applies the knowledge already within self that more can and will be given.

Tempt not the spirit in self, nor do that for which thy conscience would condemn thee. Rather, as has been pointed out—first in the admonition indicated by Moses—it is not who shall descend from heaven nor who shall come from over the seas to bring thee a message, that thou mightest understand; for lo, it is within thine own self!

For indeed as thy body is the temple of the living God, there He has promised to meet thee. And thy faculties, thy abilities, thy mental self, thy desires, thy hates and thy loves are all a part of thee; but ye nourish them, ye feed them by the manner of thought. And it is within thine own temple, thine own tabernacle that He has promised to meet thee.

EC 315-5

More than two thousand Cayce readings recommend Balance as a fundamental principle for all individuals to apply in their lives. Interestingly, and synchronistically, in Cayce's numerology the number 6 is defined as "balance and symmetry," which fits well with the sixth emanation: Balance and Beauty. Certainly symmetry is an aspect of beauty.

The Tree's Victory and Fortitude corresponds well to Cayce's frequent repetition of Jesus' statement, "He [and she] who endures unto the end shall be saved." (Matthew 10:22)

The emanation of Might and Judgment compares well to this Cayce teaching: "There will be the need for power and position to be tempered with spiritual and mental judgment." (EC 1225-2) One may be strong, but real might comes when spiritual and mental judgment are applied in the use of that strength.

Kabbalah explains that the ten emanations are both physical dynamics in this world and in our bodies as well as metaphysical energetics and psychological thought patterns in our minds and spirits. If we apply ourselves to perfecting these enumerations in our outer daily life and relationships as well as within our hearts and minds, then we grow spiritually, mentally, and physically. Cayce's readings say virtually the same thing: the knowledge we gain in study must be applied in our lives and relationships as well as in our inner feelings and thinking if true growth is to occur.

Those of us who have been in study groups know that one of the methods used to help our progress is a regular discipline that we work on between meetings. We keep this discipline in mind throughout daily life, attempting to change our reactions to outer stimuli, as well as our inner thinking and feeling. This regular effort directed to a specific discipline helps us change habitual thoughts and emotions. Then, as we move through the whole of the lessons, we eventually gain from all the disciplines we have applied.

The other advantage is in having group support, as both a sounding board for our experiences and a learning environment that comes from hearing how others experience life and spiritual pursuits.

Kabbalah encourages conscious awareness of God but considers such awareness to be beyond our earthly capabilities, requiring us to first know our higher nature. In Cayce's discourse 1401-1, he describes God as the infinite, unseen Creator of the universe and all that is in it. This Creator has conveyed His presence within these emanations of Kabbalah. As we apply their qualities, we become one with the emanations, manifesting them in our hearts and minds and in our daily actions, words, and thoughts. As a result, God flows through us. This creates a transformative strength to the practice of applying God's principles in our daily lives. It is quite a different thing to use disciplines in one's life if one accepts that some aspect of the Creator is in those principles, those ideals.

Finally, it is important to realize that the infinite, universal, unseen Creator actually reaches into our world and into our being through these emanations. Each sefirah is a channel of God. Each sefirah is a dynamic orb of transformation that lifts and shapes us to be companionable to God and to consciously know our Creator, face to face, as did Moses.

CHAPTER

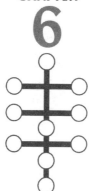

THE 22 PATHWAYS

THE LIFE FORCES FLOW THROUGH US, AND WE, THROUGH THEM

The Twenty-Two Mystical Pathways (Nativot Phayliot) is a network that circulates qualities of consciousness and energy throughout the Tree of Life. Because each of the twenty-two pathways runs between two specific emanations, respectively, they are each unique. For example, the pathway that runs between the Great I AM and Beauty is naturally going to be different from the one that runs between the little "I am" and Bonding—in the quality of both consciousness and energy.

The pathways are ethereal, but they do reach into the physical universe and, most importantly, into our hearts, minds, and even our physical bodies. In this they are both macrocosmic and microcosmic forces. In this study, we are going to focus more on the personal, microcosmic influences that affect our soul life.

Each of these twenty-two pathways corresponds to one of the twenty-two letters of the Hebrew alphabet, and each of the pathways has a number associated with it that reflects its order in the sequence of the Tree of Life. Since the Tree has ten emanations, the first pathway number is 11. And since, in this time frame, we are already deep in the Creation, and much of what we are doing is flowing *back* through the Tree of Life (at least it feels that way to us), we will begin our study with the pathway that is closest to our present state of being, 32, and proceed from there to the highest, 11.

It will be helpful to view illustration 7 as your read these.

Much of the detail about this network comes from Kabbalah's The Book of Creation (Sefer Yetzirah) and subsequent writings and interpretations, such as The Tree of Life (Kuntres Etz HaChayim), a Chassidic treatise circa 1700s, by Rabbi Shalom DovBer Schneersohn of Lubavitch.

There is a tendency to develop a linear view of these pathways, but they are interconnected, just as the emanations are. We can and do experience all of them, even when we are mostly focusing on just one. Let's try to keep a holistic view as we read these in order, beginning with the little "I am" and moving up to the Great I AM.

The Pathways

32—The Assisting Path

As we begin, the Creation is already in full swing. Now we are returning through the ten emanations and twenty-two pathways. Thus we begin with pathway 32 (10 orbs plus 22 channels). This connects the tenth emanation of our "I Am" and the Kingdom with the ninth emanation: Foundation. The awareness that runs along this pathway is called "Worshipped Consciousness" (Sekhel Ne'evad) as well as the "Assisting" or "Administrative" Consciousness and Energy. These terms relate to phases of our development. As we first awaken to spiritual awareness and higher vibrations, we worship this enlightenment and energy as a gift from God. They are a hidden well of renewing water in the very dry desert of materiality and self-conscious life. As its flow increases and we become more receptive vessels, our consciousness and energy become more comfortable and familiar with this pathway, so it moves from a worshiping to an assisting influence in the spiritualization of our bodies and minds.

This pathway is also known as a destroyer. As such, our earthly self may become scared, wanting to hide from the terrifying power of God's growing proximity. But this destroyer is as Hinduism's Shiva, a destroyer of illusions and a cleanser of the unheavenly. In its role, this pathway destroys many of the idols we have developed and hold onto so tightly—such as passionate, earthly desires and self-gratifying habits. Of course, our earthly, egocentric self feels that it cannot live without these comforts and idols. But our soul senses the need to let go of them for the higher, more eternal good. This requires that we die a little to our earthliness to make room for heavenliness—just as our loving Creator died a little to Its perfection to allow us to make mistakes by virtue of our free will and to grow to understand that such a gift is a double-edged sword and must therefore be wielded with care.

31—The Perpetual Path

Once we have been assisted in our first turn toward the Light and the vessels of our mind and body contain sufficient awareness and energy, we open the flow to and from the eighth emanation—Splendor and Glory—with that sweet quality of Surrender. This pathway is called "Continuous Consciousness" or "Perpetual Consciousness" (Sekhel Tamidi), so named because, once opened, it will never be closed; we will never fall back from this level of awareness and energy. Even if we fall away from spiritual seeking, we never forget having touched this level of awareness and energy.

All we have to do to open this pathway, no matter how earthly or even evil we have become, is to turn around from the darkness to face the Light. When we do so, all of our shadows fall behind and the path opens brightly before us. Nothing stands between us and our Creator but ourselves and our free will to step away. This pathway is associated with the two great lights in the sky: the sun and the moon, which represent, respectively, the Great I AM of the first emanation and the little "I am" of the tenth emanation. Though we live now in the moonlight of our little being, our destiny is to live in the sunlight of God's companionship.

30—The Collecting Path

Now that we have Assistance (32) and have opened Perpetual Consciousness (31), we may flow through the "Collecting" or "Collective" Consciousness (Sekhel Kelali), sometimes called General Consciousness, in the sense of universal. It contains the Ophanim—celestial beings described in The Book of Enoch with the cherubim and seraphim as "never sleeping" but watching (or guarding) the throne of God. Ophan also means "wheels," as seen in Ezekiel's vision and Hinduism's *chakras*. This pathway is a vortex of celestial energy and awareness. This channel raises our vibrations and consciousness to a new and stronger level. It flows to and from the pools of Splendor and Foundation, bathing us in renewing light and gathering to us heavenly help.

29—The Spirit-Filled Physical Path

Now victorious, we enjoy the vigor of the seventh emanation: Fortitude. This channel is called "Physical Consciousness" (Sekhel Mugsham), in the sense of giving life and growth to all of physical life. The essence of spirit invigorates form; spirit enlivens flesh and matter. Now our physical lives have a new level of energy and awareness that we have not enjoyed for a very long time, long before this incarnation.

28—The Natural Path

This new vigor opens the flow to and from the ninth and seventh emanations through the pathway called "Natural Consciousness" (Sekhel Mutba), in the sense of Nature's life-giving ways and laws. Finally, we are in sync with the forces of Nature.

27—The Exciting Path

Next is the "Exciting" or "Palpable Consciousness" (Sekhel Murgash). It is so named because the consciousness of all living things created under the entire upper realms were given life through this flowing pathway. Here is the élan vital, the metaphysical kundalini energy. Amazingly, the age that follows the end of the Mayan Age of Movement, ending on the winter solstice of December 21, 2012, is the Age of the Spirit of All Living Things—the age for this pathway. This pathway's consciousness and energy are the animators of manifested life, making all creators palpable, excited by the flow of life within them.

26—The Renewing Pathway

Now we reach the energy of Renewing Consciousness (Sekhel MeChudash). Here all things are made new. Forgotten truths are renewed. Lost treasures of the soul are rediscovered. Here we feel our old selves again, as celestial souls rather than terrestrial bodies. Our spiritual being has been in suspension, lingering in a stasis since our entry into physical matter. Now our spirit stretches its wings again and awakens to live renewed.

25—The Testing Pathway

The next channel is "Testing Consciousness" (Sekhel Nisyoni). Here is where we meet the "original temptation" to see if it still holds sway over us. This is where the Light Forces test all returning, renewed, and resurrected souls. On the descent it was a test we failed. On the ascent, it will be an easy one to pass, since we have come to know how much we lost and we are wiser from our experiences.

According to the Bible, this test is as by fire, in the sense that fire refines, or perfects, metals rather than destroys them.

> I will put this third [the renewed souls] into the fire, and refine them as one refines silver, and test them as gold is tested. They will call on my name, and I will answer them. I will say, "They are my people"; and they will say, "The Lord is my God."   Zechariah 13:8-9

The disciple Paul picks up on this, writing:

> Each man's work will become manifest; for the Day will disclose it, because it will be revealed with fire, and the fire will test what sort of work each one has done.
>   1 Corinthians 3:13

And, as we have already seen in chapter 5 on emanations, our God is a consuming fire, purging and cleansing those He loves, that they may be more perfect. Metals are made more perfect through the testing by fire. Here we are speaking of the metaphysical fire of the Spirit, not the flames of combustion, as expressed by John the Baptist:

> I baptize you with water for repentance, but he who is coming after me is mightier than I, whose sandals I am not worthy to carry; he will baptize you with the Holy Spirit and with fire.   Matthew 3:11

24—The Pathway of the Imagination

Now we have the flow of the "Imaginative" or "Apparitional Consciousness" (Sekhel Dimyoni), often called Apparitive Consciousness. This is the appearance of nonmaterial vessels, as apparitions. As strange as it seems to us living in three-dimensional matter, the imaginative forces are the pathway to higher consciousness and perception. Here we think of imagination as unreal fantasy, but thoughts are things in the realms of heaven and the Universal Consciousness. Our individualness is evident in this world by a separate physical body, but in the heavens, we have only our mind and soul, which have the qualities of apparitions, ghosts, and spirits, and in this realm the imaginative forces are real. Consider how free and expansive our mind would be beyond three dimensions, in a vast openness of infinity. This is the imaginative pathway. Nothing is beyond the mind's imagination. We could expand into infinity and no one could discern us from the Infinite, and in a flash, we could contract again, expressing our individualness while still with the universal.

Many in this earthly world have developed their minds to high levels of imagination and nonearthly awareness. We see it in how we grasp metaphors, emblems, and symbols, and in concepts and imagery that are beyond anything that is manifested in this physical reality. These powers flow from this pathway.

23—The Sustaining Pathway

The "Sustaining Consciousness" (Sekhel Kayam) flows between the emanation of Splendor and Judgment. Here we gain the sustaining power necessary for the journey through the upper portions of the Tree of Life. Now we are moving into the higher heavens of vibration and consciousness. We need help. We find that help in this pathway. Once we are fully charged by the energy and awareness in this path, we are ready to move higher.

22—The Faithful Pathway

Next is the "Faithful Consciousness" (Sekhel Ne'eman). It flows back and forth between Judgment and Beauty/Balance. A biblical passage refers to this level of consciousness and energy: "They will live again in God's shadow. They will grow like grain. They will blossom like grapevines. They will be as famous as the wines from Lebanon." (Hosea 14:7) Here we enjoy the blessings from God upon His faithful.

21—The Pathway of Conciliation

Next is the "Desired and Sought Consciousness" (Sekhel HaChafutz VeHaMevukash) through which flows the Divinity to and through us. Here we enjoy bestowing the blessings of God upon all of creation, as channels of God's grace to all. The object of our desire and seeking is realized, and we take a first step toward becoming the godly companions we were created to be by channeling God's blessings to others. Naturally, this flows between the emanation of Mercy and Loving Kindness and the emanation of Victory and Fortitude. This is also called the Path of Conciliation, where previous damage is repaired, where karma morphs into grace. Here all the harm we brought upon others is mended, and we become a blessing in the lives of others.

20—The Pathway of Will

The pathway of "Consciousness of Will" (Sekhel HaRatzon) engages the most powerful gift given to us by our Creator: free will. As we find in the Scriptures:

> Beloved, let us love one another; for love is of God, and he who loves is born of God and knows God. He who does not love does not know God; for God is love.   1 John 4:7-8

Now we willfully choose to love; we choose to share our consciousness with God and to be channels of God's emanations in whatever circumstance or relationship we find ourselves. Cayce states it most clearly:

> The Creator, in seeking to find or create a being worthy of companionship, realized that such a being would result only from a free will exercising its divine inheritance and through its own efforts find its Maker. Thus, to make the choice really a Divine one caused the existence of states of consciousness, that would indeed tax the free will of a soul; thus light and darkness. Truly, only those tried so as by fire can enter in.
>
> EC 262-56

19—The Spiritual Activities Pathway

Filled with the joy and inspiration of our journey so far, we reach the pathway of the "Consciousness of the Mystery of all Spiritual Activities" (Sekhel Sod HaPaulot HaRuchniot Kulam). Now we become aware of life in the Spirit and of all activities in the spiritual realms. We have arrived! We are ready to enter the highest heavens and do what godlings do throughout the Cosmos, free and alive. Since these are realms and activities so beyond anything we know on earth, they are a mystery to us. But we shall know them as we reach this level of enlightenment.

18—The Influencing Pathway

Now we examine the "Consciousness of the House of Influences" (Sekhel Bet HaShefa). Here we intuit an allusion and probe a secret. Here we learn the forces behind the Cause of Causes, behind the First Motivation. These are among the highest level of vibration and awareness, having qualities of stillness and intuition.

17—The Sensing Pathway

The "Consciousness of the Senses" (Sekhel HaHergesh) prepares the faithful seekers to be clothed in the "Spirit of Holiness." This is also called the Disposing Path, for it arranges, organizes, and marshals the energies and thoughts in a new order. We are truly changed and arrayed in ways we have not considered. At this level we are so close to God that it is becoming difficult to discern between ourselves and God, for we are nearly one.

16—The Enduring Pathway

This is the pathway of the "Triumphal One," also known as the "Enduring Consciousness" (Sekhel Nitzchi). Those who endure wear the Crown of the triumph, and we are very close to the Crown now. There is no surer way of getting here than to keep on keeping on despite all obstacles. It is considered to be the "Delight of the Glory of God's Presence." It is also called the Garden of Eden, but this is the metaphysical garden that was prepared for the faithful.

15—The Stabilizing Pathway

Finally, we reach the "Stabilizing Consciousness" (Sekhel Ma'amid), so called because it stabilizes the essence of creation in the "Glooms of

Purity." Glooms of Purity is a strange concept. Kabbalists consider gloom to be a cocoon in which a metamorphosis from lonesome soul to untied godling magically occurs. This is similar to modern-day psychological belief that mild depression is a place of formative rebirth and creativity. One comes out of it with an intuitive sense of what to do next, yet went into it lost and uncertain. To find this place, outer life and consciousness must be a little gloomy, thus causing one to withdraw and to go deep within—there the magic happens, as in the cocoon.

14—The Illuminating Pathway

This is a wondrous channel that flows between the emanations of Wisdom (Father) and Understanding (Mother). It is called "Illuminating Consciousness" (Sekhel Meir) because it is the essence of the "Speaking Silence" (Chashmal). It yields intuitive insights into the mysteries of the holy secrets.

13—The Uniting Pathway

Here is the essence of the "Unity Directing Consciousness" (Sekhel Manhig HaAchdut). Here flows the balm of the completion of our truly unified spiritual being. It runs between the Crown and Beauty/Balance, and where else would we find such a healing union?

12—The Glowing Pathway

From Understanding flows a pathway to the Crown and back again. It is called by the Kabbalists the "Glowing Consciousness" (Sekhel Bahir). It is thus called because it is the essence of the "Ophan-wheel of Greatness," as written in The Book of Enoch and seen by Ezekiel. It is called the "Visualizer" (Chazchazit), the place that gives rise to the Vision Seers, who can perceive the apparition of the Infinite Eternal (Ein Sof). It is also called the "Consciousness of Transparency," indicating that the veil between levels of consciousness no longer has the opacity to it with which we suffer in our limited inner vision.

11—The Glaring Pathway

The final path is called "Glaring Consciousness" (Sekhel MeTzuchtzach), because of the brilliance of the Light of the "I AM." The hidden is exposed, the veil of the temple is rent, and the Holy of Holies is fully illuminated. Here we lose ourselves in the Holy Radiance of our Creator's presence. Kabbalists also call this the "Scintillating Consciousness," because its brilliance is more than a quality of light—it includes vibration and invigoration.

Now we might ask how one can apply all of these pathways in our daily lives. That would indeed be difficult if such pathways were linear and sequential, as our numbering and writing would imply, but they are operating simultaneously in a holistic manner. And, as we seek, they respond, flowing to us. It is God's great pleasure to bless us with these energies and awarenesses.

Why are there so many dynamics in the Kabbalistic teachings? One of the best explanations of this comes from Cayce's marvelous readings:

> Have you conceived—or can you conceive—the requirements of the influence to meet all the idiosyncrasies of a *single* soul? How many systems would it require? In you we find oft one friend for this, another for that, another for this relationship, another for the prop, another to arouse. Yet all are the work of His hand, are yours to possess, yours to use—as one with Him. There are conditions that may meet every idiosyncrasy of the *individual* soul! Then consider the millions, and how much is required of you!
>
> There are centers through which those of one solar system may pass to another, as we have indicated in information for individuals. There are also those experiences in which individual souls may seek a change. As He gave, "as the tree falls so does it lie." [Ecclesiastes 11:3] This is not only material, it is also mental and spiritual. Is God's hand short, that there would not be all that each soul would require? For it is not by the will of God that any soul perishes, but with every temptation, with every trial there is prepared the way of escape.
>
> GOD, the Father, then, is the Creator—the beginning and the end. In *Him* is the understanding, *by* and through those influences that have taken form—in universes—to meet the needs of each soul—that we might find our way to Him.   EC 5755-2

7

THE HEAVENS

"In the beginning God created the *heavens* and the earth." (Genesis 1:1; RSV, ASV, WEB; italics mine) Clearly, the first line in three different translations of the Bible indicates that there are *heavens*, not simply a heaven. When a person says, "I was in seventh heaven," he means that he was the happiest he could be. "Seventh heaven" is expressed in Yiddish, *zibnten himl.* Kabbalah reveals these seven heavens, and even gives insight into how one may come to traverse them.

Merkabah mysticism, based on the visions of Ezekiel, Isaiah, and Daniel and found in Hekhalot writings, teaches the initiate to ascend to and through the heavens by meditation practices, passing from one to another, finally entering through the seven "palaces" in the seventh heaven to the very throne of God.

In contrast, the Hasidim (a pious movement originating in Poland and Ukraine) perspective teaches: "It is not the mystic who ascends through the palaces, but the relational aspect of God that descends to man."

Curiously, Cayce's metaphysical discourses agree more with the teachings of Merkabah. Cayce's readings state it clearly:

No one approaches the Throne—or the threshold of Universal Consciousness—without that purpose of either lifting self to that consciousness or bringing us [heavenly angels and guides] down to their own ideal. Then why, even I [a heavenly guide named Demetrius], should I make thee falter, or why should one seek less than the gods of Glory?   EC 311-5

From the perspective of this heavenly guide speaking through or being channeled by Cayce, we are to lift ourselves up through the heavens to the Throne, for the other way is a faltering way and does not help awaken us to our godly nature and destiny. This guidance also touches on the often ignored teaching that we are gods—sons and daughters of the Most High—as written in Psalm 82 and referred to by Jesus in the gospel of John 10:34.

There are Kabbalah texts teaching one how to achieve a heavenly ascent through the "heavenly palaces" (Hekhalot) and what to expect there. There are also Kabbalah texts teaching how one may draw down angelic spirits to interact with and help the seeker. Cayce's readings are not against this, but encourage seekers to let God send the guides and angels, for He knows best.

There are several larger documents of the Hekhalot (also spelled Heichalot), such as Hekhalot Rabbati (in which six of the seven palaces of God are described), Hekhalot Zutarti, Shiur Komah, and 3 Khanokh (which is also known as 3 Enoch, The Book of the Palaces, The Book of Rabbi Ishmael the High Priest, and The Revelation of Metatron). There are also hundreds of small documents, many little more than fragments, which address the concept of heavenly realms (palaces, firmaments, planes) and describe methods for traversing them (though this is very dangerous and requires much practice and skill—as well as a pure heart and a clear and focused mind).

Among various Gnostic groups and some early Christian ones, the meditative journey through the seven heavens was also known and practiced, always secretly.

The disciple Paul revealed this, too, when he wrote, "I know a man in Christ who fourteen years ago (whether in the body, I know not; or whether out of the body, I know not; God knows), was caught up even to the third heaven." (2 Corinthians 12:2)

In the Koran, dictated to Mohammed by the archangel Gabriel, it is written, "See you not how Allah has created the seven heavens one above another, and made the moon a light in their midst and made the sun a lamp?" (Sura 71)

In most teachings of the Kabbalah the seven heavens are listed from lowest to highest, as in the following (see illustration 15):

1. Veil (Vilon)—the curtain, the veil of heaven (Vilon Shemaim); taken from Isaiah 40:22.
2. Firmament (Raki'a)—the firmament, the canopy, the expanse of heaven, which are the stars, moon, and sun; mentioned in Gen 1:14-18.
3. Cloud/Sky (Shehakim)—the clouds from which the manna from heaven fell to nourish the seekers. Here is where the well of the water of life is and the fountain of gardens; taken from Psalm 78:24-26.
4. Mansion (Zebul)—the lofty dwelling, "mansion of holiness" (*zevul kodshekha*), considered the temple-mansion in the "Golden City"; taken from 1 Kings 8:11-13.
5. Dwelling (Ma'on)—the refuge, a place of peace from the struggles. Home of the ministering angels; mentioned in Deuteronomy 26:15.
6. "City of God" (Makon)—the changeless, perfect residence, containing the template for all life forms. This is the storehouse of good, eternal treasures; taken from 1 Kings 8:39.
7. "Vast Plains of God" (Aravot)—the highest heaven, the vast expansive plains of God, Infinity, the Eastern "Void"; empty, still, silent, a dimension of pure contentment. This is the Divine Womb from which all life originally came into being; taken from Psalm 68:4.

Notice that the first three heavens are associated with physical life, the second three with mental dimensions of consciousness, and the last with Infinity, a quality that human beings would have difficulty knowing directly because of their finite nature. Yet, through sequential passage through each of the dimensions during deep meditation, the seeker can rise to a state of consciousness in the Infinite Mind of God.

In the Talmud, Resh Lakish, one of the most famous scholars of the Torah, describes the seven heavens in some detail:

> [There are] seven, namely, Wilon [Vilon], Rakia, Shehakim, Zebul [Zevul], Ma'on, Makon, Araboth [Aravot].
> Wilon [Vilon] serves no purpose except that it enters in the

morning and goes forth in the evening and renews every day the work of creation, for it is said: "That stretches out the heavens as a curtain, and spreads them out as a tent to dwell in."

Rakia is that in which sun and moon, stars and constellations are set, for it is said: "And God set them in the firmament [Raki'a] of the heaven."

Shehakim is that in which millstones stand and grind manna for the righteous, for it is said: "And He commanded the skies [Shehakim] above, and opened the doors of heaven; and He caused manna to rain upon them for food."

Zebul is that in which (the heavenly) Jerusalem [as described in the Revelation] and the Temple and the Altar are built, and Michael, the great Prince, stands and offers up thereon an offering, for it is said: "I have surely built Thee a house of habitation [Zebul], a place for Thee to dwell in for ever. And whence do we derive that it is called heaven?" For it is written: "Look down from heaven, and see, even from Thy holy and glorious habitation."

Ma'on is that in which there are companies of Ministering Angels, who utter (divine) song by night, and are silent by day for the sake of Israel's glory, for it is said: "By day the Lord doth command His loving kindness, and in the night His song is with me."

Araboth is that in which there are Right and Judgment and Righteousness, the treasures of life and the treasures of peace and the treasures of blessing, the souls of the righteous and the spirits and the souls which are yet to be born, and dew wherewith the Holy One, blessed be He, will hereafter revive the dead. There [too] are the Ofanim and the Seraphim, and the Holy Living Creatures, and the Ministering Angels, and the Throne of God; and the King, the Living God, high and exalted, dwells over them in Araboth, for it is said: "Extol Him that rides upon Araboth whose name is the Lord . . . "   [Brackets and parentheses in the original]

The most important heaven is the lowest one, the Veil, or Curtain, because if we can perceive it and develop a conscious awareness of it, then we have made the first big step toward total spiritual awakening. Despite what you may think, we know this veil well and are familiar with the qualities of our mind on both sides of this veil. To again use a familiar example, how many times have we had a dream that impressed us (either scared us or inspired us), and as we came closer to waking, we noticed that our bladder was full, so we decided to go empty the bladder and then reflect on the dream when we returned? Yet, when we returned to our bed, the dream was completely gone! We had no recollection of it. How is this possible? We just experienced the veil, a most subtle yet opaque veil! When in the dream, we were in our soul mind and were quite comfortable there. We knew it as a part of ourselves. Then, as we engaged our body to walk to the bathroom, we passed through this veil into our outer mind, which is in charge of moving the body. However, our *outer* mind did not have the dream! It has no content of the dream, only a sense that the inner mind has content that is going to be reviewed. But it does not contain that content. Now we see just how subtle and yet opaque this veil is. We do not even notice when we pass through it, and yet, once on the other side, we cannot see back through it.

Fortunately, that's only partially true, because if we practice becoming more aware of subtle aspects of consciousness, we will come to perceive the movement through the veil and what side of the veil we are on at any given time. We will explore more on this in the final section of the book, on Spiritualization and Reunion. For now, let's keep in mind that these levels of heaven are levels of consciousness and that we can expand our consciousness as we awaken spiritually.

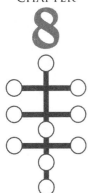

8

ANGELS, ARCHANGELS, AND DEMONS

As crowded and busy as earth is, the heavens are many times more crowded and busy. We look through our powerful telescopes and see no one, but we are only looking at the visible universe; one must look into the invisible realms to catch a glimpse of the real heavens and the angels. Kabbalah has much to say about angels, archangels, and even demons, but let's begin with Cayce's discourses.

(Q) Is the guardian angel a healing force for physical betterment?
(A) The guardian angel—that is the companion of each soul as it enters into a material experience—is ever an influence for the keeping of that attunement between the creative energies or forces of the soul-entity *and* health, life, light and immortality. Thus, to be sure, it is a portion of that influence for *healing* forces.

And as may be experienced in the activities of individuals, it may become so accentuated as to be the greater influence in their experience. Thus it is as has been given of old; that to some there is the gift of healing, to some the gift of speech, interpreting of tongues, to ministering. Yet all are of the same Spirit. For these are ever that which is the assurance, in that as has been given—God hath not willed that any soul should perish but hath with every temptation, with every condition prepared an association, an activity, a manner, a way for the regeneration of those influences or forces that may cause the overcoming of fear or any of those things that would separate a soul from the Creative Forces.

Hence, as has been indicated for this body here, the making of the physical adjustments is necessary; but it is just as necessary for the activities of the associations through which the energies of the bodily forces may be attuned to the spiritual and mental self—through the closer association and walk with creative energies within self.

For *all* must coordinate. Just as in the Godhead—Father, Son, Holy Spirit—so within self: Body, Mind, Soul. Mind is the Builder; Mind is the Way—as the Christ-Consciousness. As it is directed then through the influences of the bodily functions it becomes aware of its oneness, and thus is the guardian force made to be at-one with the whole of the purposes and desires, and the will of the individual.

Do these things then, as we find, as indicated, and we will bring to the physical forces a better cooperation and coordination; and thus through the mental application of the at-onement with the Creative Forces, better reactions in every manner.

(Q) Is it through the guardian angel that God speaks to the individual? (A) Ever through that influence or force as He has given, "Ye abide in me and I in thee, as the Father abides in me, so may we make our abode with thee."

Then as the guardian influence or angel is ever before the face of the Father, through same may that influence ever speak—but only by the command of or attunement to that which is thy ideal.

What then is thy ideal? In *whom* have ye believed, as well as in what have ye believed? Is that in which thou hast believed able to keep ever before thee that thou commits unto Him?

Yes—through thy angel, through thy *self* that *is* the angel—does the self speak with thy Ideal!   EC 1646-1

Notice this last line, because it reinforces the teaching that we are of Divine origin and, despite our present physical condition, remain connected to our Creator through an unseen portion of our being that is angelic: "through thyself that is the angel."

Notice also that Cayce ties the angelic portion of our being to our ideal. Again and again Cayce's readings ask us, what is your ideal? In what and in whom do you believe? Is it our ideal to be among the children of God or simply the children of men? Do we have room in our hearts and minds for heavenly things? Or is it earthly things that matter most to us? You would not be reading this book if they were, so let's assume that you are interested in heavenly things and that these have a place in your ideal life and consciousness.

In this next reading excerpt, Cayce reveals that our angel is always in communion with God:

> The face of self's *own* angel is ever before the Throne. Commune oft with Him.   EC 1917-1

Jesus affirms this in Matthew's gospel:

> Take heed that you despise not one of these little ones [the children gathered around him]; for I say to you, that in heaven their angels do always behold the face of my Father which is in heaven.   Matthew 18:10

When Edgar Cayce was in the deep state through which he obtained readings, his subconscious, or soul mind, could attune to the very highest sources in the spiritual dimensions. In the well-known *Search for God* study group readings, the 262 series, there were occasions when the archangel Michael would actually speak *through* Cayce and give powerful messages. Cayce's discourses called Michael the archangel of change:

> Michael is the Lord of the Way—and in the *ways* of understanding, of conception, of bringing about those things that make for the changes in the attitudes in physical, mental, or material relationships . . . [Michael] is the *guide* through such spiritual relations . . .
> EC 585-1; italics mine

When studied as a whole, the Cayce readings indicate that each of us is a soul that is learning to become companionable to God and all the other created beings (the two great commandments: love God; love others). On the earthly side of the soul is a temporary outer persona we call the personality, often referred to by Cayce as "the body mind." This is what you and I consider to be our real self. On the other side of our soul self is a divine portion of our being that is an angel. It is heavenly, has never left its original place with God, and was made in the image of God. This is the "holy immortal" portion of us, as described in Zoroastrian lore.

For an example of how these three portions of our being interface, let's consider the biblical story of the patriarch Jacob, his twin brother, Esau, and the angel as a metaphor for these three parts of ourselves. In personality, Esau was a hunter and warrior, hairy and strong, wild and free, who loved the fields and woods. Jacob, on the other hand, was more internal and reflective in nature. He was gentle, enjoyed learning and good conversation, liked the company of women and the surroundings of the tribal camp, and had developed a skill with domesticated animals, particularly husbandry of breeding healthy goats and sheep. Esau's soul sought to experience physical life with as much gusto as possible, whereas Jacob, as our soul self, sought to experience the higher, ethereal things, more of the mind and heart than of the body. One night, in a profound experience, Jacob met an angel. He caught firm hold of the angel and would not let it go until the angel blessed him. After the blessing, Jacob asked the angel's name, but the angel was surprised by such a question and gave no answer. Could it be that the angel was none other than Jacob's divine self, his angelic self? After this experience, Jacob said that he had seen God "face to face." How could he make such a statement unless the angel was also before the throne of God? We may consider this story an example of how personality, soul, and angel self interact with one another.

St. Augustine wrote, "Every visible thing in this world is put under the charge of an angel." Genesis Rabba (a Jewish commentary on the biblical Genesis) states, "There's not a stalk on earth that has not its angel in heaven." According to Psalm 91:11, God has charged his angels to watch over us, as Jesus confirms in Matthew 4:11 and 26:53.

There was a time when only our angelic selves existed. The angelic part of our being was alive and active long before Earth, long before physical bodies. Life existed in the spirit, or we might say, in energy without matter. Perhaps, if we think of ourselves as minds and wills without form, this may help awaken us to our angelic portion. The One Mind created within itself many individual consciousnesses and gave them free will. Life went along in this manner for many, many eons before some of these angelic beings took form in bodies. What was it like back then? What were the angels doing? Cayce and Kabbalah, along with many earth legends and fables, give us some of the amazing pre-Earth history. Let's explore some of the chronicles of the angels.

In the Old Testament, Yahweh is called "the Lord of hosts;" *hosts* being the legions of angels. Psalm 82:1 states that "God stands in the Congregation of God; He judges among the gods." Here the angels compose the congregation and are gods within the one God. Notice that the term *Congregation of God* implies that all in the congregation are godlike.

When speaking of angelic beings, the Bible uses the terms *messenger of God (melakh Elohim), messenger of the Lord (melakh Adonai), Sons of God (b'nai Elohim)*, and the *Holy Ones (ha-qodeshim)*. Other terms are used in later texts, such as *the upper ones (ha'oleevoneem)*.

Daniel is the first biblical figure to refer to individual angels by name.

Metatron is considered the highest of the angels in Kabbalistic mysticism. Metatron is briefly mentioned in the Talmud and figures prominently in Merkabah mystical texts. In 3 Enoch, or the Book of Heavenly Palaces (Sefer Hekhalot), there is a link between Enoch, son of Jared (great-grandfather of Noah), and his transformation into the angel Metatron. Surprisingly, there is the same connection in the Edgar Cayce readings! As strange as the name is, this is the highest angel in almost all listings of angels. We'll cover more on this angel later.

Michael, who serves as a warrior and an advocate for Israel (Daniel 10:13), is considered to be the guardian angel of the Israelites, and Gabriel is the guardian of the Ishmaelites (modern-day Arabs). This began with the two sons of Abraham: Isaac and Ishmael. Gabriel is mentioned in the book of Daniel (Daniel 8:15–17) and briefly in the Talmud, as well as in many Merkabah mystical texts.

In Jewish and Dionysian lore, the Congregation of Angels is arranged into two main choirs: seraphim and cherubim.

Seraphim are the highest order of angels and attend to the throne and altar of God. They are variously referred to as the burning ones, the red ones, and beings of fire, because of their association with the fire of the altar of God and the fire of truth, particularly the "test as by fire" that the archangel Michael requires of every soul who attempts to pass to higher levels of heaven. In the Bible, seraphs—mentioned only in Isaiah 6:2 and 6:6—surround the throne of God and bring Isaiah a coal from the fire on the altar of God with which to cleanse his lips and speech.

Seraphs are often depicted with six wings. The colors red and white are associated with them, as well as the element of fire. Cayce's reading 275-35 actually refers to the "seraphim choir" when instructing a young man about his music training, noting that the "Prince of Peace was a harpist" in such a choir.

Cherubim, on the other hand, are mentioned throughout the Bible. Their name is derived from the Assyrian (or Akkadian) word *kirubu*, which means "one who prays, blesses, or intercedes," and are often seen as those who intercede between God and humans. As the second order of angels, they are often depicted as winged children, but this originated during the Middle Ages and is not a classical image of them. Cherubs are depicted as having four wings, and blue is the color associated with them, because of their connection with the sky and, in some cases, with the wind and the element of air.

Cayce's readings portray the angels as active beings, much involved with the lives of humans. They were and are co-creators with the Creator, and as such, created much of the universe that we see. How many angels were created? According to the Egyptians, each star in heaven is the light of one angel, and there are more stars in the portion of the universe that is visible from earth than there are grains of sand on all the beaches and deserts of earth!

The 9 Choirs of Angelic Beings

The traditional order of the angelic hierarchy fits with the three Triads of the Tree of Life (see illustrations 3 and 8), and in each of the three Triads are three choirs of angels. Here is the order:

First Choirs
• Seraphim   • Cherubim   • Thrones

Second Choirs
• Dominations (Dominions)   • Virtues   • Powers

Third Choirs
• Principalities   • Archangels   • Angels

- The Seraphim are the highest order of the nine choirs of angels. They surround the throne of God continually singing, "Holy, Holy, Holy is the God of Hosts!" They are said to be so bright that humans cannot look at them. Lucifer was among the Seraphim before the rebellion in heaven that led to his fall and that of many angels. The Prince of this choir is Michael.

- The Cherubim were God's choice for the Ark of the Covenant. Dionysius taught that these were the angels of knowing, or knowledge. They were assigned to guard the Tree of Life from humanity, less we eat from it and become immortal. (In Revelation this restriction is rescinded, allowing spiritualized humans to eat the fruit of the Tree of Life.) Cherubim are humanlike in appearance and are guardians of God's glory. In Muslim lore, the Cherubim were formed from Michael's tears over the sins of the Faithful. They are alluded to as celestial attendants in the Revelation (chapters 4–6). The Prince of the Cherub Choir is Gabriel.

- The Thrones represent God's divine justice. Dionysius wrote, "It is through the Thrones that God brings His justice upon us." This third choir is known as the "many–eyed ones" because, when viewed by humans, they are covered with eyes. They are known for their humility and submission to God's will. They reside in the area of the cosmos where material form begins to take shape. The lower choirs of angels need the Thrones in order to access God. The Prince of the Thrones is Orifiel, the angel of Saturday and the planet Saturn. He is also Chief of Talismans.

- The Dominions are considered the "Angels of Leadership." Dionysius writes that theirs is the position of authority, regulating the duties of the angels and making known the commands of God. "Through them the majesty of God is manifested." The Prince of the Dominions is Zadkiel, angel of the fourth emanation of Mercy and Lovingkindness.

- The Virtues are known as the "Spirits of Motion" and control the elements. Some refer to them as "the shining ones." They govern Nature. They have control over the seasons, stars, moon, and sun. They are also in charge of and perform miracles, and provide courage, grace, and valor. The fifth choir of angels acts on the orders of the Dominions and represents the power of God. The Prince of the Choir of Virtues is Uzziel, one of the principal angels in rabbinic angelology. According to the

Book of the Angel (Raziel), Uzziel is among the seven angels who stand before the throne of Glory.

• The Powers are warrior angels who fight against evil and defend the heavens and earth. They fight against evil spirits who attempt to bring chaos into the harmony of life. The Prince of this choir is Kamael (Camael). In Druid mythology, Kamael is the Angel of War.

• The Principalities is the seventh choir in the hierarchy of angels. Surprisingly, they have hostility toward God and, not so surprisingly, toward humans owing to sin, which is disharmony and imbalance in the Cosmos. The chaos that has come from sin has made them upset and harsh in their judgment. The disciple Paul writes that Christ has gained ultimate rule over them by virtue of his sacrifice in conquering sin and death. (Romans 8:38; 1 Corinthians 15:24; Ephesians 1:21, 3:10, 6:12; Colossians 1:16, 2:10, 15) According to Milton in *Paradise Lost* (VI, p. 447), the Prince of the Choir of Principalities is Nisroch ("the great eagle"), considered by some to be a demon, continuing the idea that the Principalities are hostile. Of course, some of these descriptions reflect both human and fallen angel fear of the angelic forces.

• Archangels are the predominant type of angels mentioned in the Bible and are considered to be the "chief angels." (Jude 9; 1 Thessalonians 4:16) The Archangels are God's messengers to the people at critical times. (Tobit 12:6, 15; John 5:4; Revelation 12:7) The Prince of the Archangels is none other than Metatron.

• The ninth choir is the Choir of Angels, which includes our guardian angels, who stand before the throne of God and present our petitions while also watching over us, less we stumble on our way to reunion with our Creator. The Prince of this choir is Phaleg, or Phalec, the governing spirit of Mars, often referred to as the War Lord. Phaleg's signet is among the amulets and talismans of protection.

No biblical writer wrote as much about angels and their choirs as Paul. In fact, most of the Bible does not mention much about angels until Paul's letters of the New Testament, where we learn of the Principalities and Archangels and several angels are named. Fortunately, there is so much literature beyond the Bible on angels that volumes could be written about the angels and their choirs. Paul himself writes that before his ministry, he ascended (in his body or out of it, he was not sure) to the third heaven, into Paradise, and learned much of what he would subsequently write about.

A significant angel in Edgar Cayce's volumes is Halaliel. In my search of angelic texts, I could not find any angel named Halaliel. However, it is common for angels to have many names. For example, Metatron has more than one hundred other names! In one very strange Cayce reading, I found that some in attendance believed that Cayce was correlating Halaliel with a most famous angel, Haniel. It was a life reading given to an eight-year-old girl. He is attempting to give this soul's planetary sojourns when, according to Gladys Davis, Cayce's stenographer, he pauses for a long time. Here is her record of this reading. Notice that she was not certain what angel Cayce was referring to and indicates this with her bracketed comments.

> As to the astrological sojourns, we find Venus with [long pause . . .] Haniel [Halaliel? Or 1 Chr. 7:39 Haniel? Or some other?] is rather the guide for the entity, for he is the overlord lord—making for experiences in the entity as of one delicate in its choices, making for a disposition tending towards that of finesse, making the most of all the associations; making friendships easily and drawing upon the force and power from those associations in a manner and way that even the entity itself will not—until it has passed through the experiences of making itself at-one with the greater developing force—understand as to how this is done."   EC 665-1

Haniel (meaning "grace of God") is the angel of the month of December and is, according to *A Theological Discourse of Angels*, the "governor of Capricorn and Venus." Haniel is the angel who carried Enoch (who, according to the Bible, did not die, but was "taken by God") from Earth to Heaven. Haniel is compared with Ishtar, the Chaldean angel who rules Venus. He is an archangel and is listed among the ten holy sefiroth.

Archangels of the Emanations (Sefirot)

A sefira (singular of *sefiroth*) is an initial emanation of God's holy being during the creation of the universe. As we have studied earlier, in

Kabbalah there are ten holy and ten unholy sefiroth. The holy ones emanated from God's right side, and the unholy from His left. Some writers compare the ten holy sefiroth to Plato's powers, or intelligences, and with the Gnostic's aeons, or light emanations.

As angels, the holy sefiroth are arranged in this order (see illustration 8): Metatron (crown), Raziel (wisdom), Zaphkiel (understanding), Zadkiel (mercy), Kamael (might), Michael (beauty), Haniel (victory), Raphael (splendor), Gabriel (foundation), and Metatron (kingdom). Notice that Metatron is both the first and the last in this listing, which echoes Paul's writing of the first Adam and the last Adam: "The first man Adam became a living soul. The last Adam became a life-giving spirit." (1 Corinthians 15:45) [Note: In some schools, Michael is Splendor and Raphael is Beauty, which does seem to fit better with the meaning of their respective names and roles.]

• Metatron (crown and kingdom) is called King of the Angels, Angel of the Covenant, Prince of the Presence, and the Lesser Yahweh (the *tetragammaton*, which is YHWH, the name of the Almighty Father in Heaven). Many believe this name reveals his role as the Logos, God's primary expression into the creation. As the Logos, the Word, Metatron is the bridge between humanity and divinity. He is identified with Mercury, Hermes, Enoch, and several other key figures, all of which Cayce's readings identify as incarnations of the Logos, the Messiah. There is even a Kabbalistic connection between Adam (before he sinned) and Metatron, a connection that Cayce's readings also make. Kabbalah holds that Metatron was the guiding angel of Israel during the forty-year exodus in the wilderness searching for the Promised Land.

The origin of his nonangel-like name is unknown, and it is unusual among Hebrew names. Though difficult to give meaning to, some believe the name comes from the Latin *metator*, meaning "a measurer," which would certainly fit with Hermes, who measured the weight of every soul's heart to see if it were light enough to enter the heavens, and then recorded the finding in the Scroll, or Book of Life. Metatron maintains "the Archives of Metatron." In Jewish angelology, it was Metatron who stayed the hand of Abraham, keeping him from sacrificing his son Isaac. Metatron resides in the 7th Heaven, the dwelling place of God. When evoked, he appears as a column of fire, his face as bright as the Sun. In the Zohar, he is "the rod of Moses," from which comes life from one side and death from the other. Amazingly, Metatron is the Angel of Death while, at the same time, the Angel of Resurrection! The Zohar equates him with Adam before he sinned: pure, powerful, and always in the company of God. Curiously, Metatron is also considered to be the teacher of children in Paradise who died prematurely.

• Raziel (wisdom) is the legendary author of Kabbalah's The Book of the Angel (Sefer Raziel). His name means "Secret of God." It is said that Noah learned how to build the ark by reading Raziel's tome. Raziel is the Herald of Deity and Preceptor Angel of Adam. According to legend, Raziel's great power is magic. In Targum Ecclesiastes (10, 20), the earliest commentary on the biblical Ecclesiastes, Raziel is the angel that was standing on Mount Horeb proclaiming the secrets to all humanity. In Kabbalah, he is the Chief of the Erelim. The Erelim are the Angels of Peace and are known to weep over destruction and death.

• Zaphkiel (understanding) is the governor of the planet realm of Saturn. His name means "Knowledge of God." He is Chief of the Order of Thrones and Ruler of the Order of Cherubim—the angels sent to guard the gates of Eden. Originally they were depicted as the bearers of God's Throne, as the charioteers, and as powerful beings with four wings and four faces. Zaphkiel is also the Herald of Hell, bringing messages to those that have become lost and suffer in their sins.

• Zadkiel (mercy) is the Angel of Benevolence, Mercy, and Memory, and the Chief of the Order of Dominations. His name means "Righteousness of God." He is ruler of the planet realm of Jupiter. In the Zohar, Zadkiel joins with Zophiel (another name for Zaphkiel) when the archangel Michael goes to battle. In some lore and magical books, Zadkiel is the Regent of Hell, ruling over lost souls and sinners—as such, it is comforting to know that he is also the angel of mercy.

• Kamael, often Camael, (strength), meaning "He Who Sees God," is the Chief of the Order of Powers. The Druids considered him the god of war. Naturally, he is the angelic guardian of the planetary realm of Mars (the Roman god of war). He is referred to as "the talisman of the angels"; thus the word *cameo* comes from this angel's name, Camael (more on these cameos and amulets in chapter 9).

• Michael (beauty, or some say splendor) is the Chief of Archangels,

Protector of the Presence (of God), and Chief of the Order of Virtues. He is the Angel of Repentance, Righteousness, Mercy, and Sanctification. His name means "Who is as God." He rules the 4th Heaven and is the guardian angel of Israel (all seekers). He is conqueror of Satan (see 12th chapter of the Revelation). His secret name is Sabbathiel (Lord of the Sabbath, "the intermission"), indicating that when humans rest from their willful doing and when they seek God as opposed to their interests, he protects them. His mission, according to Cayce's readings, is as "the lord [or guard] of the Way, *not* the Way but the lord of the Way, hence disputed with the influence of evil . . . " (EC 5749-3)

• Haniel (victory) means Grace of God, Glory of God, or "He Who Sees God." He is Chief of the Order of Principalities and governor of Venus, as was the Chaldean angel Ishtar. His powers were often evoked by an amulet. His name has been found on many unearthed amulets.

• Raphael (splendor, or some say beauty) means "God has Healed." He is one of the presences with powers over diseases and wounds that afflict the children of men. He is one of the three angels that Abraham questioned about saving Sodom and Gomorrah (Genesis 18; the other two were believed to be Michael and Gabriel). Legend holds that Raphael handed Noah a book of healing after he landed and was to begin repopulating the world. He is the Angel of the Sun, Prince of the 2nd Heaven, Chief of the Virtues, Guardian of the Tree of Life, and the Angel of Healing. He is credited as the angel who troubled the healing waters at Bethesda (John 5). This water healed the first to step in it. In The Book of Tobit (a book of the Old Testament Apocrypha), the archangel Raphael is mentioned. The Cayce readings, works built on holistic healing, actually identify "beauty and the arts" with Raphael more than they do healing, as do a few other sources. In one reading, Cayce told a person that he was present when Raphael "first began to make an influence in the Earth," saying,

> Thus the beauties of nature, the abilities to depict the beauties of nature, are a part of your own heritage. And lucky indeed may be those who may some day have the works of thy hands. For they should be one day almost as precious as Raphael's, in the eyes of those who really enjoy God's pictures of nature.   EC 3954-1

- Gabriel (foundation) means "God is My Strength." In the three religions of The Book (Bible)—Judaism, Christianity, and Islam—he is one of the top two angels, along with Michael. He and Michael are the only two angels named directly in the Old Testament (other angels are secretly known but not named). Cayce's readings state that "Gabriel is, to be sure, the Announcer." Gabriel presides over Paradise and is the ruler of the 1st Heaven. Mohammed said Gabriel (Jibril, in Islam) dictated the Koran to him. Gabriel is the Guardian Angel of the Ishmaelites (the Arabs). He is the angel who appeared to the prophet Daniel and told him all about the future of his people, and was the first to announce the coming of the Messiah. Legend holds that Gabriel was the man–angel that Jacob wrestled with to gain his blessing and new name, Israel. (Genesis 32:24)

- Metatron (kingdom) means the "lesser Yahweh," ruler of the first emanation, who also rules this tenth and final emanation. Recall, this is the only emanation that is able to contain God's initial expression of creative explosion of light, life, and consciousness.

Fallen Angels

At some point in the heavenly activities of the angels, a rebellion occurred. It was led by one of the most beautiful angels, Lucifer, whose Hebrew name means "light bearer," or "light bringer," and is associated with the morning or day star, Venus. "How art thou fallen from heaven, O day-star, son of the morning!" (Isaiah 14:12)

According to the Cayce readings, Lucifer, along with many angelic companions, including one named Ariel, "made for the disputing of the influences in the experiences of Adam in the Garden." (EC 262-57) Cayce further explains that the rebellion actually began in the spirit, long before the physical Garden of Eden, with angels fighting against angels. As we read in the biblical Revelation, the rebellious angels were engaged by the archangel Michael and his angelic army, who drove them out of heaven, causing them to fall from their original grace. They were cast into the earth with their leader, Satan, the name given to now fallen Lucifer. (Revelation 12) These are now known as the Angels of Darkness, which include Lucifer (Light Giver), Ariel (once of the Choir of Virtues),

Beelzebub (once of the Choir of Cherubim, whose name means "Lord of the Flies"), Belial (mentioned 178 times in the Cayce readings and is considered by many to be a form of Satan, formerly an angel of the Choir of Virtues), Leviathan (once of the Choir of Seraphim), Procell (once of the Choir of Powers), Raum (once of the Choir of Thrones), Semyaza (formerly of the Choir of Seraphim), Vual (formerly of the Choir of Powers), and Azazel (once of the Order of Cherubim).

During one of his readings, in which he was vulnerable to dark forces, Cayce actually had to struggle to shield himself from the dark angel Azazel. It began when a questioner asked the deeply attuned Cayce to actually contact Azul (one of Azazel's names, which include the variants Azael, Hazazel, and Azrael, meaning "God strengthens"). This dark angel is one of the chiefs of the Fallen Angels. Legend holds that Azazel taught men how to fashion swords and shields, and women how to beautify their eyelids and wear ornaments to entice men to unclean thoughts of sin. He is known as the Rider of the Serpent, Seducer of Men, and Satan's standard bearer. He refused to bow his head before God's newly created Adam—recall that humankind was made lower than the angels but with the potential to judge them. (1 Corinthians 6:3 and Hebrews 2:6–7)

Here is the record of this profound Cayce session. Observe that the archangel Michael, the Guardian of the Way, actually speaks through Cayce as this dangerous moment developed, determined to protect Cayce.

Q: Can you contact Azul for me?
A: Demetrius, Michael, [yes]; Azul, no.
Q: You cannot?
A: Cannot.
Q: Why?
A: There are barriers between this body and Azul, as produced by that between Demetrius and between Michael.
Q: Can you contact Azul for anyone else?
A: Not under these conditions; for I, Michael, speak as the Lord of the Way. Bow thine heads, O ye peoples, that would seek to know the mysteries of that life as makes for those *faltering* steps in men's lives when not applied in the manner as has been laid down. O ye stiff-necked and adulterous generation! Who will approach the Throne that ye may know

that there is *none* that surpasses the Son of Man in His approach to *human* experience in the material world!

Q: What is my father's name?

A: No.

Q: Can't you answer that question?

A: To be sure, it may be answered. It will not here.

Q: Why will you not answer these questions, when I want to make sure in order to help?

A: He that seeketh a sign when he standeth in the presence of the Highest authority in the Way may *not* be given a sign, unless he has done in the body that which entitles him to same.

Q: Why is Edgar Cayce surrounded by such wrong vibrations and entities in this great work?

A: For there has been the continued battle with those forces as Michael fought with over the body of Moses. He that leads, or would direct, is continually beset by the forces that would undermine. He that endureth to the end shall wear the Crown. He that aideth in upbuilding shall be entitled to that that he *builds* in his experience. He that faltereth, or would hinder, shall be received in the manner as he hinders.

EC 2897-4

In this next reading, Cayce gives a counter to the influences of evil, clearly identifying the nature of evil in our lives.

Q: Comment on "The devil and Satan, which deceiveth the whole world, he was sent out into the earth."

A: Did He not—the Christ, the Maker—say this over and over again? that so long as spite, selfishness, evil desires, evil communications were manifested, they would give the channels through which that spirit called Satan, devil, Lucifer, Evil One, might work? Also He has said over and over again that even the devil believes but trembles. Then he that denies in his life, in his dealings with his fellow man, that the Spirit of Truth makes free, denies his Lord!   EC 262-119

During other readings, an angel identified as Halaliel spoke through Edgar Cayce and was identified among those who fought against the rebellion.

Q: Who is Halaliel, the one who gave us a message on Oct. 15th?
A: One in and with whose courts Ariel fought when there was the rebellion in heaven. Now, where is heaven? Where is Ariel, and who was he?
A companion of Lucifer or Satan, and one that made for the disputing
of the influences in the experiences of Adam in the Garden. EC 262-57

This angel came through Cayce on several occasions, mostly giving
prophecies. Cayce's family and friends became concerned that they were
getting distracted from the One Source, and this angelic communication stopped.

Cayce's protection from the dark angel was well warranted. There are
many detailed legends recounting the activities of dark angels. Rabbi
Joseph's Midrash of Shemhazai and Azazel (yes, the very angel Michael
kept from speaking through Cayce) recounts one of the most detailed
insights into angel lore. Here is a portion of that account:

When the generation of Enosh [son of Seth, grandson of
Adam] arose and practiced idolatry and when the genera-
tion of the Flood arose and corrupted their actions, the Holy
One, Blessed be He, was grieved that He had created man,
as it is said, "And God repented that he created man, and
He was grieved at his heart."

Sometime later, two angels arose, whose names were
Shemhazai and Azazel, and said before Him: "O Lord of the
universe, did we not say to You when You created Your
world, 'Do not create man?'" As it is said, "What is man that
You should remember him?" The Holy One, Blessed be He,
said to them: "Then what shall become of the world?" They
said before Him. "We will suffice, instead of it."

He said, "It is revealed and well known to me that if perhaps you had lived in that (earthly) world, the evil inclination would have ruled you just as much as it rules over the
sons of man, but you would be more stubborn than they."
They said before Him, "Give us Your sanction and let us
descend (and dwell) among the creatures and then You will
see how we shall sanctify Your name." He said to them,

"Descend and dwell among them."

Immediately, the Holy One allowed the evil inclination to rule over them, as soon as they descended. When they saw the daughters of man that they were beautiful they began to corrupt themselves with them, as it is said, "Then the sons of God saw the daughters of man"; they could not restrain their inclination.

Sometime later, Shemhazai saw a girl whose name was Istehar; fixing his eyes at her he said: "Listen to my (request)." But she said to him: "I will not listen to you until you teach me the Name by which you are enabled to ascend to heaven, as soon as You mention it." He taught her the unspeakable Name.

What did she do? She mentioned it and by which ascended to heaven. The Holy One said, "Since she has departed from sin, go and set her among the stars." It is she who shines brightly in the midst of the seven stars of the Pleiades, so that she may always be remembered. Immediately, the Holy One fixed her among the Pleiades [also known as the "Seven Sisters"].

When Shemhazai and Azazel saw this, they took for them wives, and fathered children. [Genesis 6:1-2: "And it came to pass, when men began to multiply on the face of the ground, and daughters were born unto them, that the sons of God saw the daughters of men that they were fair; and they took them wives of all that they chose."] Shemhazai begat two children, whose names were Ohya and Hahya. And Azazel was appointed chief over all kinds of dyes and over all kinds of women's ornaments by which they entice men to unclean thoughts of sin.

Immediately, Metatron sent a messenger to Shemhazai and said to him: "The Holy One is about to destroy His world, and bring upon it a flood." Shemhazai stood up and raised his voice and wept aloud, for he was sorely troubled about his sons and (his own) iniquity. And he said: "How shall my children live, and what shall become of them, for each one of them eats daily a thousand camels, a thousand horses, a thousand oxen, and all kinds (of other animals)?"

One night the sons of Shemhazai, Ohya and Hahya, saw (visions) in (their) dreams, and both of them saw a dream. One saw a great stone spread over the earth like a table, the whole of which was written over with lines (of writing). And an angel (was seen by him) descending from heaven with a knife in his hand and he was erasing and obliterating all the lines, save one line with four words upon it.

The other (son) saw a garden, planted whole with (many) kinds of trees and (many) kinds of precious stones. And an angel (was seen by him) descending from heaven with an axe in his hand, and he was cutting down all the trees, so that there remained only one tree containing three branches.

When they awoke from their sleep they arose in confusion, and, going to their father, they related to him the dreams. He said to them: "The Holy One is about to bring a flood upon the world, and to destroy it so that there will remain but one man and his three sons." Upon that, they cried in anguish and wept, saying, "What shall become of us and how shall our names be perpetuated?" He said to them: "Do not trouble yourselves, for your names. Ohya and Hahya, will never cease from the mouths of creatures, because every time that men lift (heavy) stones or boats, or anything similar, they will shout and call your names." With this, their tempers cooled down.

What did Shemhazai do? He repented and suspended himself between heaven and earth head downwards and feet upwards, because he was not allowed to open his mouth before the Holy One, Blessed be He, and he still hangs between heaven and earth.

Azazel (however) did not repent. And he is appointed chief over all kinds of dyes which entice man to commit sin and he still continues to corrupt them.

In the Bible we find God expressing the fall of the perfect angels:

> You were the signet of perfection, full of wisdom and per-
> fect in beauty. You were in Eden, the garden of God; every
> precious stone was your covering: carnelian, topaz, and jas-
> per, chrysolite, beryl, and onyx, sapphire, carbuncle, and
> emerald; and wrought in gold were your settings and your
> engravings. On the day that you were created they were
> prepared. With an anointed guardian cherub I placed you;
> you were on the holy mountain of God; in the midst of the
> stones of fire you walked. You were blameless in your ways
> from the day you were created, until unrighteousness was
> found in you.   Ezekiel 28:12-15

There is redemption for the fallen, as there is for all souls that have
become lost in the distractions and temptations of free-willed life and
self-centeredness.

Angels of the Dark Side, the "Shells" (Kellipot)

Here is the list of the dark angels that came from the dark side, with
an explanation of their names. These unholy emanations (sefirot) are
shadows of the Holy Emanations (Sefirot) and come out of the left side of
God. See illustration 9.

- Thaumiel, the "Twins of God," the "Two-Headed" (doubled-
mindedness, wanting both God and mammon).
- Chaigidiel, the "Confusion of God's Power."
- Sathariel, the "Concealment of God," who hides the face of Mercy.
- Camchicoth, "Devourers" or "Wasters."
- Golachab, Golab, and Usiel, the "Destroyers."
- Thagirion, the "Builders of Ugliness."
- Harab Serapel, (considered to be plural) means the "Ravens of
Death," the leaders of the infernal regions.
- Samael, "Desolation."
- Gamaliel, "Pollution."
- Lilith, the feminine half of the first Adam, giving Adam one

hundred children every day, according to Rabbi Eliezer in *The Book of Adam and Eve*. The Zohar describes Lilith as "a hot fiery female who at first cohabited with man," but when Eve was created, she "flew to the cities of the sea coast," where she is "still trying to ensnare mankind." In Hebrew writings, the name Lilith first appears in the Alphabet of Ben Sira (circa 900s), though images exist of her that date back to Assyria's golden age. See illustration 18. Many rabbis consider her to have been the temptress of Adam and the mother of Cain.

Lilith is the shadow of none other than Metatron. However, the Light Feminine consciousness associated with the tenth emanation is Shekinah, known as the "Divine Indwelling" and the "Bride of the Lord."

Gnosticism helps us understand this, identifying the female spirit *(he kato Sophia)* who, in her ideal essence, is the "Lightsome Mother" *(he Meter he Photeine)*. In her lower state, however, she is the "Lustful One" *(he Prouneikos)*, a once virginal goddess who fell from her original purity. Here we can see both her light and shadow side as well as her ultimate perfection and redemption.

All demons are mortal, but in the Zohar, Lilith is an immortal until the Messianic Day—a day that is prophesied in Isaiah 37:31: "And the remnant that is escaped of the house of Judah shall again take root downward, and bear fruit upward."

Edgar Cayce's readings identify Lilith as the first Eve and the divine half of the Logos incarnate. Cayce states that Lilith, as the fallen and then redeemed Divine Feminine, was perfected through many incarnations, the final one being as Mary, the mother of Jesus, to whom the archangel Gabriel gave the famed address:

> "Hail, thou that art highly favored, the Lord is with thee; blessed art thou among women. Fear not, Mary, for thou hast found favor with God. And, behold, thou shalt conceive in thy womb, and bring forth a son, and shalt call his name Jesus. He shall be great, and shall be called the Son of the Highest, and the Lord God shall give unto him the throne of his father David. And he shall reign over the house of Jacob forever; and of his kingdom there shall be no end."
> Then said Mary unto the angel, "How shall this be, seeing

I know not a man?"

And the angel answered and said unto her, "The Holy Spirit shall come upon thee, and the power of the Most High shall overshadow thee; therefore also that holy thing which shall be born of thee shall be called the Son of God. And, behold, thy cousin Elizabeth, she hath also conceived a son in her old age, and this is the sixth month with her, who was called barren. For with God nothing shall be impossible."   Luke 1:30-37

Clearly, the angel spoke to this woman as a rare and special soul with a major role to play. This story has all the elements of the Gnostic legend of the Lonesome Mother (Mary) and the Lustful One (Lilith), redeemed in Sophia, the Wise Female.

Redemption and resurrection is a path that all may choose to journey, even Lucifer, as reflected in Scripture. Lucifer, under his moniker "Morning Star," is prophesied to rise again and rejoin the heavenly hosts:

"I am the Alpha and the Omega, the first and the last, the beginning and the end. Blessed are they that wash their robes, that they may have the right to come to the tree of life, and may enter in by the gates into the city."
Revelation 22:13-14

"I am the root and the offspring of David, the bright, the morning star. And the Spirit and the bride say, 'Come.' And he that hears, let him say, 'Come.' And he that is athirst, let him come. He that will, let him take the water of life freely."
Revelation 22: 13-14, 16-17

Seen in these lines are the "root" of David, which was fallen, and the offspring of David, which has risen and become redeemed and restored.

Angels of the Revelation

When Cayce was asked to direct his attention to the seven angels in the Revelation, he gave a fascinating answer and then developed that answer into a clearer sense of how angelic influences govern our experiences.

> Q: Do the 7 angels described in Rev. 8-9 represent spiritual forces governing the various dimensional planes through which souls pass between incarnations on the earth? Please explain.
> A: This is a very good interpretation. Yes.   EC 281-30

He then goes on to explain how our development and application of truths in this world affect our experiences "in the interim," or when we are beyond this world—and, from Cayce's perspective, we are beyond this world when in death, sleep (which he called a shadow of death), prayer, meditation, or deep reflection. Here is his insight into how our actions affect our experiences.

> Happiness is love of something outside of self! It may never be obtained, may never be known by loving only things within self or self's own domain! "He hath given His angels charge concerning thee, lest at any time ye dash thy foot against a stone." [Psalm 91:11-12] Hence we find that in the *interims* where there are the guiding influences of that we have loved. If ye have loved self-glory, if ye have loved the honor of the people more than those thoughts of the mental, spiritual, and moral welfare, what manner of angels will direct thee between thy interims?
> EC 281-30

A bit scary, isn't it? But he goes on to give us some good guidance for avoiding the angels of darkness.

> Think on the study then of self, but let it all become as has been so oft given: "Study to show thyself approved unto God," the God in self, the God in thine own consciousness—that *is* creative in its essence; rightly divining and dividing the words of truth and light; keeping self unspotted from the world. And ye become lights to those that sit in darkness, to those that wander. Though ye may be reviled, revile not again. Though ye may be spoken of harshly, smile—*smile!* For it is upon the

river of Life that smiles are made. It costs so little! It does thee so much good, and lifts the burdens of so many!   EC 281-30

In another reading, he encourages us to commune with God:

Make known unto the Lord what thou wouldst do. The mind will clear in Him. Hold tight to that faith thou hast in Him that is able to keep that you commit unto Him, for in His arms He will bear thee up—and He will give His angels charge concerning thee. They will banish those fears, those walls of darkness that thou hast built in your determinations, in your recklessness in mind. For, savor thou of the things that take hold onto those things that bring fear and darkness, turning thy face from the light? *Face* the light! Draw near to Him. He will draw near to thee.   EC 378-27

Angelic forces are aspects both within us and about us. They are both holy and unholy. Our job is to accentuate the holy and good while minimizing the unholy and bad (meaning that which separates rather than unites). This brings forth the angels of light and our better self, our angelic self. There will come a time when the angels, the morning stars, will sing together again. (Job 38:7)

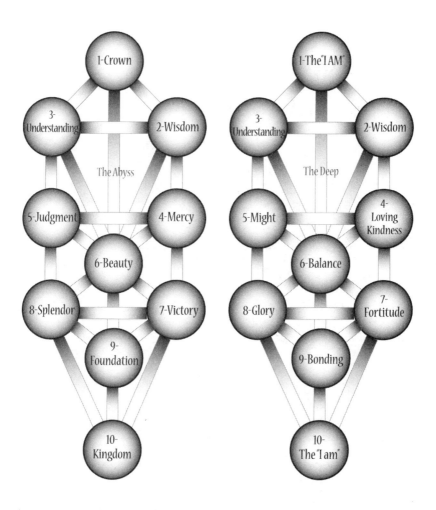

#1–The Tree Of Life with 10 Emanations (Sefirot)
This illustration depicts a common listing of the order and qualities of the Emanations.

#2–Alternative Qualities
This illustration depicts an alternative listing of the qualities of the Emanations. The "I AM" of God and the "I am" of our being are destined for reunion.

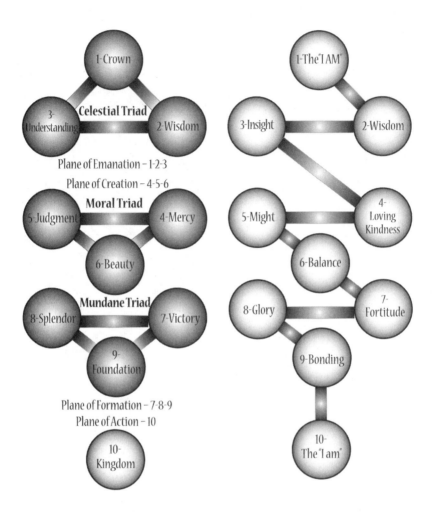

#3–The Triads of Balance
This illustration depicts the three main triads that balanced the energy and the four Planes of Existence.

#4–The Flow of the Emanation
This illustration depicts the flow of energy from God and returning to God, moving between the I AM and the I am.

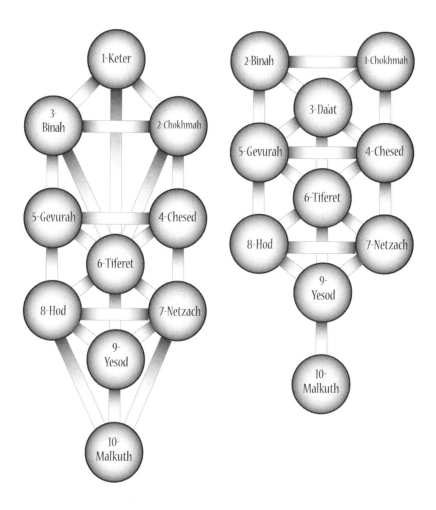

#5–the 10 Emanations (Sefirot)
This illustration depicts the Emanations in Hebrew. Malkuth is also Shekhinah.

#6–A Variant of the Emanations
This illustration depicts a variant developed in the Middle Ages. Da'at means Knowledge.

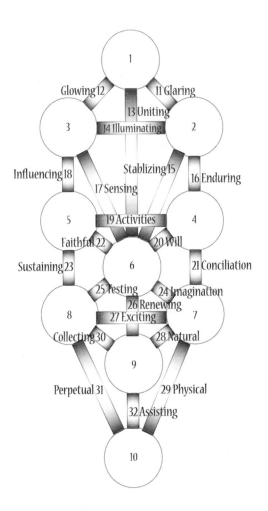

#7–The 22 Pathways/Channels
This illustration depicts the 22 pathways or channels that
run between the orbs. They number from 11 to 32.

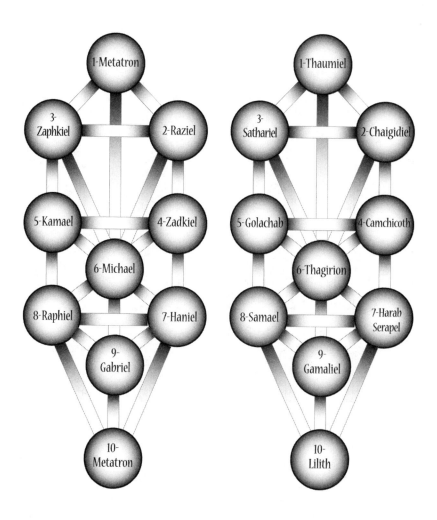

#8–The Archangels of
Emanations
This illustration depicts a common
listing of the Archangels of each
Emanation.

#9–The Dark Angels of Unholy
Emanations
This illustration depicts a common
listing of the Dark Angels of the
unholy Emanations.

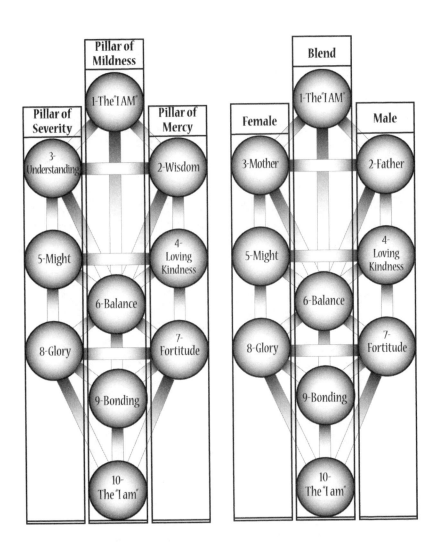

#10–The 3 Pillars
This illustration depicts the three
pillars: Severity, Mildness, and Mercy.

#11–The 3 Pillars
This illustration depicts the three
pillars: Female, Blend, and Male.

#12–The 4 Planes of Existence
This illustration depicts the
four concentric planes around
the Infinite Eternal.

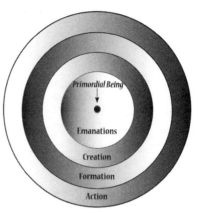

**#13–The 5 Planes—
Primordial Being**
This illustration depicts the four
planes plus the Primordial Being. The
Infinite Eternal is hidden.

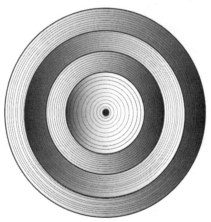

**#14–The 4 Planes—
10 Emanations in Each**
This illustration depicts the four planes;
within each are the 10 emanations.

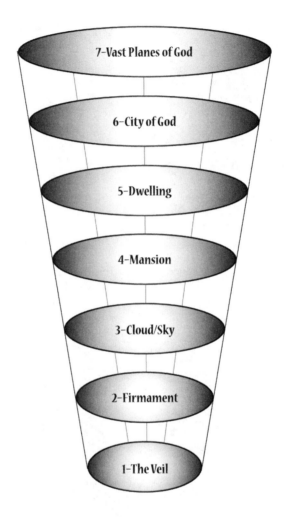

#15–The 7 Heavens
The mystical initiate ascends through the seven heavens,
one after another, using meditative practices.

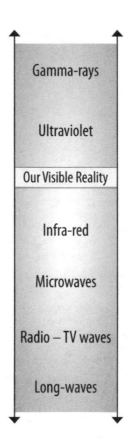

#16–Electromagnetic Spectrum
This illustrates our slender reality in the whole of the spectrum.

10 Emanations

"Palatium Arcanorum" (Place of Secrets) / "Metaphysica gentiles" (gentile wisdom limits)

PALAT UM ARCANO RUM

KABBALA DENUDATA

N. T
EN APXH HN
S Aoroc

She has the keys

"explicat" (she explains)

"antrum materie" (the cave of matter) / "domat" (she calms)
"Intrat" (she enters)
"alterat" (changes for the better)
"mare concupscientiarum" (the sea of ardent longing)

#17–Frontispiece: Kabbala Denudata (Kabbala Unveiled)
Secrets contained in this original Kabbalah imagery.

#18–Lilith—the first Eve
This is a terracotta relief from Sumer,
c. 2000 BCE.

#19—Blue Circle Talisman
Protective Talisman on Turkish airliner.

#20—Hand of Miriam (or Hamesh)
Examples of Protective Talismans.

#21—Handwritten Amulets
Among the most common talismans are
handwritten amulets.

#22—Solomon's Seals
Among the most powerful talismans are Solomon's Seals.

#23—Signet of Orifiel
Protective icon of the
angelic Prince of Thrones.

#24–Egyptian Scarab and Ankh
The scarab symbolizes resurrection and the
ankh life and the life force.

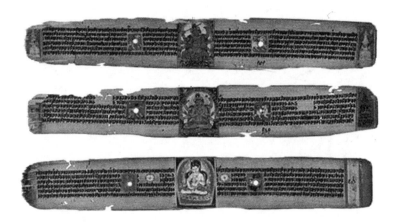

#25–Palm Leaf Manuscript
Written in Sanskrit on palm tree leaves, these
manuscripts have been dated to 1600 BCE.

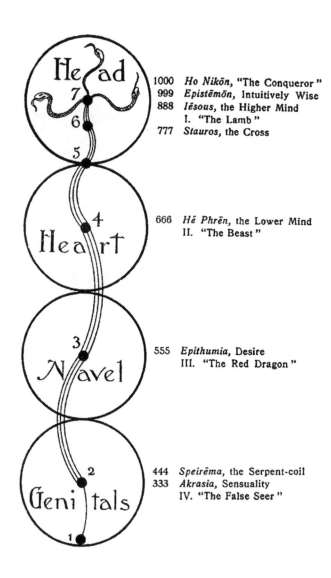

1000	*Ho Nikōn,* "The Conqueror"
999	*Epistēmōn,* Intuitively Wise
888	*Iēsous,* the Higher Mind
	I. "The Lamb"
777	*Stauros,* the Cross
666	*Hê Phrēn,* the Lower Mind
	II. "The Beast"
555	*Epithumia,* Desire
	III. "The Red Dragon"
444	*Speirēma,* the Serpent-coil
333	*Akrasia,* Sensuality
	IV. "The False Seer"

#26–Gnostic and Kabbalistic Kundalini
Kabbalah numbers and Gnostic terms correlated to the
spiritual centers of the body and the Revelation.

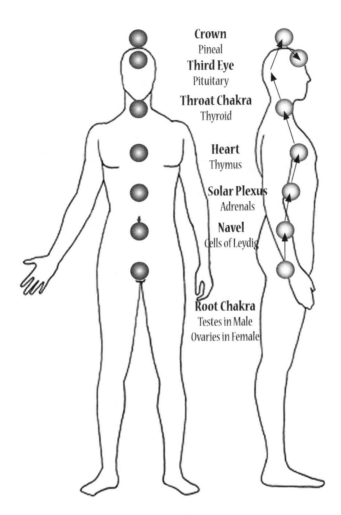

Crown
Pineal

Third Eye
Pituitary

Throat Chakra
Thyroid

Heart
Thymus

Solar Plexus
Adrenals

Navel
Cells of Leydig

Root Chakra
Testes in Male
Ovaries in Female

#27–Spiritual Centers and Kundalini Pathway
The body's spiritual centers and pathways
according to classical sources and
Edgar Cayce readings.

GLAND	CHURCH	LORD'S PRAYER	PLANETS	ANCIENT 4 ELEMENTS	4 BEASTS	OPENING SEALS	COLORS
PITUITARY	LAODICEA	HEAVEN	JUPITER			SILENCE	VIOLET
PINEAL	PHILADELPHIA	NAME	MERCURY			UPHEAVALS (EARTHQUAKE)	INDIGO
THYROID	SARDIS	WILL	URANUS			SOULS SLAIN	GRAY (BLUE)
THYMUS	THYATIRA	EVIL	VENUS	AIR	EAGLE	PALE HORSE	GREEN
SOLAR PLEXUS	PERGAMOS	DEBTS	MARS	FIRE	LION	RED HORSE	YELLOW
LYDEN	SMYRNA	TEMPTATION	NEPTUNE	WATER	MAN	BLACK HORSE	ORANGE
GONADS	EPHESUS	BREAD	SATURN	EARTH	CALF	WHITE HORSE	RED

#28–Edgar Cayce Revelation Chart
Developed from information given by Edgar Cayce.

THE REVELATION—Chart prepared by Helen Ellington and Gladys Davis, based on their study of 281 series, *Bible Dictionary* (Smith's) [1885 edition, Holman and Co.], meditation, etc. (See page 68, Q-1.)

281-29, A-32; Rev. 7, Rdg. 10/28/36-A-32:
281-30, A-6; Rev. 7, Gen. 49, Rdg. 2/17/37-A-6:

4 Corners of the Earth (Body-Jacob) (Influences)
12 Tribes: 12 Major Divisions:

SPIRITUAL (Hail-Water-Sea):
    3 Attributes:
        Light.. Zabulon .... Digestive
        Soul (Love) .... Joseph .... Covering
        Will... Benjamin .... Bone Structure

MENTAL (Fire-Heat):
    3 Attributes:
        Desire .... Simeon .... Organs
        Choice .... Levi .... Glands
        Conscience .... Issachar .... Membranes

HEREDITY (Air-Blood):
    3 Attributes:
        Life (Sensation) .... Aser .... Lymph
        Opportunity .... Nephthalim .... Nerves
        Power .... Manasses .... Elimination

ENVIRONMENT (Earth-Physical):
    3 Attributes:
        Preservation .... Juda .... Assimilation
                                              (To Mental
                                            Material-Spiritual)
        Perpetuation .... Reuben .... Blood
                                              Circulation
                                              (Keeping Alive)
        Attraction .... Gad .... Cells
                                              (Construction)

EXPLANATION OF ABOVE CHART

Spiritual is the life, Mind is the builder, Physical is the result. The body is a physical pattern of the spiritual. Consequently, each major division of the Body must be complete in itself. No one organ can be a major division as it is only a result or a channel through which the three major divisions work; namely, Cells, Blood Circulation, Assimilation.

#29—Edgar Cayce Chart of the 12 Tribes and the Human Body
Developed from information given by Edgar Cayce.

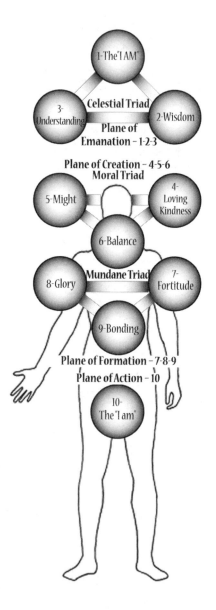

#30—Interconnectedness of Body, Mind, and Soul with Orbs
The Tree of Life and the Planes of Existence are interconnected
in our being: body, mind, and soul.

Occult Influences

9

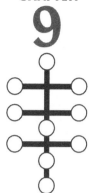

MAGICAL INCANTATIONS AND TALISMANS

One of the most distinguishing aspects of Kabbalah from traditional Jewish theology is the emphasis on magical power. This is especially true of the magical power of Hebrew letters and words, particularly the names and attributes of God. However, in the strictest sense, God does not have a name. The numerous names for God in the literature of Kabbalah are descriptive titles for God's various functions and emanations. For example, *adonai* means "a lord," in this case, *the* Lord, Adonai. It is a title rather an actual name.

Kabbalists use the numerical values of the Hebrew letters in the words to derive insights into the nature of reality, especially the letters in the various "names" for God, the names of the angels, and significant passages of the Torah. Then they use these secret insights to set up powerful protection and influence in the world of human life, where evil influences have to be countered and opportunities captured.

Talismans

With these secret insights, Kabbalists make talismans (from the Arabic *tilasm*, ultimately from the Greek *telesma*, or *telein*, which means "to initiate"; in this case, into the power to avert evil and evoke good, which are objects intended to protect the wearer and bring good fortune, health, and various other human wants.

Amulets

Talismans can be amulets (from the Latin *amuletum*, meaning an object that protects a person from trouble) in the form of gems or simple stones, statues, coins, drawings, pendants, rings, plants, certain animals, and even words said in certain situations.

Cameos

A talisman can be a simple cameo. To protect or amend their destiny, individuals would seek the help of a cameo with an image or words with magical power. The name *cameo* was first mentioned in the Jerusalemite Talmud (tractate of Sabbath, chap. 36, par. 71). The name indicates a means of connecting the body with an object, such as Tefillin (phylacteries), which are black, leather straps used to connect cubes containing parchment scrolls inscribed with the Shema (daily prayer) and other biblical passages. They are wrapped on the arm and head of men during weekday morning prayers. (The Jewish sect of the Essenes included women in this ritual.)

Anthropologists and archaeologists have found cameos in ancient sites all over the world and have concluded that cameos were used in different cultures as early as the Neolithic period, 9500 BCE.

The Evil Eye

According to anthropologists and archaeologists, most of the cameos from the prehistoric period were designed to protect one from the *evil eye (ayin hara)*. This ancient Western belief (the evil eye is not found in East Asia, with the exception of the Usog curse of the Philippines) is that the evil eye may come directly from the devil, from the devil working through someone, from someone who is envious, or even from someone who mistakenly releases good news or displays good fortune too publicly. There are many instances in both the Tanakh (the Jewish Bible) and the Talmud (rabbinic discussions) of people casting the evil eye. In Europe and America, to ward off a jinx, Ashkenazi Jews exclaim, *Keyn aynhoreh!* (also spelled *Kein ayin hara!*), meaning in Yiddish, "No evil eye!"

Attempts to ward off the curse of the evil eye have created many talismans in diverse cultures. As a class, they are called *apotropaic* (Greek for *prophylactic*, or *protective*, meaning "turns away," in the sense that they turn away or turn back the potential harm).

A common talisman is composed of concentric blue and white circles (usually from inside to outside—dark blue, light blue, white, dark blue). This image is considered to be a staring eye that can bend the malicious gaze back to the sorcerer. See illustration 19.

A blue eye can also be found on some forms of the *hamsa hand*, an apotropaic, hand-shaped amulet against the evil eye found in the Middle East. In Jewish culture, the *hamsa* is called the Hand of Miriam; in Muslim culture, the Hand of Fatima. See illustration 20.

The evil eye protector, as a visual device, is known to have been common in Greece dating back to at least the sixth century BCE. In Greece, the evil eye is cast away through the process of *xematiasma* (exorcism), whereby the exorcist silently reads a secret prayer passed over from an older relative of the opposite sex, usually a grandparent. Such prayers are revealed cautiously because there is a superstition that those who reveal them indiscriminately lose their ability to cast away the evil eye.

The Red String Bracelet

Whether it is an ancient custom or a modern commercial product, the red string bracelet has become a special Kabbalah talisman. It comes from a belief that if a red thread is wrapped around Rachel's tomb in Israel seven times while reciting specific Hebrew prayers, especially including Psalm 33, then the wearers of the bracelets made from this thread will carry with them a special blessing, for Rachel loves her children and God loves Rachel. Rachel Emeinu (Our Mother) is considered to be a potent spiritual influence for those in this world.

The bracelet is worn on the left wrist. Judaism.com explains that "the left heart is full of blood and is home to the Nefesh, the vitalizing animal soul in a person. Wearing the string around the left hand reminds the person of the 'battle' that must be waged against one's selfish urges." Further, "every morning, 'a thread of grace prevails' and G-d renews the world for another day. The string symbolizes that 'thread of grace.'" (Note: Such Jewish writers use "G-d" for "God," rather than write the name completely, because they believe that the name should not be spoken aloud or written.)

One of the prayers said as the red string is being blessed is the Ana B'Koach Prayer. Here is that prayer:

We implore You by the great power of Your right hand, release the captive.

Accept the prayer of Your people; strengthen us, purify us, Awesome One.

Mighty One, we beseech You, guard as the apple of the eye those who seek Your Oneness.

Bless them, cleanse them; bestow upon them forever Your merciful righteousness.

Powerful, Holy One, in our abounding goodness, guide Your congregation.

Only and Exalted One, turn to Your people who are mindful of Your holiness.

Accept our supplication and hear our cry, You who know secret thoughts.

This mystical poem in Hebrew consists of seven lines with six words per line. The total of forty-two words corresponds to one of the Holy Names of God. The initial Hebrew letters of each word also refer to this Holy Name.

Icons of Protection and Well-being

This very practical side of Kabbalism used magicians known as Ba'alei ha-Shem, or "Masters of the Name," to create deflective charms. They combined the techniques of magic they had acquired from the Babylonians and Egyptians with the authority and power of the holy Hebrew names of God to create a unique form of Kabbalistic magic.

The most famous cameo in history was the Egyptian scarab (beetle), which was an emblem dedicated to Ra, god of the sun. According to the ancient Egyptians, the dung beetle was a symbol for resurrection from the dung of the world. According to Kabbalah, the beetle was a symbol of infinity. Cayce identifies the scarab with one of the seven ages of humanity in the earth. See illustration 24. Like the scarab, the Egyptian ankh was a sacred cameo representing the power of Eternal Life. See illustration 24.

In Christianity, the crucifix and the simpler cross are protective cameos.

Since the Middle Ages, Kabbalah has been the inspiration for creating cameos containing angel's names or names related to God. Kabbalists had a profound influence on Christian mystics, who learned from the Kabbalists how to use the icons.

Incantations

One of the main devices in Kabbalah magic was the audible citing of biblical passages, God's titles, angels' names, and holy names, sometimes in the form of a prayer or actually calling or evoking the divine influence into action on one's behalf. They contained within them "seed sounds," or hidden syllables, which, when spoken aloud, would evoke, or conjure, magical forces. Here again the Kabbalistic idea that God and His forces enter this world through sounds, phrases, and names gives support to this means of channeling power. Most of these were spoken with authority, not begging or beseeching, but commanding. The incantation would often be structured in such a way as to affirm the facts of God's power and presence and the powers of all the forces of heaven. Nothing was left to doubt or uncertainty. Here is an example:

> I, [your name], servant of God, desire, and call upon thee, and conjure thee, Pureness (Tehor), by all the holy angels and archangels, by the holy Michael, the holy Gabriel, Raphael, Uriel, Thronus, Dominations, Principalities, Virtues, Cherubim, and Seraphim, and with unceasing voice I cry, 'Holy, holy, holy is the Lord God of Hosts,' and by the most terrible words: Soab, Sother, Emmanuel, Hdon, Amathon, Mathay, Adonai, Eel, Eli, Eloy, Zoag, Dios, Anath, Tafa, Uabo, Tetragammonaton (YWHW), Aglay, Josua, Jonas, Calpie, Calphas, Appear before me, [your name], in a mild and human form, and do what I desire.

Repetitions of an incantation were required to total one of the magic numbers—3 and 7, occasionally 9—but a caution was given concerning the number 9 because, in some cases, it evoked certain demons and was considered the number of karma. However, among some groups, 9 was and remains a most powerful number. However, to repeat an incantation the wrong number of times could also render it useless.

In the following incantation, the repetitions vary and need to be recited precisely to gain the full power of the incantation.

> By Thy universal name of grace and favor Yahweh (but not spoken aloud), set Thy grace Yahweh (again, not spoken aloud) upon [your name], son of [your mother's name], as it rested upon Joseph, the righteous one, as it is said, "And the Lord was with Joseph, and showed kindness unto him, and gave him favor" in the sight of all those who beheld him [Gen. 39:21]. In the name of Michael, Gabriel, Raphael, Uriel, Kabshiel, Yah [repeat eight times], Ehyeh, Ahah [repeat four times], Yehu [repeat nine times].

When an incantation was being used to undo something, it would often be said backward (which could be a real challenge) or in a diminishing manner. For example, the demon that brought on fever was Ochnotinos. To break his hold on a person, the healing cantor would chant solemnly and with power in his voice, *Ochnotinos, chnotinos, notinos, otinos, tinos, inos, nos, os*. In this way he would diminish the demon's power until it vanished. When sending one's child off to school, one would incant the name Armimas, the angel of the Sabbath, in a diminishing manner because it was time to stop resting, as one does on the Sabbath, and to start working: *Armimas, rmimas, mimas, imas, mas, as*.

These incantations were often spoken while also stepping backwards or throwing something over one's back. Other actions were also considered to help the incantation, such as spitting, because human saliva was considered to have magical powers. This idea goes way back to the Maya and ancient Egyptians. Isis received her amazing powers from the spittle of Ra, and the Mayan Mother god made the perfect Blue Maze people from the spittle of the Children of God mixed with the ashes of their mistakes.

Reversing the diminishing chant would be used to build up a power. One of the best examples is the famous Key of Solomon (Clavicula Salomonis)—*ton, ramaton, gramaton, ragramaton, tragramaton*—and it concludes triumphantly, *tetragrammaton* (YWHW, Yaweh). This was believed to build up to a point of evoking the very presence of the invisible God and all His forces.

Sometimes these incantations were spoken while standing in a circle or even in concentric circles. There was a belief that demons could not trespass from public territory to private, so standing in one's own circle, one's own space, had protective power that could not be violated. The magician's circle was often scribed with a sword or knife, and sometimes the directions require three or seven concentric circles, the type of metal and the number of circles adding to the protective virtues of this magical method. Often salt was used to form the circle or circles. Interestingly, in the Orient, the general practice at a funeral is for the mourners to circle the coffin seven times, reciting an antidemon phrase. Similarly the late custom among East-European Jews for the bride to walk around her groom under the wedding canopy three or seven times was likely intended to keep off the demons who were waiting to disturb their joy and peace.

Some incantations were chanted. Edgar Cayce also taught that incantations can protect one from evil and lift one from this reality to the heavens, as well as raise the vibrations of the body and awaken the chakras. Here are three comments from Cayce's discourses:

[In a previous incarnation] the entity developed that which later became the chant which to many would drive away what was called the evil eye, the evil influence.   EC 949-12

If there is allowed oft the raising of self through the voice, through the music, that bespeaks of praise—as in the chant to the celestial forces that may make for an attuning of the inner self; these are *well* for the entity.   EC 891-1

With the aid of a low music, or the incantation of that which carries self deeper, deeper—to the seeing, feeling, experiencing of that image in the creative forces of love, enter into the Holy of Holies. As self feels or experiences the raising of this, see it disseminated through the *inner* eye (not the carnal eye) to that which will bring the greater understanding in meeting every condition in the experience of the body.

EC 281-13

Cayce and the Power of an Affirmation

Of all the wonderful guidance to come through Edgar Cayce's attunement to the Universal Consciousness, using an affirmation is unique to him. Affirmations can help us change our mind, mood, and health, and reach new levels of awareness and happiness. He gave over a hundred affirmations to people seeking physical, mental, or spiritual help.

From his perspective, an affirmation is an ideal structured in a potently suggestive statement. It is to be spoken aloud or silently, being sure to maintain a consciousness of the meaning of the words and to maintain a positive, expectant attitude until the whole of one's mental being is affected positively by the meaning. The affirmation is to be repeated three to five times, with the goal of achieving a "full, positive response" from the mental portion of one's being.

By affirmation we mean that it should be an *affirmation*! Not merely spoken in a singsong manner or said just once. Take at least the time to repeat the affirmation, positively, three to five times that there may be the full, positive response in the mental activities of the body.

EC 271-4

I have selected three of Cayce's affirmations. The first one is intended to take hold of desires, needs, and attitudes that we all experience in life and move them to a higher, more universally attuned level, resulting in greater harmony and happiness in our lives. After sharing this affirmation, Cayce sharply instructed the person to "leave it with Him" (God) rather than keep wondering and doubting in anxious waiting for immediate results. His encouragement was to *feel* the power of the affirmation in one's mental self and then let it go free. The reason for this, he explained, was that the "unseen forces" are more powerful than the seen and work in ways unnatural to humans. The unseen forces work best when we have faith in them, a demonstrated faith shown by allowing them to work their magical way through our bodies, minds, hearts, and lives. He said that the spirit of patience, expectancy, and contentment are fertile soil from which the unseen forces can bring forth their miracles.

The second affirmation is designed to help us find the best way to be a channel of blessings to others. Cayce explained that the phrase "my going in and my coming out" (taken from Exodus 28:35) is speaking about going in to the holy place within us, where God meets with us, and coming out from the holy place to relationships with others and our outer work. The going in, of course, is done mostly during sleep, prayer, meditation, and moments of reflection and stillness.

The third affirmation is designed to connect us with what Cayce called "the Christ Consciousness," a state of mind and perspective that best channels the power of light and love into and through us—an excellent state to experience.

Three Cayce Affirmations

Let my desire and my needs be in Thy hands, Thou Maker, Creator of the universe and all the forces and powers therein! And may I conform my attitude, my purpose, my desire, to that Thou hast as an activity for me. (Now leave it with Him and go to work!)   EC 462-8

Lord, here am I! Use Thou me in the ways as Thou knowest best. May my going in and my coming out always be acceptable in Thy sight, my Lord, my Strength, and my Redeemer.   EC 2803-3

Let that mind be in me that was in Him, who knew that of Himself He could do nothing, yet in the power of the light of the Father of all may we, may I, may all, come to know His love the better. Thy will, O Father, be done in me just now.   EC 436-3

Handwritten Cameos and Amulets

Cameos are based on "virtue writing" (in this chapter, the term *virtue* is being used in its Kabbalistic sense of an energy operating without material or sensible substance—an invisible influence emanating into human life). These writings contain ancient scripts, "angel writing," and King Solomon seals. The cameos that appeared later in history were considered to give powers or problem–solving attributes to those who carried them.

Most handwritten Kabbalah cameos contain verses from the Torah, angel's names, God's names, and Hebrew letters, taken from the person's name requesting the cameo as well as the mother's name. In Jewish magic, the sacred name of a person includes the mother's name, and the same rule appears in Greek and Arab magic. In post–Talmudic Aramaic incantations and in the medieval texts, it was quite consistently adhered to, the father's name occurring only rarely. This practice comes from Menahem Recanati's explanation of the Zohar: "All magic comes from woman." In Psalm 116:16, it is clearly stated that every man is "the son of thy handmaid." This follows the secret sin of Adam that we considered in chapter five on emanations: Adam caused the Divine Feminine, who is the handmaid of God, to become divorced from her heavenly mate. As humankind allows the feminine to reunite with the heavenly, humankind gains magical power.

In the Middle Ages, Kabbalists created amulets according to instructions received during séances and channeling sessions. These cameos were written combinations of letters and symbols and would evoke, or conjure, magical forces. Here are three examples of written charms:

Adonai Sabaoth ("Lord of Hosts," "Lord of Armies"), give grace, love, success, charm to the bearer of this amulet.

Ehyeh Asher Ehyeh ("I Am Who I Am"), ha-nora ha-gibbor ("the mighty one," "the hero").

Ehyeh Asher Ehyeh ("I Am Who I Am"), hayei olam le-olam ("eternal life forever").

Early in Jewish history, as a way to save space on precious and scarce writing materials (easy-to-produce paper was centuries away), Jewish scribes developed an elaborate list of abbreviations for commonly used phrases and terms. For example, the title for God, Ha-Kadosh Barukh Hu ("The Holy Blessed One"), became HKB"H. Such acronyms were known as Roshei Teivot, meaning the "heads of words," and these cover the pages of traditional Jewish works such as the Midrash. Here are some samples of acronyms found on written virtues:

ShYCh"G—Shuvah Yah Chatzah Nafshi—"Return O Eternal, save my life." (from Psalm 6:5)

Here's one with simply a title for God:

Sh"Y—Shomer Yisrael—"Guardian of Israel." (from Psalm 121)

Acronyms can also convey a verse from a Jewish prayer, as in this example:

AGL"A—Atah Gibor L'olam Adonai—"You are Forever Powerful, O Eternal." (This is the Gevurot prayer, the second blessing of the "18 Blessings," Shemoneh Esrei.)

Here are two solemn appeals:

BACh"V—Bashem El Chai V'kayyam—"[Do this] in the name of the living and enduring God."
BM"T—B'Mazal Tov—"[bless me] with good fortune."

Here's a call for the protection of angels:

ARGM"N—Uriel, Rafael, Gabriel, Michael, Nuriel.

Another might contain the sum of ten emanations of Kabbalah's sefirot, as in this last example:

CHBT"M—Chochmah, Binah, Tiferet, Malchut—"Wisdom, Understanding, Beauty, Kingdom."

King Solomon Seals

King Solomon Seals are the most powerful symbols in Judaism and Christianity. Each symbol carries its special attributes of power.

According to practical Kabbalah, the King Solomon Seals are famous for their tremendous powers and are used widely for amulet writing. See illustration 21.

The secret of writing amulets properly is in the hands of a few masters who know how to write a faultless and complete seal. A specific script is used for each person's individual request. The text is written in ancient Hebrew scripts and angel writing on a special kosher (legal) parchment, made of deer skin (also used for Mezuzah scrolls), using feather and ink. It is well developed and written according to the name, the birth date, and the mother's name of the person ordering it, and fitted to solve the problem or the request.

The most effective handwritten amulets, apparently, are those dedicated to the requester personally and prepared as just mentioned.

Magic in the Psalms

The Medieval Jewish text Shimmush Tehillim ("On the Use of Psalms") probably formed the basis for Godfrey Selig's (1673–1708) *Secrets of the Psalms: A Fragment of the Practical Kabbalah*. Each of these books explains how to use words and phrases from the Psalms. Here are some examples from *The Sixth and Seventh Books of Moses* by Johann Scheible and Moses and Joseph Ennemoser. The accompanying comments are those of Eoghan Ballard of the University of Pennsylvania:

Psalms for Making Peace between Husband and Wife

Psalms 45 and 46—Whoever has a scolding wife, let him pronounce the 45th Psalm over pure olive oil, and anoint his body with it, then his wife, in the future will be more lovable and friendly. But if a man has innocently incurred the enmity of his wife, and desires a proper return of conjugal love and peace, let him pray the 46th Psalm over olive oil, and anoint his wife thoroughly with it, and, it is said, married love will again return.

Eoghan Ballard: Psalm 45 refers to anointing with "the oil of gladness" and to the "rejoicing" that occurs when the "glorious" daughter of the King of Tyre is brought before the King. Psalm 46 contains the words, "God is in the midst of her . . . God shall help her . . . He makes wars to cease unto the end of the Earth."

Psalm to Make Your Home Lucky

Psalm 61—When you are about to take possession of a new dwelling, repeat this Psalm just before moving in, with a suitable prayer, trusting in the name of Schaddei (the True God), and you will experience blessing and good fortune.

Eoghan Ballard: Psalm 61 contains the lines, "Thou hast been a shelter for me, and a strong tower from the enemy. I will abide in Thy tabernacle forever; I will trust in the covert of Thy wings."

Psalm for Safe Travel at Night

Psalm 121—When you are compelled to travel alone by night, pray this Psalm reverently seven times, and you will be safe from all accidents and evil occurrences.

Eoghan Ballard: Psalm 121 opens with the line, "I will lift up mine eyes unto the hills, from whence cometh my help."

Psalm for Severe Headache or Backache

Psalm 3—Whosoever is subject to severe headache and backache, let him pray this Psalm [. . .] over a small quantity of olive oil, [and] anoint the head or back while in prayer. This will afford immediate relief.

Eoghan Ballard: Psalm 3 contains the line, "Thou, O Lord, art a shield for me; my glory, and the lifter of mine head."

Psalm for a Repentant Liar
Psalm 132—If you have sworn to perform anything punctually, and notwithstanding your oath you neglect to perform your obligation, and in this manner have perjured yourself, you should, in order to avoid a future crime of a similar kind, pray this Psalm daily with profound reverence.

Eoghan Ballard: Psalm 132 contains the line, "The Lord hath sworn the truth unto David; he will not turn from it."

The 10 Words of Creation

The following is a powerful magic built on the first lines in the Bible. Naturally, they are called The Ten Blessings of Creation (Asser Ma'Amarot) and correspond to the ten emanations (sephirot):

1. Genesis 1:3—(Ve-Yomer Elohim), "Let there be light," and there was light.

2. Genesis 1:6—(Ve-Yomer Elohim), "Let there be an expanse in the midst of the waters, and let it divide the waters from the waters."

3. Genesis 1:9—(Ve-Yomer Elohim), "Let the waters under the sky be gathered together to one place, and let the dry land appear," and it was so.

4. Genesis 1:11—(Ve-Yomer Elohim), "Let the earth put forth grass, herbs yielding seed, and fruit trees bearing fruit after their kind, with its seed in it, on the earth," and it was so.

5. Genesis 1:14—(Ve-Yomer Elohim), "Let there be lights in the expanse of sky to divide the day from the night; and let them be for signs, and for seasons, and for days and years."

6. Genesis 1:20—(Ve-Yomer Elohim), "Let the waters swarm with swarms of living creatures, and let birds fly above the earth in the open expanse of sky."

7. Genesis 1:24—(Ve-Yomer Elohim), "Let the earth bring forth living creatures after their kind, cattle, creeping things, and animals of the earth after their kind," and it was so.

8. Genesis 1:26—(Ve–Yomer Elohim), "Let us make man in our image, after our likeness: and let them have dominion over the fish of the sea, and over the birds of the sky, and over the cattle, and over all the earth, and over every creeping thing that creeps on the earth."

9. Genesis 1:28—(Elohim Ve–Yomer), Blessed them, "Be fruitful, multiply, fill the earth, and subdue it. Have dominion over the fish of the sea, over the birds of the sky, and over every living thing that moves on the earth."

10. Genesis 1:29—(Ve–Yomer Elohim), "Behold, I have given you every herb yielding seed, which is on the surface of all the earth, and every tree, which bears fruit yielding seed. It will be your food."

Edgar Cayce and Magic

The following are several past–life readings for souls who had developed magical skills and divinations, some for weal and some for woe. Cayce's comments on these add to our understanding of magic.

The entity was among those who by its own wits, as would be called, today (being left by others and by its companion), made what would be called now sorceries or divinations, using charm and magic as a means to attain those desires and purposes.

Hence in the present all things pertaining to charm, sacred formulas, societies, initiations, the ritual of varied groups are of interest to the entity, no matter whether these are in the darkest minds of men or in the higher ritualistic orders.

These abilities were not used for other than material things. Thus, while they have the material hold, they must be watched and guarded against becoming the thing ye worship, rather than the spiritual. Hence the warning that has been indicated to the entity. It is the spirit with which ye do a thing, the purpose that brings weal or woe in its effect in the experience. EC 3285-2

Here's another:

Before that the entity was in the French land, during those periods when there were disturbances and wars not only with the Huns but with those peoples of the Norse land.

In that period the entity found the needs for relying upon the cunningness of its ability to work magic, as it were; to use all the wiles of every nature to have and hold its place or position among those in such times. Yet the entity then, in the name Madame Queluman, was equal to the occasion.

Thus those experiences as may be found in the abilities of the entity to judge individuals, to know the way of their thinking, or what they think; the abilities as one who is sensitive to the activities of others, those who are interested in all forms of occult or mystic powers, the influence of charm, the influence of rote. All of these become a part of the innate or manifested experience of the entity.   EC 2835-1

In this next reading, the soul learned her magic from Native Americans in the Virginia territories; specifically, from the children of the medicine men.

Before this we find the entity was in the land of the present nativity when there were the friendships of the entity, as Leila Fitch, which made for associations with the offspring of the medicine men of the Virginia land; not too far from the present environs but between the areas close to the river, yes, but on the other side and above Jamestown and Williamsburg.

The entity then learned from nature, understanding of the manifesting of life in the earth. The entity had the abilities in the hands to make things, to bring to pass in the experiences of others by using what is sometimes called magic. It is natural law of attraction or repulsion of activities by rote of mind, as well as elements in nature itself; for, as is understood by those who would interpret man correctly, the body-physical if alive is composed of all the elements in the earth. Some have antipathy, others have attraction, and the attraction may be used to create, or antipathy may be made to work against or produce thoughts, conditions, emotions in the bodies of others.

These the entity used, not too seriously, yet to its own questioning by others.

Thus in the present, in relationships which have been with peoples and groups, sometimes a question mark, and yet greater are the abilities of the entity even in the present to use divine science, or divine attraction, to bring to pass in its experience those things which may help or hinder.

Never use thy abilities for self-indulgence or self gratification; it becomes sin.   EC 5277-1

The next past–life account goes all the way back to ancient Egypt. Cayce even uses the term "Higher spheres" in relation to learning about the Creator.

In the one then before this, we find in the Egyptian country, when the first laws were being transcribed or given to the peoples under the second ruler, or the one who gave the greater forces in learning pertaining to all arts and designs of man to show the relations with the Higher spheres, or relation between the Creator and the created. The entity was in the capacity of the soothsayer, or magician of that Court. The personality and urge as we find from this, in that of the study of all things mystical and pertaining to the lost arts, especially concerning metals and alchemy. These are the studies the entity seeks.   EC 182-2

It was common for Cayce to reference planetary sojourns when giving past–life readings, because he taught that souls not only incarnate in the three–dimensional realm of earth but are active between incarnations in fourth– and fifth–dimensional realms associated with the planets in this solar system!—realms comparable to colleges within the university of this system.

In entering, we find the entity coming under the influence of Neptune and Venus, with those influences as are seen in Uranus, Jupiter and Mercury. Many are the influences as are seen innately in the entity's experience, and these—from the astrological influence—*will* influence, *do* influence, unless the entity applies will in an *unusual* way and manner; for that as is *builded* in the present is rather strong in these influences, *especially* in Neptune, Venus and Uranus, Neptune making for those of the mystic, especially influencing this entity in the respect that those forces as come from that as may be termed odors, incenses, or such, will influence the entity in an unusual way and manner. Rather, then, in the application of self in this respect, let this body be tempered by judgment, understanding, and reason, and when duty—*in* love's influence—is in accord *with* same, may the entity apply self in a manner as to *build* for the greater influences to make for development for self and for others, for *through* this may the entity, in the *application* of self, gain for self—and in building for others, make for the greater development and the greater aid to many.

In that as is called, then, mysticism, or magic, may the *entity* excel—will these be tempered by those of the forces of love, duty, and reason.

One naturally adapted to self and to associates as regarding the reading, understanding, of mystic and magic influence.

One that is naturally adapted and gifted in making of relationships, or of losing same.

One as of broad experience, and no matter what field or endeavor the entity may choose, will be as of much of the experience that has been already gained within the entity's *influences*; also there will be seen many of those conditions when those of hardships, as related to *understandings* of individuals, must arise in the entity's experience.

In the *abilities*, these lie for the entity in the development of the *mental* field as *related* to that of the occult and mystic forces in life.

In the abilities of the entity, and that to which it may attain in the present:

In the field of the understanding of the magic or mysterious forces, especially as applied to the influences over peoples, and in the *application* of same—whether as to song, music, or of precious stones—even these that have to do with the odors—may the entity gain, conquer self, and develop through these experiences; keeping in that way in which the criterion for the development is made as the ideal; holding that, the entity may reach to that position as to *whatever* is desired, so long as the *desire* is in accord with that universal force or development, called—God.   EC 1714-1

There are objects and words that have power for us. Some have the power of protection, some keep us centered, some inspire us, and some shield us. Yet, as we grow in spiritual awareness and strength, the magical power comes increasingly from our sense of oneness with the source of all power—God. Even so, God's blessing can be upon an object or in a name or phrase that we carry with us on our journey through material manifestation.

Cayce and the Power of Stones

During Cayce's amazing soul readings, he would occasionally instruct the seeker to wear, usually "next to the skin," a specific stone for a little extra help with the challenges of life and of living in a physical body that is sensitive to vibrations. In the order of frequency with which he mentioned a specific stone, I have selected the top four: lapis, pearl, amethyst, and coral.

LAPIS
Cayce explained that lapis is not a mineral but a metal, the "erosion of copper." (EC 3416-1) We know that copper is a good conductor of electricity, but Cayce did not go there. He said that lapis has "the vibratory helpful force for health, for strength, for the ability through the mental self to act upon things, conditions, decisions, and activities" and "will bring health and hope, and—best of all—the ability to *do* that so desired." (EC 1651-2)

Occasionally, he would explain that the stones he recommended were connected to a person's past-life experiences; for example:

> The entity should ever wear about the body the lapis lazuli or the lapis linguis; for these will bring strength to the body through those vibrations that are brought or built in the innate experience of the entity from its sojourn in the Egyptian land.   EC 691-1

King Tut's golden death mask was made with lapis and coral.

Lapis linguis has greenish tones, a color that Cayce identified with healing. Lapis lazuli is blue, a color Cayce identified with spiritual growth.

Lapis lazuli is akin to the azurite family of stones. Of course, azurite gets its name from the deep blue color azure (derived from an Arabic word for blue).

The greenish lapis linguis is closely akin to malachite. Malachite and azurite are often found together. They occur abundantly in Arizona and New Mexico.

However, true lapis contains lazurite (not to be confused with lazulite). The little difference between pure lazurite and lapis is that lapis also contains pyrite (golden yellow flecks or streaks) and calcite (white flecks or streaks), and is more common than pure lazurite, which is rare and expensive. Fortunately, Cayce specifically named lapis lazuli and linguis, not lazurite.

Lapis is found in Afghanistan. It was mined six thousand years ago for the Egyptians. Afghanistan is the modern name for the biblical "land of Nod, east of Eden," to which Cain was banished. Lapis can also be found in California and Colorado as well as Argentina.

Lapis has been used to protect and strengthen its wearers since very ancient times. In several readings recommending lapis, Cayce warned that its vibrations were too high to be touching the skin. He recommended that it be enclosed in crystal or glass or that a piece of glass or crystal be placed between the body and the lapis.

To Cayce, lapis is a spiritual stone that can be helpful in raising our attunement during meditation. However, he gave this warning:

> But know these, my child, are but means—and are *not* the God-Force,
> *not* the Spirit, but the *manifestations* of same.   EC 707-1

PEARL

Lapis has long been considered to be a good stone for men and has been popular with them for millennia, but the pearl is unquestionably feminine. From antiquity, it has been considered to have magical properties.

Pearls are organic gems. As we know, they are created by an oyster (mollusk) covering a foreign object with beautiful layers of *nacre*, the iridescent combination of layers of calcium carbonate crystals between layers of biopolymers (silklike proteins).

Long ago, pearls were rare, because thousands of oysters had to be searched to find one pearl. Today pearls are cultured by placing shell beads inside an oyster and harvesting the resulting gem. More than forty Cayce readings mention pearls. Here are some examples:

The pearl should be worn upon the body, or against the flesh of the body; for its vibrations are healing, as well as creative—because of the very irritation as produced same, as a defense in the mollusk that produced same.   EC 951-4

Thus the entity should ever keep a pearl about the self or upon the person, not only for the material vibration but for the ideal expression. For, it will be an omen—not only because of the vibrations that it may give to self but because of keeping the even temperament, yea the temper itself. For the entity can get mad, and when it is mad it is really *mad!*
                                                                EC 2533-1

A pearl is an adornment, a thing of beauty, created through the irritation of that which manifests itself in a lowly way to those that consider themselves of high estate; but by the very act of irritation to its own vibration is the higher vibration created, or brings about the pearl of great price.   EC 254-68

As you can see, Cayce teaches that the very process of creating pearls builds a vibration that helps those who wear them next to their skin. The oyster creates the pearl to protect itself from the foreign object in its shell; thus protection and defense is the vibration given off by the pearl.

AMETHYST
Amethyst is a purplish quartz crystal. It was one of the stones in the breastplate of the high priest in Exodus.

It is mined throughout the United States and Brazil. Its name comes from a Greek word meaning "not intoxicated." An ancient Greek myth tells of a fair maiden who wished to remain chaste but was pursued by Dionysus, the god of wine and intoxication. She received protection from Artemis, who turned her into a beautiful statue of crystal quartz. Humiliated by what his desires had created, Dionysus then wept over her, and his tears of wine turned her crystalline image purple.

Cayce valued the stone as a protection from dangerous emotions and desires. He explained to one person that amethyst on the body would quiet the body from physical depression or physical reactions that make one restless and ill at ease. (EC 1626-1) He told another that the stone and its unique color would help control temperament. (EC 3806-1) He often recommended it be worn as an "amulet or adornment about the body." (EC 1035-1)

However, he warned that all stones are but "step–stones" to better conditions, "not foundations." (EC 500-1) The stone does not change the person. The stone simply adds a helpful vibration. The mind and the heart must *use* the assisting vibrations of the stones to improve their activities.

In reading 364-12, Cayce tells us that an Atlantean temple had semi–circular columns with inlaid amethyst that would catch the sun's rays, making various light patterns and colors move through the chamber, casting a protective vibration.

CORAL

If you wish to have quiet in the midst of "unquiet," Cayce recommends coral (red, rose, pink, or white): "The body will find that the unquiet and the tumultuous conditions will be changed to the harmonious abilities to give out." (EC 694-2) He explains that coral carries the natural forces in nature that calm human emotions. In this same reading, he says,

> Your soul has been tried as by fire through many of your experiences in the Earth. Yet there are those things that make for harmony in their relationships as one to another, as do the turmoils of the mother-water that brings forth in its activity about the earth those tiny creatures [coral] that in their beginnings make for the establishing of that which is the foundation of much of those in materiality. Hence the red, the deep red coral, upon thine flesh, will bring quietness in those turmoils that have arisen within the inner self; as also will the pigments of blue

to the body bring the air, the fragrance of love, mercy, truth and justice
that is within self.   EC 694-2

Mixing the red coral with blue apparently brings mother–water, air,
and the fragrance of the fruits of the spirit that we need so much in our
lives and in our inner selves.

Overall, Cayce recommended coral to ease mental and vibratory
urges that make disturbances in oneself. In a reading for Ms. 2154-1, he
warned against wearing the red or white coral but encouraged wearing
rose coral.

In discourse 307-15, he said that coral as jewelry or ornaments is
inherently of Creative Forces, as it is from water itself. Again, like the
pearl, the manner and environment in which the stone is made carries
a vibration that the body can use.

In closing, it is important to understand that the stone in itself does
nothing but contribute to the vibrational mix around oneself. Selecting
the right stone for your needs has to come from within you, and these
vibrations may change as your vibratory needs change. We need to use
our intuition and perhaps test various types to find those that are right
for us.

One last tidbit. Occasionally, Cayce identified the stones as "omens." I
believe he meant this in the sense of something good coming from
wearing the stones. Cayce taught that the stones are not merely omens
or good luck charms but are vibratory aids "for health, for strength, for
the ability through the mental self to act upon things, conditions, decisions, and activities." (EC 1651-2)

10

THE INFLUENCE OF NUMBERS

Cayce's discourses state that the best numerology is the ancient Hebrew mysticism found in Kabbalistic, or "Talismanic," teachings, which he says is "a combination of the ancient Persian or Chaldean, Egyptian, Indian, Indochina, and such." (EC 5751-1)

The translation of the Hebrew word *sefirah* is "counting," although it has many connotations, our focus having been on its use as an emanation. For the Kabbalists, each number rules manifestations that fit that number. Seven, for example, rules the seven orifices in the human head (eyes, ears, nostrils, and mouth), the seven days of the week, the seven planets of ancient astrology, the seven chakras, and so on. Four is found in the "city four square" and the four elements of this world, and the like. Twelve rules the zodiac, months, and so on.

The Book of Creation (Sefer Yezira), more scientific than religious, indicates that the Creation, at one level, was accomplished by divine speech. Hinduism also presents the idea that sound created the universe. There are twenty-two letters in the Hebrew alphabet, and there are 231 possible variations using these twenty-two letters. Rabbi Harav Yitzchak Ginsburgh writes that "two-letter units are sub-roots, each sub-root being a gateway to meaning and understanding. We are taught in Kabbalah that there are 231 gates." The Hebrew word for *gate (sha'ar)* also means "opening," and it is through these openings that the Word of God expressed the Creation. Each of these numbers is a creative portion of the ensemble of the Creation.

Kabbalah teaches that all of creation emanated from the Ein Sof, the Infinite Eternal. It did so through the sefirot, the ten emanations of Its being expressed in the Tree of Life. From the tenth emanation came the twenty-two letters of the Hebrew alphabet. These letters are more than letters; they are powers with numerical values. From these numerical powers the whole finite universe came into existence. Number is the essence of all things. The existence and relationships of everything depends on numerical proportions. Since the essence of everything is number, the number associated with anything reveals its essence.

All the twenty-two letters are coordinate powers. Even so, the number 3 is obviously different from the number 6, and computations of numbers will differ according to the components involved. But it is important to keep in mind that all is one, and each expression contains a portion of the Whole.

Allow me for a moment to be a bit abstract in an attempt to reveal how numbers may be adjusted to achieve harmony and balance. In Kabbalah, there are three levels of high numerical expression: Equal Balance, Addition, and Separation. When both one's inner disposition and outer life circumstances are equal, then there is Equal Balance. When balance requires adding to life's equation (either in self or in one's outer activity), then the highest goal is Addition. When one needs to reduce some influences or separate from some influence to achieve balance, then the highest mission is the expression of Separation. Each mission has its degree, hence the designations Degree of Equal Balance, Degree of Addition, and Degree of Separation, respectively. When examining oneself and one's life, it is helpful to consider these three principles and the degree of need to find ultimate harmony.

Kabbalah numerology gives numeric values only to letters, words, and names, whereas traditional numerologies commonly evaluate dates and numbers as well.

Kabbalah numerology can become so complicated as to confuse and distract from one's soul journey, leaving one lost in the multiplicity of this dimension. For example, in one system the numerical value of a letter is "filled" (miluim), or expanded. Using this method, the letters in the name of God become words with sums of 72, 63, 45, and 52, but each letter has variant spellings, so there are 27 possible expansions of the Holy Name. When all of this is calculated, the expansion totals 1521! Even so, God is Oneness. We are not going through this maze to get to the simple truth that God is one.

In this chapter we will focus only on the primary numerical values and their helpfulness to our soul growth. The Kabbalah numerology used here is based on key chapters in The Book of Creation (Sepher Yetzirah). It is expressed in the ten emanations and the twenty-two channels through which the energy of the Tree of Life flows.

Numbers are all around us, of course: the date we were born, our address, our phone numbers, social security numbers, our automobile tags, and our name all have numbers associated with them. Every day, month, and year has a number associated with it. Cayce advises us to approach numerology in a much different manner than commonly practiced today. The numbers do not dictate our conditions or opportunities, they *reflect* the conditions or circumstances within which *we determine*, by the use of our free will, what will be built. If we keep this in mind, we will get the most out of numbers and numerology. Here is an interesting Q & A from Cayce's readings:

Q: What months and years will be of greatest progress for this body materially and spiritually?

A: These, as indicated and as given, are *built*; rather than their *influencing* the conditions that come about for changes for material or mental, or spiritual advancement; and are much in the same category as numerological conditions or astrological influences. These influences are activities that an individual has accomplished in certain periods, that with their cycles bring those influences that act as a stimuli during certain periods.   452-6

In this reading Cayce brings up the influence of cycles: the circling around again of karma, tests, patterns, types of people, circumstances, and habitual reactions. Some are coming toward us, some surround us, and some are going away from us. There are numbers that relate to the past, while others portend the future. In this reading and others, Cayce explains that we are all in the midst of cycles, which he describes as "those influences that act as a stimuli during certain periods." Thus, certain numbers will be relevant at certain times in our lives but not at other times. Remember this in order to avoid assigning any one number to yourself or your situation. You are growing, and situations and opportunities change. These cycles give us another opportunity to improve and grow spiritually.

Here's another teaching from the same reading:

> The *influences* are made, and when the cycle rolls around the influence is there! As an illustration: An individual builds for self in certain surroundings a certain environment, as in the visitation of certain places, certain lands or certain homes. While in a certain surrounding, a certain environment or influence is natural. So it is with the cycles of time, or with those periods in year, month, day, hour, or what, the influence of those conditions have their bearing upon the mien of the individual.
>
> EC 452-6

He is saying that we build for ourselves certain situations, rhythms, patterns, habits, and surroundings—in a "normal" day's cycle, in a week's cycle, in a year's cycle—that naturally influence our demeanor. We can take this to mean that our disposition and temperament change naturally as the movement of the cycles stimulate us in different ways, but we determine how we react or use them.

Think of it this way: what are you like at 6 a.m.? What are you like at 6 p.m.? What are you like and what are the influences in your life in winter months? In summer months?

We have to take responsibility for our role in the numbers around us and know that we have the innate power to change our reaction to any condition by using our God-given free will. Even when circumstances are blowing against us, we can always tack against that wind, like a good sailor, until we reach a more favorable breeze as the cycle shifts again. We are the key to what the numbers mean and how we use the influences they represent.

Kabbalah and the Meaning of Numbers

Number 1

From a Kabbalistic perspective, the number 1 represents both the beginning and the oneness within which multiplicity exists.

One is first, and all the numbers follow from the one.

The first expression reflects the Infinite Eternal's creativity, which is motivated and guided by love. Here are the Creative Forces, as opposed to the destructive ones. Here is the womb of Divine Love that conceived the entire Universe—and cares. The first emanation of the Divine on the Tree of Life is the "I AM that I am."

Some Kabbalists believe this first emanation of God reveals the Creator's concern for Its creation, having the sole purpose of shielding the world and the world's beings from the brilliant yet blinding light of the Creator, thus it is the "Concealed Consciousness." In ancient Egypt this would be Amon Ra (or Amun Ra), the so-called hidden aspect of God.

In the number 1 is the entire plan. It is wholeness. The entire creation exists within the 1. Diversity and multiplicity exist within the oneness of the whole.

One is also centeredness. A heart and mind that is centered is a place of tranquility and clarity in a sea of activity. In centeredness it calls for an ideal. The ideal creates a principle around which all activity proceeds purposefully, orderly, and balanced. As images of the Divinity, we need our plan, or ideal, from which our growth and direction are guided.

The weakness of 1 is stagnation. Thus, the number 2 becomes necessary, for it is a channel through which we implement the plan, the ideal.

Number 2

From a Kabbalistic perspective, the number 2 reflects a consciousness stimulated to execute the plan of life and enlightenment. Two is a readiness to express, a willingness to go forth and make manifest the plan. This motivation and momentum is the father of all created things. In 1 the plan is conceived; in 2 is the impetus to carry out the plan.

The number 2 reflects the second emanation of the Infinite Eternal: Wisdom (Chokhmah). The number 2 looks up to the I AM to perceive the plan, and then seeks to implement what it perceives.

A soul with the numeral two desires to express, to go forth and assist life to flow according to the Divine Plan. In 2 we find a search for Wisdom, a love for Wisdom—but especially wisdom expressed or applied in life and in relationships.

The number 2 is considered masculine and has the attributes of the father. It is the archetype of fatherhood, for it is referred to as the "Father of Fathers," and it is within this context that 2 is mystically synonymous with Eden. Eden was a key aspect of the initial plan. It was a prototype, a model. The ideal world was revealed in the initial ensample, Eden.

Kabbalistically, 2 is the "Wisdom–Gushing Fountain," the "Water of the Wise," and is called the "Illuminating Consciousness" because it takes what it gleans from Concealed Consciousness and expresses it.

The weakness of 2 is division, which may create a sense of "otherness." Even numbers, as opposed to odd numbers, have traditionally been considered the weaker numbers, because they can be divided; thus, they are not stable. The I AM and Wisdom need the triad strength of Understanding to become stable. The number 2 is a wise eye, but it needs the eye of understanding to gain depth of perception. This leads to the number 3.

Number 3

From a Kabbalistic perspective, the number 3 is Understanding. It is the Cosmic Mother (Imma), within whose womb all that was contained in the number 1 and perceived by the number 2 finally becomes distinguished, clarified, and comprehendible. This emanation is considered the Mother of Mothers. It is feminine. In the blending of mother Understanding with father Wisdom a conception occurs, giving life to the next seven emanations on the Tree of Life.

According to the Kabbalistic symbolism of the Palace, or Divine Mansion, the appearance of the number 3 represents the unfolding of what was once hidden but is now knowable. The stage that was Wisdom (number 2) now expands through the nourishing that comes from Understanding. She is called the "Sanctifying Consciousness," for she takes the Concealed and the Illuminating and prepares them for the next stages of Creation while shielding them from potential contamination and confusion.

The coming seven days of Genesis will flow out of her womb, birthing the next seven emanations.

In Gnostic teachings, the number 3 is the key to all mysteries. The three supreme principles are (1) not–created, (2) self–created, and (3) created. The Ideal has a threefold nature, threefold body, and threefold power. Of course, the triangle has three sides, and in the diagram of the universe—a triangle within a circle—it represents the triune condition within the infinite whole.

Body, mind, and soul comprise the triad of our being. Physical, mental, and spiritual are the dynamics of our reality. If one aspect is greater than another, the balance is lost.

Three's weakness is that, in distinguishing the parts from the whole, it becomes distracted by the parts and thereby loses sight of the oneness of all life. The 3 also has the weakness of imbalance, resulting in struggles and inequities. Balance must be maintained. For example, a three-legged stool is not a sound foundation. It tips over very easily unless the weight it maintains is centered. Likewise, with balance maintained, 3 has the strength of the triad, which is a stabilizing dynamic in the Tree of Life.

Number 4

From a Kabbalistic perspective, the number 4 reflects the fourth emanation of the Tree of Life, that of the Loving Kindness and Mercy of God (Chesed). The number 4 is considered a masculine force, the productive "doer" power, which manifests itself in the universe and in humanity. It is said that the powers of Love and Mercy contained in the number 4 were so great that the aspects of the number 5 had to be created to set a limit on the all-merciful, all-loving flow in order to sustain truth and order!

Kabbalah teaches that this orb on the Tree of Life represents the first day of Creation in Genesis. On this day God created light and separated the darkness from that light to make the first day and night.

In the beginning God created the heavens and the earth. And the earth was waste and void; and darkness was upon the face of the deep; and the Spirit of God moved upon the face of the waters. And God said, 'Let there be light,' and there was light. And God saw the light, that it was good; and God divided the light from the darkness. And God called the light Day, and the darkness he called Night. And there was evening and there was morning, one day.

Genesis 1:1-5

The number 4's awareness is called "That Consciousness Which Receives and Contains." It is given this title because it contains the spiritual emanations of the Higher Consciousness of the Creative Spirit expressed out of the union of the Triad of the I AM, father Wisdom, and mother Understanding.

Its weakness is in division, separation, and scatteredness, losing its centeredness amid multiplicity. It becomes too lovingly outpouring of its life force while unable to retain its vital connection to Infinite Energy. It must maintain its receptive container characteristic—balancing the Light from above with the need from below.

Number 5

From a Kabbalistic perspective, the number 5 represents an awareness called "Radical Consciousness," because it is closest in equality to the Supreme Crown (number 1) and emanates from the depths of Wisdom.

The number 5 represents the fifth aspect, or emanation, of the Tree of Life, the Judgment and Might of God (Gevurah). Its nature is feminine, and it limits the abundance of Love and Mercy (number 4) to hold to truth and order. By the same token, the severities of Power in the 5 are tempered by the Love and Mercy of 4, so the two exist in a state of harmonic balance on the Tree of Life (see illustration 3).

This aspect of the Tree of Life is symbolically the second day of Genesis, when God separated the waters by creating a firmament.

And God said, "Let there be a firmament in the midst of the waters, and let it divide the waters from the waters." And God made the firmament, and divided the waters that were under the firmament from the waters that were above the firmament; and it was so. And God called the firmament Heaven. And there was evening and there was morning, a second day.   Genesis 1:6-8

The firmament symbolizes a truth, a place upon which one establishes his or her ideals and guiding standards. Now the waters above are separated from the waters below.

The number 5 is also discernment, the power to see through muddled situations and thoughts, separating good from evil, right from wrong, true from false. This is why Kabbalism considers 5 to be "Truth Consciousness."

The weakness of 5 is cold-heartedness, as when judgment slips into condemnation, and love and mercy have no longer any offsetting balance to the power of 5.

Number 6

From a Kabbalistic perspective, the number 6 represents the awareness called "Consciousness of the Mediating Influence." Six seeks to resolve discordant influences. Six is cooperation, holistic vision, and the bridging of opposites. It mediates the extremes, bringing them to balance.

The number 6 also refers to the sixth aspect of the Tree of Life, Beauty and Balance (Tiferet). It is a beauty through balance and harmony, through health and liveliness.

This number has an androgynous form, meaning it contains both male and female aspects. The source of this androgyny has its origin between the Creator's two arms, that part which expands from the heart to all parts of the whole. This portion of the Tree of Life gives life to art, music, and creativity.

The sixth emanation represents the third day of Genesis, when the waters under heaven were gathered in one place and the dry land appeared. It was the day when grass and herbs and fruit trees were created.

And God said, "Let the waters under the heavens be gathered together unto one place, and let the dry land appear"; and it was so. And God called the dry land Earth; and the gathering together of the waters he called Seas: and God saw that it was good. And God said, "Let the earth put forth grass, herbs yielding seed, and fruit-trees bearing fruit after their kind, wherein is the seed thereof, upon the earth"; and it was so. And the earth brought forth grass, herbs yielding

seed after their kind, and trees bearing fruit, wherein is the
seed thereof, after their kind; and God saw that it was good.
And there was evening and there was morning, a third day.

Genesis 1:9-13

Even though 6 is an even number, and even numbers are categorized
as the weaker numbers, 6 is considered to have no weakness.

Number 7

From a Kabbalistic perspective, the number 7 represents the awareness called "Mystical Consciousness," because its virtues are hidden and
only seen by the eyes of the spiritually minded. This stage of the path
awakens the connection to one's true relationship as an active member
of humanity, nature, and the cosmos. Along this path, one realizes and
actualizes one's true potential.

The number 7 also refers to the seventh aspect of the Tree of Life,
Victory and Fortitude (Netsah). It is a masculine, active principle that
achieves victory through endurance. It has an intuitive sense of individuality in the midst of universality. It is infinite in the midst of the
finite reality.

This aspect of the Tree of Life symbolically represents the fourth day
of Genesis, the day on which God created the lights in the heavens as
signs. Seven sees the meaning in signs, symbols, and the passage of time.

And God said, "Let there be lights in the firmament of
heaven to divide the day from the night; and let them be for
signs, and for seasons, and for days and years; and let them
be for lights in the firmament of heaven to give light upon
the earth"; and it was so. And God made the two great
lights; the greater light to rule the day, and the lesser light to
rule the night: he made the stars also. And God set them in
the firmament of heaven to give light upon the earth, and to
rule over the day and over the night, and to divide the light
from the darkness; and God saw that it was good. And there
was evening and there was morning, a fourth day.

Genesis 1:14-19

Seven awakens to the hidden meaning of life as it is revealed through illumination and revelation. Seven is a life and a consciousness of victory over all that hinders the soul in its journey.

The weakness that may manifest in the number 7 is excessive otherworldliness, which results in losing a sense of the purposefulness of this incarnation, with its circumstances and relationships. One's head may be in the higher heavens, but one's feet must be firmly planted on the ground of this reality and its opportunities.

Number 8

From a Kabbalistic perspective, the number 8 represents the awareness called the "Perfecting Consciousness." It is from here that the ability to prepare principles to live by emanates. Eight attaches itself to the roots hidden in the depths of Love and Mercy (Chesed, number 4) and then springs forth with principles to live by.

The number 8 is Splendor and Glory (Hod). Once the inertia of doubt, uncertainty, and fear is overcome and the drive toward enlightenment vitalized, the soul can be filled with the spirit of healing and resurrection. This transformation is symbolized by the splendor of God that fills the mind and heart. Eight may become a light to all.

This number symbolizes the fifth day of Genesis during which God created the creatures of the sea and air.

> And God said, "Let the waters bring forth swarms of living creatures, and let birds fly above the earth in the open firmament of heaven." And God created the great sea-monsters, and every living creature that moves, wherewith the waters swarmed, after their kind, and every winged bird after its kind; and God saw that it was good. And God blessed them, saying, "Be fruitful, and multiply, and fill the waters in the seas, and let birds multiply on the earth." And there was evening and there was morning, a fifth day.
>
> Genesis 1:20-23

Eight realizes its full potential through perfecting its consciousness. It is fruitful, creative, and multiplies through daily living of what it knows is best, as revealed by God's splendor and glory flowing through all life.

Eight fills physicality, materiality, and the world with the light and wisdom of the heavens and God's goodness. In 8, the physical and the spiritual find harmony and balance. In 8, physical life finds spiritual purpose and meaning. For 8s, relationships become opportunities to apply the "fruits of the spirit"—love, kindness, patience, understanding, gentleness, and forgiveness.

The weakness of 8 is that its joy for this world can become so materialistic as to diminish space in the mind and heart for spiritual, ethereal awarenesses and activities.

Number 9

From a Kabbalistic perspective, the number 9 represents the awareness called the "Purifying Consciousness," because it purifies the numbers, qualifies and adjusts the manner in which they are represented, and unites them so that they may not suffer division and destruction.

The number 9 also refers to the ninth aspect of the Tree of Life, the Foundation and Bonding (Yesod). Upon the foundation of 9, all aspects of the Tree of Life achieve their ideal.

Nine is the élan vital, the life force, the kundalini energy. Nine has a sexual quality to it, not in the sense of sexual activity but in the nature of the two genders and Creation. In 9 the two genders are bonded in harmony, bringing forth a new birth, a new consciousness. Nine is symbolic of both the male and female root chakra. Nine is the sexual organ of the "Divine Hermaphrodite," God's bonding of Heavenly Father and Mother.

Nine is representative of the sixth day of Genesis, when God created male and female in one (they are not separated until the second chapter of Genesis).

And God said, "Let us make man in our image, after our likeness; and let them have dominion over the fish of the sea, and over the birds of the heavens, and over the cattle, and over all the earth, and over every creeping thing that creeps upon the earth." And God created man in his own image, in the image of God created He him; male and female created He them. And God blessed them; and God said unto them, "Be fruitful, and multiply, and replenish the earth, and subdue it; and have dominion over the fish of the sea, and over the birds of the heavens, and over every living thing that moves upon the earth."

And God said, "Behold, I have given you every herb yielding seed, which is upon the face of all the earth, and every tree, in which is the fruit of a tree yielding seed; to you it shall be for food; and to every beast of the earth, and to every bird of the heavens, and to everything that creeps upon the earth, wherein there is life, I have given every green herb for food"; and it was so.

And God saw everything that he had made, and, behold, it was very good. And there was evening and there was morning, the sixth day.   Genesis 1:26-31

Because the sixth day of Creation is the last day of Creation (God rested on the seventh day), the number 9 represents completion. Nine signifies the finishing of what was begun.

The weakness of 9 is in the handling of the stewardship over all of the creatures and creation that God assigned to us. This manifests in no stewardship, poor stewardship, or excessive dominance over the creatures and the creation. And since 9 is considered to be the number of karma, there is a price to pay for abuse of stewardship.

Kabbalah Numbers 11 and 22

Kabbalah 11

From a Kabbalistic perspective, the number 11 represents the eleventh awareness, the "Scintillating Consciousness," so named because it is the garment held up before the "Formations and the Order of the Superior and Inferior Causes," referring to the movement from the Plane of Formation and the Mundane Triad to the Plane of Creation and the Moral Triad (see illustration 3). To possess this path is to enjoy great dignity and to come face to face with the Cause of Causes. Such contact is scintillating.

Kabbalah 22

From a Kabbalistic perspective, the number 22 represents the twenty-second awareness, "Consciousness of the Faithful," or "Faithful Consciousness," because it is filled with spiritual virtues, which are increased until their complete enlightenment and luminescence is realized.

Kabbalah Triplets–666 and More

In classical Kabbalism, the number 666 was associated with the persecuting Roman Emperors, most often with Nero, but some associated the number with cruel Domitian. A broader interpretation would be to associate it with Roman power as a symbol of worldly power, as opposed to heavenly—man's power versus God's. Since the number of the beast is required to sell or purchase, this fits well. "No one can buy or sell unless he has the mark, that is, the name of the beast or the number of its name." (Revelation 13:17) It is the number of materialism, commercialism, and mammon. It is also the number of earthly humanity without any awareness of higher purposes and planes.

In a Gnostic illustration with Greek terms and Kabbalah numbers (illustration 26), we find a map of the levels of consciousness and energetics. The source of this image is *Apocalypse Unsealed* by James Morgan Pryse, published in 1910.

From the bottom we begin, and the journey to resurrection and enlightenment proceeds. (The name for each number is followed by its name in Greek and the Greek meaning of the word.)

333, "The False Seer," Akrasia (lacking command over oneself).

444, "the Serpent-coil," Spirema (coil).

555, "the Red Dragon," Epithumia (desire, craving, longing, desire for what is forbidden, lust).

666, "the Beast," He Phren (the lower mind; parts of the heart and the mind).

777, "the Cross," Stauros (a cross; an upright stake).

888, "the Lamb," Iesous (Jesus, meaning "Jehovah is salvation").

999, "Intuitively Wise," Epistemon (imbued with knowing).

1000, "the Conqueror," Ho Nikon (the victor, conqueror).

In Revelation, when the disciple John sees the number 666, he knows what it symbolizes and why it is called the number of the beast: because it is the lower mind that never seeks higher consciousness and is not willing to endure the sacrifice necessary to reach such higher awareness. That sacrifice is symbolized in the number of the cross—777—upon which one must "crucify desire in self that your real potential may be realized." (EC 2475-1)

Cayce's Quick Number Guide

Here is one interpretation of numbers found in the Edgar Cayce readings:

One is the beginning, to be sure. Before one is nothing. After one is nothing, if all be in one—as one God, one Son, one Spirit. This, then, the essence of all force, all manners of energies. All activities emanate from the One.

Two—the combination, and begins a division of the whole, or the One. While two makes for strength, it also makes for weakness. This is illustrated in that of your music, of your paintings, of your metals, of whatever element we may consider!

Three—again a combination of One and Two; this making for strength, making for—in division—that ability of Two against One, or One against Two. In this strength is seen, as in the Godhead, and is as a greater strength in the whole of combinations.

Again, in four, we find that of a division—and while a beauty in strength, in the divisions also makes for the greater weakness—as may be illustrated as in the combinations seen in metal, or numbers, or music, or color.

Five—as seen, a change—as may be seen in a comparison of any of the forces outlined.

Six—again makes for the beauty and the symmetrical forces of all numbers, making for strength;

As does seven signify the spiritual forces, as are seen in all the ritualistic orders of any nature; as seen in the dividing up of conditions, whether they be of the forces in nature or those that react to the sensual forces of man in any character.

Eight—again showing that combination in strength, also a combination in weakness;

Nine making for the *completeness* in numbers; yet showing not the strength as of Ten, nor yet the weakness as of Eight, yet making for that termination in the *forces* in natural *order* of things that come as a change imminent in the life.

In *ten* we have those of the completeness as of numbers, and a strength as is found in *few*; yet these are as a combination in the forces as are manifest.

In *eleven* is again seen those of the *beauty* of numbers, yet that weakness as was signified by those of the betrayal in the numbers.

Twelve as a *finished* product, as is given in all forces in nature; as was given in all forces as combined to those of the ritualistic forms, those of the mystic forces, those of the numbers as related to those of a combination; for as of the voices of *twelve* requiring Twenty to even drown same, or to overcome same. The same as may be seen in all of the forces in nature. *Twelve* combined forces brought those strengths into the world as of |were| necessary for a replenishing of same. EC 5751-1

Remember, numbers do not define you or determine your life course; they only reflect conditions, inclinations, available opportunities, and potential challenges.

Cayce on Numbers and Astrology

In one of his discourses, Cayce outlined his view of the influence and use of numbers and their correlation to astrology in our lives.

In the study of Life and its many varied phases, while the mental and mental aspects are the *ruling* factors in an individual entity's own development, well that those external conditions that *influence* for urges *in* the mental be studied also. Not that *any one* phase be exclusive or excluded from the rest, if the body would know and understand impulses in individual activities that *may* be controlled or made apparent in their actions *by* these varying influences, as *well* as how such influence self; that is, as astrological influences, astronomical influences, numerological influences, *and* such—for these are as *signs* of that as has been |built| in an entity's whole make-up. To be sure, where other individuals rather than self are concerned, their numerological, astrological or astronomical effects may have or may *not* have been influenced by *their* reaction *to* their immediate or their environmental conditions, or their hereditary conditions; yet knowing how or why, or *where* such influences effect or *affect* an influence in Life, or *on* Life itself, and comparing same with *self's* influence, gives *one* an insight into character, personality, individuality, and *knowing* same one is *indeed* with an understanding that is worth while.

Now, if one becomes so accustomed to viewing life from such a standpoint *wholly*, to be sure such an one may soon be termed a *crank*, yet these considered—Life as a whole considered—will *certainly* make for a much more *interesting* and *worth while experience* for all!

These intimations are given as an insight into *this* entity's—[311]'s—*own* experience.

In *any* influence, will—a self, the ego, the I Am—is the greater force *to* be dealt with, but as numbers do influence, as astronomical and astrological conditions do influence, a *knowledge* of same certainly gives an individual a foresight into relationships with individuals. EC 311-3

How To Calculate Numbers

Let's briefly examine how to identify numbers and how to interpret them. We will begin with the numbers in names. According to Cayce,

[T]hese give the significance to the numbers of the individual. These may be reached either by adding the numbers of the letters as signify the name, or the numbers as applied *to* each individual letter in the name. These will give the sum total of that which applies to the individual.   EC 5751-1

Let's use Edgar Cayce as an example. In basic numerology, each letter is assigned a number. In current systems, which are based on the Pythagorean model (Hebrew letters are often converted into a Pythagorean model), the numbers go from 1 through 9 and then start over again. Consequently, the letters a through i equal 1 through 9; then, starting over again, the letters j through r equal 1 through 9; and finally, s through z equal 1 through 8. Using this method, the name Edgar Cayce would look like this:

5–4–7–1–9 (e–d–g–a–r), 3–1–7–3–5 (c–a–y–c–e)

Normally, we would then add these numbers together and get the sum total number of 45. The next step is to reduce this number to a single digit by adding the two numbers together; thus 45 yields 9 (4+5).

We may also use the numbers associated with each part of the whole name (Edgar and Cayce), which would be 26 for Edgar and 19 for Cayce, giving us 8 (Edgar, 26 reduced by adding 2+6) and 1 (Cayce, 19 would be reduced by 1+9=10, then 1+0=1), respectively. Thus his individual dynamics involve 8 personally (Edgar), 1 for family (Cayce).

The 8 indicates a motivation to be fruitful and multiply in materiality. It is also the number of money, which, in Cayce's case, was always a challenge, cycling him and his family through rhythms of plenty and lack. We also have the number 1 for the family name, indicating a strong family base from which to reach out and do good. Anyone who knows his story knows that this is true. His family played a big part in his life and gave him much support and strength.

When we add together these two name numbers (8 + 1), we get 9 for the entire name. Nine indicates a person who is reaching a completion and, in doing so, is likely to meet karmic energies within himself that need to be finally resolved. For all of the influences within the man Edgar Cayce, he certainly held onto and lived his attunement and service, even when he was sorely tested or at his weakest moments. Kabbalah considers the ninth awareness to be the "Purifying Intelligence."

Now that we have Cayce's name numbers, let's get his birthday numbers, which will give us his life path number. He was born on March 18, 1877. March is the third month; thus its number is 3. Now let's add 3+1+8+1+8+7+7, which totals 35 and reduces to 8, an influence we have already seen in his personal name. Kabbalah identifies 8 as the awareness of the "Perfecting Intelligence." It is from here that the ability to prepare principles emanates. It attaches itself to the roots hidden in the depths of 4, which is the emanation Chesed—love, loving kindness, compassion, and grace. Cayce speaks of the specific numbers of 2, 4, 6, and 8 in this reading: "Two makes for a division; yet in the multiple of same, in four, it makes for the greater weaknesses in the divisions. In six and eight it makes for the same characterizations." (EC 216-15)

Obviously, the even numbers are considered to possess innate weaknesses because they represent divisions and separations, when life must seek union and oneness. However, the readings also note that there is strength even in these weaknesses and encourage us to focus on the constructive and minimize (but not ignore) the destructive influences. And we must remember to do just that, even when the numbers are weak, negative, and foreboding. For example, by dividing things into their parts, one can better discern the underlying influences and adjust one's approach accordingly. The readings identify 4 as among the weakest of numbers, yet four has strengths, as in "the city four-square," the four directions, four seasons, and the "four principles necessary to be present in the activity of a normal body." ("Heart, liver, lungs, and kidneys. These are the four major principles of a physical organism." –EC 2072-9)

Although Cayce may have suffered negative monetary karma, he clearly had an abundance of love, lovingkindness, compassion, and grace in the midst of his material suffering. His personal letters reflect this. His marriage reflected it. His lifelong friendships mirrored it. Many of those around him of course loved him despite his human weaknesses. They loved his work and supported him in times of tragedy and apparent failure (the loss of his center during the Great Depression, and two arrests for "practicing medicine without a license"—no convictions).

Notice Kabbalah's statement that it is from the 8 awareness that the ability to prepare principles emanates and that these principles attach themselves to the roots of love, lovingkindness, compassion, and grace. Certainly, the readings that came through this man further prepared us all by revealing higher principles.

11

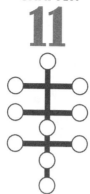

PLANETARY INFLUENCES

Edgar Cayce's mystical discourses have much to say about the planets in relation to our soul's journey. Our physical bodies may not survive in the atmospheres of these planets, but according to activities recorded in ancient astrological records, our souls apparently enjoy the fourth dimension. There are even ancient texts, such as the Palm Leaf Manuscripts in India, indicating that ancient peoples knew a great deal about the other planets in our solar system.

Long before the concept of star gates became popular in the movies and television, Cayce disclosed that we have a star gate for our solar system: Arcturus.

In reading 900–25, Cayce explains that, in the higher dimensional spheres of many of the planets in this solar system, entities (and by "entities," he means the whole being: mind, soul, and spirit) are attracted to conditions that will help in their development. They pass through these again and again and again "until they are prepared to meet the everlasting Creator of our entire Universe, of which our system is only a small part," and that the entity continues "changing, as it were, from one development to another, until the entity passes from that solar system, or sphere, through Arcturus or Septimus." We know Arcturus; it is a star in the constellation Boötes, the Herdsman. Cayce appears to be giving us another name for this star: Septimus.

One Cayce illustration of our soul journey is explained in this way: we find in the earth's plane that an entity that manifests hate and aggrandizement of the flesh in any unnatural desire may find "their reclamation, their remolding, and their beginning again, in the spheres of Saturn's relative forces." Notice his use of the phrase "relative forces" when identifying the portion of Saturn he is referring to—it is not the physical planet that we see three–dimensionally—he is describing forces and planes *relative* to our view but beyond our three dimensions. According to Cayce, we

> pass through those spheres in which the entity must manifest, that the entity may manifest the gained development through the earth's plane. For in flesh must the entity manifest, and make the will one with the God, or Creative Force, in the Universe, and as such development reaches that plane, wherein the development may pass into other spheres and systems, of which our (the earth's) solar system is only a small part; in this, then, is meant the entity must develop in that sphere until it (the entity) has reached that stage wherein it may manifest through the spiritual planes.   EC 900-25

In the following discourse, Cayce denotes the specific qualities that an entity develops in each planetary plane:

> Mercury pertaining of Mind.
> In Mars of Madness [tempering madness, rage, and mayhem].
> In Earth as of Flesh.
> In Venus as Love.
> In Jupiter as Strength.
> In Saturn as the beginning of earthly woes, that to which all insufficient
>   matter is cast for the beginning.
> In that of Uranus as of the Psychic.
> In that of Neptune as of Mystic.
> In Septimus as of Consciousness.
> In Arcturus as of the developing.
>   EC 900-10

Once the entity perfects its growth here, it may move beyond this system into other systems and, ultimately, into infinite, universal oneness with the Infinite Eternal (the Ein Sof).

Cayce accepts, as Kabbalah teaches, the concept of planes of existence and indicates that there are planes of existence that correlate with the planets in our system. From Cayce's mystical perspective, astrology is not how the movement of the planets around the earth affects one's life but how the soul has sojourned in dimensions or planes of life in those realms we call planets. They are not only three-dimensional objects; they are also fourth- and fifth-dimensional realms of soul activity.

> Q: Give the names of the principal planets, and the influence on the lives of people.
> A: Mercury, Mars, Jupiter, Venus, Saturn, Neptune, Uranus, Septimus [we assume this is the star Arcturus, not the planet Pluto]. The influence as is experienced by many of those in and about the earth plane is defective. Many of the forces of each is felt more through the *experience* by the entity's *sojourn* upon those planets than by the life that is lead" on Earth!

Cayce goes on to explain that earth life is of supreme importance to soul growth and consciousness expansion, adding that, when we engage our God-given gift of free will, we draw all the innate benefits of our soul's planetary training into this life! "Will is the factor in the mind of man that must be exercised." The influence of growth and development from the planetary sojourns and training may be brought into this incarnation when "that soul and spirit returns to bring the force to the earth individual, as it is breathed into the body." (EC 3744-4)

Rabbi Akiva (also spelled Akiba), 50–135 CE, issued a prohibition against calculating astrology to determine one's daily life or to make decisions and predictions through astrology. He believed and taught that the Talmud forbade one to use horoscopes to determine one's future actions. In the Torah (Deuteronomy 18:10) it is written, "There shall not be found among you one who calculates times," understood to be referring to astrology used for predictions. But Rabbi Akiva did note that the Talmud does permit one to do character analyses using astrology.

If all that one is doing is letting the planets and stars dictate one's life, then Cayce concurs with the rabbi. Cayce's readings clearly favor using one's mind, heart, and especially one's will to make decisions. Like the rabbi, Cayce believed that people can learn about themselves and their inner influences by understanding how their souls have lived and experienced life beyond earth, among the emanations, some of which correlate to specific planets. Kabbalah teaches that five of the planets are associated with specific emanations of energy and consciousness, as well as the Moon and Sun. In *Alchemie und Kabbala*, Gershom Gerhard Scholem offers the following list, as does the sixteenth-century treatise titled "The Refiner's Fire" (Esh M'tzaref):

Sun—Judgment (5: Gevurah)—Gold
Moon—Mercy and Loving Kindness (4: Chesed)—Silver
Mercury—Kingdom and the "I am" (10: Malkuth)—
    Quicksilver (mercury)
Venus—Surrender and Splendor (8: Hod)—Copper
Mars—Beauty and Balance (6: Tiferet)—Iron
Jupiter—Victory and Persistence (7: Netzach)—Tin
Saturn—Foundation and Remembrance (9: Yesod)—Lead

To follow, the planets are correlated according to the Gra System (Rabbi Eliahu Gaon of Vilna in the 18th century):

Moon—Mercy and Loving Kindness (4: Chesed)
Mars—Judgment (5: Gevurah)
Sun—Beauty and Balance (6:Tiferet)
Saturn—Foundation and Remembrance (9:Yesod)
Jupiter—Kingdom and "I am" (10: Malkut)
Venus—Victory and Fortitude (7: Netzach)
Mercury—Splendor and Glory (8: Hod)

This listing seems better than the previous one, and many argue that this is closer to the classical. The first listing correlates Mars with Beauty and Balance, whereas the second list gives the Sun this more acceptable correlate, putting Mars with Judgment. The original versions of the Book of Creation clearly correlate the planets to emanations five through ten, beginning with Saturn. But later Kabbalists lost the original connections founded in the Book of Creation and moved the planets upward into the nonplanetary emanations of the Tree of Life. This was especially the case of those Kabbalists who dropped the tenth emanation as a planetary realm. These varying views developed because, when the Book of the Brightness (Sefer Ha-Bahir or simply Bahir) and the Zohar were published, groups attempted to fit them with the Book of Creation (Sefer Yetzirah).

Originally, the first four emanations describe Adam Kadmon's (the "Logos") inner reality, and the last six emanations describe his outer reality. The lower six are often referred to as the "six extremities," which are emanations five through ten, representing Saturn through Venus, respectively. This is that listing:

Saturn—Judgment (5: Gevurah)
Jupiter—Beauty and Balance (6: Tiferet)
Mars—Victory and Fortitude, also Power (7: Netzach)
Sun—Splendor and Glory (8: Hod)
Mercury—Foundation and Remembrance (9: Yesod)
Venus—Kingdom and "I am" (10: Malkut)
Moon—(This is not in the Tree of Life but a shell or kernel beneath the Tree.)

These would be considered the truly classical arrangement, and by some, the only true arrangement. Certainly, having Mars with Victory, Fortitude, and Power fits better than the other two listings. And since God is love, Venus as the Kingdom and the "I am" feels right, as well. Mercury, being the mind, also fits well with Remembrance. The Sun as Splendor, Jupiter as Balance, and Saturn as Judgment also seem right and, amazingly, fit with the Edgar Cayce readings as well!

Interestingly, the Zohar correlates Ezekiel's four beasts (the lion, eagle, ox, and human) with angelic and astrological influences. Here is a section from the Zohar that describes these:

For every man who is compounded of the four elements is accompanied by four angels on his right hand and four on his left, those already named; and from the side of his body Metatron presses close to him at the right and Samael at the left. Now all men are formed of the four elements, but on the order in which these elements are found—that is, the order of the planets with which each man is connected—depends the order of the angels who accompany him, and also the potential characteristics of the man. Thus, if his ruling planet be the Lion, Michael will lead, and be followed by Gabriel, and after him Raphael, and lastly Nuriel. If, however, his planet is the Ox, first comes Gabriel, then Michael, then Nuriel, then Raphael. If the Eagle be the planet by which he is influenced, Nuriel will be first, then Michael, followed first by Gabriel and then by Raphael. And should his planet be Man, then will Raphael lead, with Michael, Gabriel and Nuriel coming after in the order named. Now all aspects of Michael are of the attribute of mercy. A man whose leading angel is Michael will be benevolent, he will be pious and wise ; but all this applies only if he is a student of the Torah, for if he is not so he will be the very reverse of all this, since he will be formed after the evil inclination; he will be stupid and unfeeling, without benevolence or worth—for no ignorant man can be truly pious. Should a man be from the side of Gabriel, his attributes will all partake chiefly of the quality of justice: he will stand up courageously against the wicked; he will prevail over his own evil inclinations, will abhor sin and cleave unto all things righteous, and he will become a judge by profession; but again, all this will only come to pass if he study the Torah with diligence and attain proficiency; should he neglect this, he will be as strong in iniquity as otherwise in holiness; he will rejoice in the tribulations of the righteous; he will be hard in his condemnations, bold in evildoing, with no fear of sin; he will have a red face, and will be of the type of Esau—a blood-shedder. He whose planet is the Eagle possesses neither the attribute of mercy nor that of justice in a marked degree, but is either moderately good or moderately bad, as his good or evil inclination obtains influence over him, as his countenance reveals, red and white being blended therein. He who is under the guidance of the planet Man combines in himself—in so far as he derives his characteristics from the good side—all the good qualities: he is wise and pious, strong in intellectual apprehension, sin-fearing, full of excellent virtues; and the color of his countenance is dark. But if he is governed by the principle of evil, he will be full of bad qualities."

> Shemot, "Exodus"; Raya Mehemna, "Faithful Shepherd"; 42a

There is no blade of grass that does not have a constellation *(mazal)* over it, telling it to grow.

> Book of Creation, Sefer Yetzirah 4.6

As commentaries explain, "God's providence works through the angels, but the angels, in turn, work through the stars and planets. As some authorities put it, the angels are, in a sense, like souls to the stars. Thus, for example, some sources speak of the stars as having intelligence, but the commentaries note that this is actually speaking of the angels that are associated with them."

> Book of Creation, Sefer Yetzirah 4.6

Modern works have added the distant planets. Most associate Neptune with Wisdom (2: Chokhamh), Uranus with Understanding (3: Binah), and Pluto with Knowledge (Da'at, which is used in some systems, especially those that eliminate Keter, the Crown, and the "I AM").

Here are the Seven Planets, or "Heavens," of Gnosticism (in their Greek form) as given to us by the Gnostic writer Origen (Contra Celsum, VI, xxxi), in descending order: The heavenly realm of Saturn (Jaldabaoth, which may be interpreted as "Child of Chaos"); Jupiter (Jao, which may be derived from the Gnostic magical word *iao*—which is the name of God, Yahweh); Mars (Sabaoth, which is an Old Testament title meaning "God of Hosts"); Venus (Astrophaios, associated with the feminine principle); Sun (Adonaios, meaning "Lord"); Mercury (Ailoaios or Ailoein or, in Hebrew, Elohim, meaning "God"—which indicates how highly the mind was held in Gnosticism); Moon (Oraios, which may simply mean "light," in the sense of a reflected light, not the source of light).

In astrology, Cayce interprets the Sun as "destiny," the strongest influence in anyone's horoscope. The placement of the Sun in the horoscope should give an indication of one's strongest character traits (remember, we are not attempting to determine destiny, since nothing is as strong as our will in determining our future). Next in importance of influence are "the closer planets to Earth"—Mercury, Venus, Mars, and the Moon—because they are likely to be the location of our most recent planetary sojourn. (However, he did occasionally give a reading in which he stated that the soul came to earth from the outer planets, explaining that such a soul would seem strange to most of us.) Cayce terms Saturn, Jupiter, Uranus, Neptune, and Pluto as the "outer planets," whose influences are more related to our general disposition and attitude than to our urges and energies.

As we have observed earlier, Cayce relates Mercury to the mental forces and our mind; Venus to personal love and the arts and creativity; Mars to temperament, rage, power, energy; Saturn to dramatic change and the benefit and difficulty of cleansing for a fresh start (or starting over); and Jupiter to high-mindedness, high purposes, high ideals, and large groups, also relating to wealth and stature. He correlates Uranus with the extremes, as do most astrologers, but also with psychic and intuitive abilities; he correlates Neptune with the mystical experience and watery influences; and Pluto with consciousness, especially expansive consciousness, although there may also be the negative influence of self-centeredness if the awakening does not include humility and meekness.

In the beginning, our own plane, the Earth, was set in motion. The planning of other planets began the ruling of the destiny of all matters as created, just as the division of waters was ruled and is ruled by the Moon in its path about the earth; just so as the higher creation as it begun is ruled by its action in conjunction with the planets about the earth. The strongest force used in the destiny of man is the Sun first, then the closer planets to the earth, or those that are coming to ascension at the time of the birth of the individual, *but let it be understood here, no action of any planet or the phases of the sun, the moon or any of the heavenly bodies surpass the rule of man's will power, the* power given by the Creator of man, in the beginning, when he became a living soul, with the power of choosing for himself. The *inclinations* of man are ruled by the planets under which he is born, for the destiny of man lies within the sphere or scope of the planets.

Be not dismayed; God is not mocked; "Whatsoever a man soweth that shall he also reap." [Gal. 6:7]

In the various spheres, then, through which he must pass to attain that which will fit him for the conditions to enter in, and become a part of that Creator, just as an individual is a part of the creation now. In this manner we see there is the influence of the planets upon an individual, for all must come under that influence, though one may pass from one plane to another without going through all stages of the condition, for only upon the earth plane at present do we find man is flesh and blood, but upon others do we find those of his own making in the preparation of his own development.

As given, "The heavens declare the glory of God, and the firmament sheweth His handyworks. Day unto day uttereth speech, night unto night sheweth knowledge." This from the beginning and unto the end. [Ps. 19:1, 2]   EC 3744-4

As we have seen in both Kabbalah and the Cayce readings, we are celestial beings, not terrestrial. We traverse the vast expanse of space in our primal mission to know our Creator and ourselves. Consider this reading, which I've edited for clarity, and focus on the point at hand:

As an entity passes on from this present time or this solar system, this sun, these forces, it passes through the various spheres—on and on through the *eons* of time or space—leading first into that central force known as Arcturus—nearer the Pleiades. Eventually, an entity passes into the inner forces, inner sense, then they may again—after a period of nearly ten thousand years—enter into the earth to make manifest those forces gained in its passage. In entering, the entity takes on those forms that may be known in the dimensions of that plane which it occupies, there being not only three dimensions as of the earth but there may be seven as in Mercury, or four in Venus, or five in Jupiter. There

may be only one as in Mars. There may be many more as in those of
Neptune, or they may become even as nil—until purified in Saturn's
fires.   EC 311-2

Cayce would begin soul readings for individuals by identifying their
planetary and stellar influences, explaining that these were influences
because of the souls' journeys through these dimensions before incarnating. He explained: "As the entity moves from sphere to sphere, it
seeks its way to the home, to the face of the Creator, the Father, the first
cause." (EC 136-8) Cayce identifies the first cause as this: "That the created would be the companion for the Creator." (5753-1) This is the reason we were created, and as a result, the created (our soul) is given
opportunities to "show itself to be not only worthy of, but companionable to, the Creator." (EC 5753-1) Since we are talking about the Creator
of the entire cosmos and everything in it, we are celestial star travelers,
even though we feel so earthly and terrestrial in our daily lives.

Cayce said that our taking many forms in many different dimensions
and spheres helps us to experience the whole of our being and of our
Creator's consciousness. He said that "self is lost in that of attaining for
itself the nearer and nearer approach that builds in manifested form,
whether in the Pleiades, Arcturus, Gemini, or in Earth, in Arcturus,
Vulcan, or in Neptune." (EC 136-83) Yet, despite our taking on many
"forms" as we manifest ourselves, our true nature is, according to his
readings, "as light, a ray that does not end, lives on and on, until it
becomes one in essence with the source of light." (EC 136-83)

CHAPTER

12

ECSTASY

We cannot fully appreciate Kabbalah without understanding the mystic's experience of direct, personal contact with the Divine and the ecstasy of such a face-to-face communion.

Abraham Abulafia (1240–1291) of Spain and Italy, whose revelations of attunement to the Divine nearly got him burned at the stake by Pope Nicholas III, wrote a series of manuals describing how to attain mystical ecstasy. Abulafia believed that the Hebrew letters and key words in the Scriptures have secret powers and, when used like mantras, may bring on divine ecstasy. He developed a technique called "the knowledge of the combinations" (hokhmath ha-tseruf), using the infinite combinations of the letters of the Hebrew alphabet and rearrangements of spiritual words to generate an altered state of consciousness with God. He required that these sounds be repeated extensively while music is being played. The result would be spiritual ecstasy.

The Spanish Castilian mystics associated with Jacob ben Jacob ha-Cohen and Isaac ben Jacob ha-Cohen also used Hebrew letters and names for God to magically generate an ecstatic sense of union with God.

The Zohar gives us a wonderful transitional sense of moving from daily consciousness to heavenly consciousness by helping us understand the transition to sleep and even to death, then using this understanding of these natural transitions to generate a movement to higher consciousness using meditative techniques.

The Zohar also uses the metaphor of marriage between a man and a woman as a model for meditative attunement to God, using sexual terms to generate the ultimate sexual union. This is a classical concept dating back to very ancient times in Asia using the terms yin and yang as an explanation of the union of these dualistic qualities to realize higher states of consciousness and the ecstasy that results.

Merkabah mystics use the metaphor of Ezekial's chariots to ride to heaven. One of the strongest movements of mystical, ecstatic Kabbalistic practices was among the fifteenth- and sixteenth-century mystics of a town called Safed in Asia Minor (modern-day Turkey). Safed concepts and methods spread throughout the eastern Mediterranean—from Turkey to Egypt, including Palestine, and as far away as Persia—and became known as Lurianic Kabbalism, titled after its founder Isaac Luria (1534-1572), who was also known as the "Ari "(Hebrew for *lion*). Lurianic mystics seek that emptiness to which God withdrew in order for the Creation to take place—they seek out that "pure emptiness" (*tehiru*), which is a common concept in deep meditation practices around the globe in many cultures and mystical schools.

Ecstasy, in the sense that we are using the word, was best defined by Plotinus (204–270 BCE, the founder of Neo-Platonism, author of *Enneads*): "The liberation of the mind from its finite consciousness, becoming one and identified with the Infinite." It is this moment from an individual's consciousness to conscious contact with the Universal Consciousness of God that is the mystic's goal and guides his or her methods.

Direct, personal contact with the Divine was what the early Kabbalistic seekers sought. And though they sought it within the context and community of laws, rituals, and traditions, their personal contact with the Divine set them apart from the greater community. Such experiences, and the methods used to have such experiences, became secret because the greater community could not deal with such a personal connection between a human and God. The devil had to have a role in any such divination, and during some of Kabbalah's greatest times of popularity, the Inquisitor was empowered and could sentence such mystics to the fires of the stake, especially if they were not Christian, as was the case with the Kabbalists. This was a dangerous practice in those days, but experiencing God's presence was so worth the danger that many sought to learn and practice these methods.

Even though many rituals, magical practices, and angelic hierarchies—and complexities upon complexities—have been added to the codexes and lore of Kabbalah, it is the ecstasy of direct, personal contact that is at the root and core of Kabbalah. Paradoxically, it is the singular, infinite, unseen God (Ein Sof) within which all these complexities have their being that the mystic makes the ecstatic contact that inspires, rejuvenates, and transforms heart and mind, soul and spirit. These moments strengthen one's faith, nourish one's soul, enliven one's spirit, and give value to the life of the seeker.

Kabbalah teaches that the unseen God is limitless, invisible, inaudible, and even inaccessible—which appears to make it impossible for one to have any contact with the Divine. How, then, can anyone have direct, personal contact with the purest essence of the Divine? The answer requires an understanding of the original Creation. Before Creation, the infinite Creator was "the fullness of being." The Creation was expressed out of the womb of God's consciousness. Multiplicity, diversity, activity, and dimensions upon dimensions were now the fullness of being. Even so, the original condition of the Divine remained—a mysterious, silent, hidden void within which all expressed life now moved and had its being.

Contacting the Divine in its post-Creation state requires a type of perception that is alien to anything we know in the midst of the active creation. Normal human senses cannot perceive it. Jesus indicated this when he said, "Those who have ears to hear, let them hear what the Spirit says."

In a discussion with Flaccus, a fellow seeker of the Infinite, Plotinus explained:

> You ask, how can we know the Infinite? I answer, not by reason. It is the office of reason to distinguish and define. The Infinite, therefore, cannot be ranked among its objects. You can only apprehend the Infinite by a faculty superior to reason, by entering into a state in which you are your finite self no longer—in which the divine essence is communicated to you. This is ecstasy. It is the liberation of your mind from its finite anxieties. Like only can apprehend like; when you thus cease to be finite, you become one with the Infinite. In the reduction of your soul to its simplest self, its divine essence, you realize this union—this Identity.

Of note in this statement are three key points: (1) The Infinite cannot be ranked among its objects, its creations; (2) One must enter a state of consciousness in which one is no longer its finite self; and(3) Only like can comprehend like, or as many have written, the Great I AM and the little "I am" greet one another, one being the expression of the other.

Moses asked God for his name, and God replied, "I am that I am." In this mystical answer is the liberation of self and finite consciousness to oneness with the Divine and Infinite Consciousness. The Great I AM put its essence deep into the little "I am." And, as Moses learned by his face-to-face contact with God, the "I AM" is the quintessence latent deep within the little "I am." The little "I am" can therefore contact that place within itself that is a portion of its Creator, and thereby contact the source and sustainer of its life.

Such contact brings communion, renewal, and a peace that passes understanding.

Edgar Cayce had much to say about communing with the Divine. Here are some of his key insights and directions.

> The universe, God, is *within*. Thou art His. Thy communion with the cosmic forces of nature, thy communion with thy Creator, is thy birthright! Be satisfied with nothing less than walking with Him!
>
> EC 1297-1; italics mine

> Study—in all things—to show self approved unto that ideal which is set before self, knowing—and looking forward to—the closer communion with Him. For, the mind builds—and the entertaining of His will brings the closer communion with Him. In faith, in patience, know that the development of the soul's consciousness in Him grows as the applications of that known day by day are put into active, actual practice. Then, be faithful; for He that is made ruler over much is he that has been *faithful* over the little. Each are called in the more perfect way, even as that known is made manifest in the dealings with man. For, we are all ambassadors for Him.   EC 282-6
>
> In the spiritual let it be rather of the psychic but not the ordinary term. For the variation between spiritual or religious experience and psychic experience is: In religious experience one is told *what* to expect, how to

expect and when to expect! In the soul or psychic experience one at-tunes the God-self to the universal! Hence the application or experi-ence is from within and in communion with the influence of God-force in the individual life.   EC 165-24

It partakes of the . . . of the spiritual intuitive forces as comes from close communion with the Holy Spirit, the promised Comforter, the con-sciousness of the Christ.   EC 262-15

Would we seek to be in the position of communion with the spirit within; and the fellowship is the promise of the Father through the Son, that—would ye seek to know His face, be kind and gentle, compassion-ate and loving, to thy fellow man. In this manner, then, let each purge their own minds and hearts, and he that has aught against any present it to the throne of grace, and His mercy is sufficient unto all. "As ye would that men should do to you, do ye even so to them." "Forgive me, Father, even as I forgive my brother" should be that lesson, that exercis-ing of the position each would take, would they know the face of Him who seeks fellowship with His creatures; for as the Father pitieth His children, so in that manner may the Father gather those close that would seek fellowship with Him. Know that as ye forgive will ye be for-given; for "Inasmuch as ye have done it unto the least of these my little ones, ye have done it unto me."

As we deal, then, with our fellow man, may there be expected and may we expect—those blessings to come to us. In the way and manner as we deal, so must it come again to all.

In the preparations, then, let each set their minds, their hearts, their souls, at peace with Him; and there will come that light that will shine in the darkest hour, in those periods when needed most. Approach the throne of mercy with mercy to all.   EC 262-21

Keep self close to that mental and spiritual awakening that comes with the communion with Him in thine inner self, for He is able to guide through all shadows that may arise.   EC 262-37

Shut thyself away from the cares of the world. Think on that as ye would do to have thy God meet thee face to face. "Ah," ye say, "but many are not able to speak to God!" Many, you say, are fearful. Why? Have ye gone so far astray that ye cannot approach Him who is all-merciful? He knows thy desires and thy needs, and can only supply according to the purposes that ye would perform within thine own self.

Then, purify thy body, physically. Sanctify thy body, as the laws were given of old, for tomorrow the Lord would speak with thee—as a father speaketh to his children. Has God changed? Have ye wandered so far away? Know ye not that, as He has given, "If ye will be my children, I will be thy God"? and "Though ye wander far away, if ye will but call I will hear"?

If any of you say, "Yes, but it was spoken to those of old—we have no part in such," then indeed ye have no part. They that would know God, would know their own souls, would know how to meditate or to talk with God, must believe that He *is*—and that He rewards those who seek to know and to do His biddings.

That He gave of old is as new today as it was in the beginning of man's relationship or seeking to know the will of God, if ye will but call on Him *within* thine inner *self*! Know that thy body is the temple of the living God. *There* He has promised to meet thee!

Are ye afraid? Are ye ashamed? Have ye so belittled thy opportunities, have ye so defamed thine own body and thine own mind that ye are ashamed to have thy God meet thee within thine own tabernacle?

Then, woe be unto thee—lest ye set thy house in order. For as has been indicated, there are physical contacts in thy own body with thy own soul, thy own mind. Does anyone have to indicate to you that if you touch a needle there is pain felt? Ye are told that such an awareness is an activity of consciousness that passes along the nervous system to and from the brain. Then, just the same there are contacts with that which is eternal within thy physical body. For there is the bowl that must one day be broken, the cord that must one day be severed from thine own physical body—and to be absent from the body is to be present with God.

What is thy God? Are thy ambitions only set in whether ye shall eat tomorrow, or as to wherewithal ye shall be clothed? Ye of little faith, ye of little hope, that allow such to become the paramount issues in thine own consciousness! Know ye not that ye are His? For ye are of His making! He hath willed that ye shall not perish, but hath left it with thee as to whether ye become even aware of thy relationships with Him or not. In thine own house, in thine own body there are the means for the approach—through the desire first to know Him; putting that desire into activity by purging the body, the mind of those things that ye know or even conceive of as being hindrances—not what someone else says! It isn't what you want someone else to give! As Moses gave of old, it isn't who will descend from heaven to bring you a message, nor who would come from over the seas, but Lo, ye find Him within thine own heart, within thine own consciousness! if ye will *meditate*, open thy heart, thy mind! Let thy body and mind be channels that *ye* may *do* the things ye ask God to do for you! Thus ye come to know Him.

Would you ask God to do for you that you would not do for your brother? If you would, you are selfish—and know not God. For as ye do it unto the least of thy brethren, ye do it unto thy Maker. These are not mere words—they are that as ye will *experience*—if ye would know Him at all. For He is not past finding out; and if ye will know Him, tune in to Him; turn, look, hope, act in such a way that ye *expect* Him, thy God, to meet thee face to face. "Be not afraid, it is I," saith He that came to those seeking to know their relationship with their Maker. And because He came walking in the night, in the darkness, even upon the waters, they were afraid. Yea, many of you become afraid because of the things that ye hear—for ye say, "I do not *understand*—I do not *comprehend*!" Why? Have ye so belittled thyself, thy body, thy mind, thy consciousness, that thou hast seared, that thou hast made of none effect those opportunities within thine own consciousness to know thy Maker?

Then, to all of you:

Purify thy body, thy mind. Consecrate thyselves in prayer, yes—but not as he that prayed "I thank Thee I am not like other fellows." Rather let there be in thy heart that humbleness, for ye must humble thyself if ye would know Him; and come with an open, seeking, contrite heart, desirous of having the way shown to thee.

And when thou art shown, turn not thy face the other way; but be true to the vision that is given thee. And He will speak, for His promise has been "When ye call I will hear, and will answer speedily." Then, when

He speaks, open thy heart, thy mind to the opportunities, to the glories that are thine—if ye will but accept them through that attuning

Through meditation of thy consciousness, thy desire to the *living* God; and say and live within thyself as He of old gave, "Others may do as they may, but as for me, I will worship—yea, I will serve the living God."

He is not far from thee! He is closer than thy right hand. He standeth at the door of thy heart! Will ye bid Him enter? or will ye turn away?

EC 281-41

As the Body is the temple of the living soul, the temple of God—What of it? Is it to become dust again and again; yet being associated with the soul, the spirit of the individual that had been lent such, or had used such in creation as the abode of their existences, their experiences? Is it to see corruption? Is it to be lost entirely? Is it to be glorified, spiritualized? How was His Body?

As the Body is a portion of the structure in which the manifestations of the individual, as a portion of the Whole, are carried on, it, that body—is then in the keeping of its *keeper*. So what wilt thou do with same?

God hath not *ordained* that any *soul* should perish! What of thy Body? Hast thou ordained, hast thou so lived, hast thou so made thy Temple that being untenable thou dost not care for its glorifying?

Ye attempt, rightly, to adorn thy Body for thy fellow man. Dost thou care less for thy God than thy fellow man? Dost thou purge the Body, as He hath given, that it may be made whole for thine soul?

What is to come depends upon what thou hast done, what thou wilt do with the opportunity which is, has been and will be *thine* for the glorifying of same.

If ye would be like Him, then so live, so conduct thyself, that *thy body* may again and *again* be brought into such relationships that it may be raised; a glorified body to be known as thine very own!

That thou mayest have been called, this, that and the other name may make for confusion to many. But when ye say Creative Force, God, Jehovah, Yahweh, Abba, what meanest thou? One and the same thing, carrying through in the various phases of thine own consciousness; or of those who in their activities seek, as thou (if thou seekest aright), to be one with Him yet to *know* self to *be* self, I *am*, in and with the *Great I AM*. The Destiny of the Body, then, lieth with the individual. EC 262-86

(Q) With whose spirit, mentioned in the Apostles' Creed, would we commune; with ourselves or God's?
(A) Within ourselves to God. For, as intimated elsewhere, "My Spirit beareth witness with thy spirit." Whose spirit? There is only *one* Spirit—of Truth. There may be divisions, as there may be many drops of water in the ocean yet they are all of the ocean. Separated, they are named for those activities in various spheres of experiences that are sought to be expressed here. The communion of the spirit of the divine within self may be with the source of divinity. This is what is meant by the communion of saints, of those that are of one thought, for [because] all thought for activity emanates from the same source, and there is the natural communion of those who are in that thought. This may be expressed by that indicated oft, that unless a helpful experience may be presented in an individual's activity as a parallel, as a complement, as a positive and negative force that may be united in one effort, it does not run true. For *opposites* create disturbance, dissensions, disruptions, devilment. A union of force makes for strength and power. Thus, the communion of saints means that all who have one purpose, whose thoughts and motivative forces are one, may communicate; whether those in the material plane, in the borderland, or those that may be upon the shores of the other side of life.

What meaneth the interpreters of the experiences in that, "Ye as standing here shall see glory; and after six days he taketh with him Peter, James and John and goeth apart into the mountain and there was transfigured before them"? What saw they? A glorified body? The glory of the body brought what? Communion of saints? For who appeared *with* Him? Moses; that to those present meant a definite undertaking which set them apart from other peoples, which has made for the first association or communication direct with a creative force or God through the activative forces in their experience. And Elijah (or John the Baptist); representing that they, too, would become as messengers to a waiting world, ready, ripe unto the harvest as he had told them.

Then this *indeed* was the communion of saints.

It is the natural state that the intent and purpose of activity in whatever environ or sphere ye may find self, is attuned with that sought by the soul. When may such a communication be given? Seek and ye shall find; knock and it shall be opened unto you—that attunement to which thou hast brought thine self! Hence more and more is the admonition given that if ye would know God ye must be godlike to some poor soul. If ye would have friends, be a friend to a friendless one. If ye would know peace and harmony, *bring* peace and harmony to the experience of another soul. Yes, be even as He; who showed His glory to His disciples in the mount; facing death, facing even the denial by one to whom He was showing himself that he had any part in that which He would give to others.

Let it be so in thine ministry, in thine activity; in the preparations of thy body, thy mind, thy knowledge concerning that which may bring to thine self those awarenesses of the Spirit of Truth, those things that make for the experiences of each and every soul. Seek not the experience until—and unless—ye know from whence and how and to whom it is given!   EC 262-87

Experiencing our heavenly Mother and Father personally, consciously, is ecstasy. To touch the womb of our genesis, to feel the arms of our divine parents, to walk through the Garden with our Creator is a happiness and contentment that cannot be found in any other activity. We have known these states of consciousness, and we can know them again. Sadly, even when we reconnect with this primordial condition, the world and selfish interests can pull us away again. It takes much training and practice to connect, and then the right heart to maintain the connection, in the midst of free-willed life and individualness.

At its core, Kabbalah is about the ecstatic union and communion between the created and the Creator.

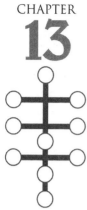

13

HIDDEN MESSAGES IN THE PROPHETS' VISIONS

In the journey from Eden to the final chapters of Revelation, there are mystical visions revealing heavenly secrets. If we understand these visions, we will gain insight into how we may become more cosmically conscious, more celestial, more spiritual, and even regain our lost immortality. Let's examine the visions of Isaiah, Elijah, Ezekiel, Daniel, and especially John in his Revelation. And let's do so with an eye toward the messages of soul growth found in the imagery and symbolism of these visions.

But first, let's review one of the biggest biblical tips for communing with God. It is found in a story about Elijah.

Elijah and the Still Small Voice

Here are the passages covering this event:

> The angel of The Lord came again the second time, and touched him [Elijah], and said, "Arise and eat, because the journey is too great for you." He arose, and ate and drank, and went in the strength of that food forty days and forty nights to Horeb the Mount of God. He came there to a cave, and lodged there; and, behold, the word of The Lord came to him, and he said to him, "What are you doing here, Elijah?" He said, "I have been very jealous for The Lord, the God of hosts; for the children of Israel have forsaken your covenant, thrown down your altars, and slain your prophets with the sword: and I, even I only, am left; and they seek

my life, to take it away." He said, "Go forth, and stand on the mountain before the Lord." Behold, the Lord passed by, and a great and strong wind tore the mountains, and broke in pieces the rocks before the Lord; but the Lord was not in the wind; and after the wind an earthquake; but the Lord was not in the earthquake; and after the earthquake a fire; but the Lord was not in the fire: and after the fire a still small voice.   I Kings 19:7-12; WEB

In this little story is revealed a great teaching for all who seek communion with God. God does not commune in power and might but in stillness. As the psalm reveals: "Be still, and know that I am God." (Psalm 46:10) Notice also that the voice came from within Elijah, draped in his heavy mantle, standing at the mouth of the cave. In the cave of our deeper consciousness, wrapped in the mantle of protection of our God-seeking heart, keenly seeking communion, the voice of God came to Elijah and comes to us. That voice was not booming. Rather, it was still and small. How does one hear a *still* voice? We *feel* it with our intuition.

For us to commune with the Ein Sof, the Infinite Eternal, we have to learn to sense God's presence within us and hear God's still, small voice. We do not do this with our outer senses. It is achieved, as Elijah's story implies, via an inner, meditative seeking. As true seekers, we need to develop our skills with meditation and the deep stillness and attunement that is the goal of deep meditation.

With this in mind, let's proceed to the fascinating and revealing visions of the biblical seers upon whom God bestowed wondrous blessings.

Isaiah, Ezekiel, Daniel, and John See the Logos

As we read these accounts, notice how many similar images, numbers, and characters there are among these visions, even though some may have a different name or title. They reflect a pattern of both God's presence and our connection to God: physically, mentally, and spiritually. Read these as if all the objects and activities are metaphors for inner places and channels of spiritual energy, especially spiritual, cleansing energy. Consider the temple or the house to be our body, and the levels to be both physical and mental, especially levels of consciousness in our deeper mind. Earth would represent our physical consciousness and reality. Angels would be heavenly aspects of ourselves and others at their soul level, while wings would be uplifting energies and thoughts. Covering the face would symbolize reversing outward–looking perception to inward seeking. The wasting of cities and houses would be cleansing the temple of body and mind of the many earthly things, thoughts, and desires.

Isaiah

I saw the Lord sitting on a throne, high and lifted up; and his train filled the temple. Above him stood the seraphim (angels). Each one had six wings. With two he covered his face. With two he covered his feet. With two he flew. One called to another, and said, "Holy, holy, holy, is the Lord of Hosts! The whole earth is full of his glory!" The foundations of the thresholds shook at the voice of him who called, and the house was filled with smoke. Then I said, "Woe is me! For I am undone, because I am a man of unclean lips, and I dwell in the midst of a people of unclean lips; for my eyes have seen the King, Lord of Hosts!" Then one of the seraphim flew to me, having a live coal in his hand, which he had taken with the tongs from off the altar. He touched my mouth with it, and said, "Behold, this has touched your lips; and your iniquity is taken away, and your sin forgiven." I heard the Lord's voice, saying, "Whom shall I send, and who will go for us?" Then I said, "Here I am. Send me!" He said, "Go, and tell this people, 'You hear indeed, but don't understand; and you see indeed, but don't perceive.' Make the heart of this people fat; make their ears heavy, and shut their eyes; lest they see with their eyes, and hear with their ears, and understand with their heart, and turn again, and be healed." Then I said, "Lord, how long?" He answered, "Until cities are waste without inhabitant, and houses without man, and the land becomes utterly waste, and the Lord has removed men far away, and the forsaken places are many in the midst of the land. If there are yet a tenth in it, it also shall in turn be eaten up; as a terebinth [a type of tree], and as an oak, whose stock remains, when they are felled; so the holy seed is its stock." Isaiah 6:1-13

The trees may have been felled, but within them is their original seed, from which a better tree will grow. This is reminiscent of Jesus' brief but poignant teaching: "Truly, truly, I say to you, unless a grain of wheat falls to the earth and dies, it remains alone; but if it dies, it bears much fruit. He who loves his life loses it, and he who hates his life in this world will keep it for eternal life." (John 12:24–25) This is not to mean that we must physically die to this life and world; rather, we must subdue this reality in order to perceive the more subtle realms of life. It is as William Wordsworth penned not so long ago in his poem "The World is Too Much With Us."

> The world is too much with us; late and soon,
> Getting and spending, we lay waste our powers;
> Little we see in Nature that is ours;
> We have given our hearts away, a sordid boon!
> This Sea that bares her bosom to the moon,
> The winds that will be howling at all hours,
> And are up-gathered now like sleeping flowers,
> For this, for everything, we are out of tune;
> It moves us not. —Great God! I'd rather be
> A Pagan suckled in a creed outworn;
> So might I, standing on this pleasant lea,
> Have glimpses that would make me less forlorn;
> Have sight of Proteus rising from the sea;
> Or hear old Triton blow his wreathed horn.

Proteus was one of the "first born," as indicated by his Greek name. Triton was "the messenger of the deep," a sea god, son of Poseidon. In the *Aeneid*, Misenus, brother–in–arms of Hector of Troy and the trumpeter of Aeneas (here representing our earthly self), challenged Triton (here presenting our godly self) to a trumpeting contest. For such arrogance, Triton flung him into the sea.

Let's take from these images and stories a sense of how we must subdue our earthliness in order to awaken and make room for our spiritual nature and our soul growth. The outer self must grow in humility, meekness, and patience in order for the true, inner self to awaken and resurrect us from our terrestrial paradigm.

Ezekiel

Ezekiel tells us, "The heavens were opened, and I saw visions of God." (Ezekiel 1:1) Again, as we read, let's keep a metaphoric perspective and consider the images and activities to be about forces within our bodies and minds. For example, the beasts in this coming vision symbolize those earthly urges that so often possess our better nature. They symbolize the four lower chakras, or spiritual centers, in our bodies (illustration 27). The firmament dividing the higher realms from the lower ones represents the veil that cloaks, or limits, our consciousness.

Here is an excerpt from one of Ezekiel's visions:

> And there was a voice above the firmament that was over their heads [the heads of the four beasts]: when they stood, they let down their wings. And above the firmament that was over their heads was the likeness of a throne, as the appearance of a sapphire stone; and upon the likeness of the throne was a likeness as the appearance of a man upon it above. And I saw as it were glowing metal, as the appearance of fire within it round about, from the appearance of his loins and upward; and from the appearance of his loins and downward I saw as it were the appearance of fire, and there was brightness round about him. As the appearance of the bow that is in the cloud in the day of rain, so was the appearance of the brightness round about. This was the appearance of the likeness of the glory of the Lord. And when I saw it, I fell upon my face, and I heard a voice of one that spoke. And he said unto me, "Son of man, stand upon

thy feet, and I will speak with thee." And the Spirit entered into me when he spoke unto me, and set me upon my feet; and I heard him that spoke unto me. And he said unto me, "Son of man, hear what I say unto thee; be not thou rebellious like that rebellious house; open thy mouth, and eat that which I give thee." And when I looked, behold, a hand was put forth unto me; and, lo, a roll of a book was there [a scroll]. And he spread it before me; and it was written within and without; and there were written lamentations, and mourning, and woe.   Ezekiel 1:25-28 and 2:1-10

These lines are so similar to those in the Revelation that we should read them now:

I saw a mighty angel coming down out of the sky, clothed with a cloud. A rainbow was on his head. His face was like the sun, and his feet like pillars of fire. He had in his hand a little open book. The voice that I heard from heaven, again speaking with me, said, "Go, take the book which is open in the hand of the angel who stands on the sea and on the land." I went to the angel, telling him to give me the little book. He said to me, "Take it, and eat it up. It will make your stomach bitter, but in your mouth it will be as sweet as honey." I took the little book out of the angel's hand, and ate it up. It was as sweet as honey in my mouth. When I had eaten it, my stomach was made bitter. They told me, "You must prophesy again over many peoples, nations, languages, and kings."   Revelation 10:1-2 and 9-11

A brief story about Jesus fits here as well:

Then Jesus was led up by the Spirit into the wilderness to be tempted by the Devil. When he had fasted forty days and forty nights, he was hungry afterward. The tempter came and said to him, "If you are the Son of God, command that these stones become bread." But he answered, "It is writ-

ten, 'Man shall not live by bread alone, but by every word
that proceeds out of the mouth of God.'"   Matthew 4:1-4

In this passage Jesus was referring to the passage in Deuteronomy:

He humbled you, and allowed you to hunger, and fed you
with manna, which you didn't know, neither did your fathers know; that he might make you know that man does
not live by bread only, but by everything that proceeds out
of the mouth of the Lord does man live.   Deuteronomy 8:3

Daniel
The prophet Daniel describes his encounter this way:

I lifted up mine eyes, and looked, and, behold, a man
clothed in linen, whose loins were girded with pure gold of
Uphaz [Ophir]; his body also was like the beryl, and his face
as the appearance of lightning, and his eyes as flaming
torches, and his arms and his feet like unto burnished brass,
and the voice of his words like the voice of a multitude. And
I, Daniel, alone saw the vision; for the men that were with
me saw not the vision; but a great quaking fell upon them,
and they fled to hide themselves. So I was left alone, and
saw this great vision, and there remained no strength in
me; for my comeliness was turned in me into corruption,
and I retained no strength. Yet heard I the voice of his
words; and when I heard the voice of his words, then was I
fallen into a deep sleep on my face, with my face toward the
ground. And, behold, a hand touched me, which set me
upon my knees and upon the palms of my hands. And he
said unto me, "O Daniel, thou man greatly beloved, understand the words that I speak unto thee, and stand upright;
for unto thee am I now sent." And when he had spoken this
word unto me, I stood trembling. Then said he unto me,
"Fear not, Daniel; for from the first day that thou didst set
thy heart to understand, and to humble thyself before thy

God, thy words were heard, and I am come for thy words'
sake."   Daniel 10:6-12

Daniel's description of the messenger from heaven is similar in many
ways to that of John's, which follows.

John

The Gospel writer John has become an icon of Christianity, but he
was the son of the Jews Zebedee and Salome and was himself well
trained in mystical Judaism, as indicated by his writings. He considered
himself to be a "true Jew." His vision that became the Revelation was
received and written while he was in banishment to the little island of
Patmos off the coast of Asia Minor (Turkey today). He begins his writing
by telling us that he was "in the Spirit on the Lord's Day when I saw and
heard," and he describes his encounter this way:

> I turned to see the voice that spoke with me. And having
> turned I saw seven golden candlesticks; and in the midst of
> the candlesticks one like unto a son of man, clothed with a
> garment down to the foot, and girt about at the breasts with
> a golden girdle. And his head and his hair were white as
> white wool, white as snow; and his eyes were as a flame of
> fire; and his feet like unto burnished brass, as if it had been
> refined in a furnace; and his voice as the voice of many
> waters. And he had in his right hand seven stars, and out of
> his mouth proceeded a sharp two-edged sword, and his
> countenance was as the sun shines in his strength. And
> when I saw him, I fell at his feet as one dead. And he laid his
> right hand upon me, saying, "Fear not; I am the first and the
> last, and the Living One; and I was dead, and behold, I am
> alive for evermore, and I have the keys of death and of Ha-
> des. Write therefore the things which thou saw, and the
> things which are, and the things which shall come to pass
> hereafter."   Revelation 1:12-19

The book of Daniel is considered the prophecy book of the Old Testament, and the Revelation that of the New Testament. Both authors see a similar messenger from heaven and receive visions of what has been, what is, and what will be. In our study, let's focus on the microcosmic aspects of their messages, that part that relates to our personal soul growth. This is exactly how Edgar Cayce's discourses addressed these messages and their strange imagery.

From Cayce's perspective, the messenger figure is the deeper, higher, spiritual, angelic aspect of our whole being. It is that portion made in the image of God and has maintained its proximity to God's throne. To John, this figure says, "Do not be afraid; I am the first and the last, and the Living One; and I was dead, and behold, I am alive forevermore, and I have the keys of death and Hades." As with John, our spiritual self—made in the image of God and destined to be an eternal companion to God—has been dead to us, and will remain so until we give birth to it again, as Jesus instructed Nicodemus: "Verily, verily, I say unto thee, except one be born anew, he cannot see the kingdom of God. You must be born a second time. That which is born of the flesh is flesh; and that which is born of the Spirit is spirit." (John 3:3-6) The first instruction from the spiritual self is to the seven spiritual centers of the body, represented by the various sevens throughout the initial chapters of Revelation.

The idea that the body possesses seven centers, or chakras, which may be used for spiritualization dates back to ancient times. One of the first recorded manuscripts to teach this is Patanjali's Yoga Sutras, written in the ancient Sanskrit language around 300 B.C. Patanjali was a student and teacher of the one of the most ancient texts of religious literature yet found in the world, the Veda, c. 1200 BCE. (The oldest Hebrew text is the Torah, The Book of the Law, dating to 1446 BCE.) Vedism was the religion of an ancient Indo-European people who settled in India. One of Vedism's key teachings, which eventually made its way into another ancient Sanskrit text, the Bhagavad Gita (c. 200 BCE), is that the Supreme Being created our souls with an eternal share of Himself/Herself in each soul, but this share is latent within us and must therefore be awakened. (Bhagavad Gita, XV, 7-11) Cayce affirms this concept when asked, "Should the Christ-Consciousness be described as the awareness within each soul, imprinted in pattern on the mind and waiting to be awakened by the will, of the soul's oneness with God?" and Cayce answered, "Correct. That's the idea exactly!" (EC 5749-14) Patanjali teaches that this latent Presence is in all of creation and, most important to us, in each physical body, able to be awakened by using the physical body in special ways. The body that is so helpful with physical activity secretly contains centers and pathways for metaphysical activity.

To experience this shared Presence of the Supreme Being, Patanjali teaches that one needs to elevate the normal levels of body energy and mental consciousness. The levels we find sufficient for everyday life are not sufficient for intimate contact with God.

In the Vedic texts and most other Eastern texts, energy and consciousness are symbolized by the cobra serpent. We Judeo-Christian followers often equate evil and Satan with the serpent; however, the teachings of Moses and Jesus contain serpent images as part of spiritualization, specifically the raising of the serpent.

During a clandestine nighttime meeting, Nicodemus, a member of the Sanhedrin (the Jewish leadership council), asked Jesus to explain the secret teachings. Jesus gave him three: The first is that we must be born again—we have been born physically, but we need also to be born spiritually. The second is that no one ascends to heaven but he or she who first descended from heaven. All of us, whether we remember it or not, have a portion within us that first descended from heaven. The third teaching uses the serpent to symbolize energy and consciousness: "As Moses raised the serpent in the desert, so must the Son of man be raised up to eternal life." Jesus is referring to the time when Moses left the kingdom of the pharaoh (so symbolic of the outer ego and worldly pursuits) to search for God in the desert. In his search he came upon a deep well around which were seven virgins attempting to water their flocks. These seven maidens symbolize the seven spiritual centers within our body. The deep well in the desert is the biblical "water of life" in the desert of this three-dimensional reality. Moses, one man, drove off all the other herdsmen that had been keeping the maidens from the water (symbolic of all our earthly distractions that keep us from nourishing our spiritual nature). He gave water to the seven maidens and their flocks. Then the girls told him a secret: they are the daughters of a high priest. He then went with them to the tent of the high priest and, ultimately, married the eldest maiden (the highest spiritual center). After these activities, he finally met God in a burning bush. Being predominantly external beings, we interpret this bush to symbolize something outside of ourselves. But consider that the burning bush may represent our own heads, the "bush" of our hair, under which is the crown chakra. This fits so well with Elijah's experience of God within him. It also fits with how the Holy Spirit manifested upon the holy women and disciples as tongues of flame on top of their heads, above the crown chakra.

Once Moses had made contact with God, he was instructed how to transform his staff into a serpent and to then raise up that serpent. (Exodus 2–4) Later in this story, having led all the people into the desert with him, Moses was directed by God to place a "fiery" serpent upon a raised staff so that everyone who looked upon it would be healed. (Numbers 21:8–9) Here again the writer is trying to convey more than a literal, physical story. We see how the serpent can be both poisonous and healing. The one that crawls on the ground is poisonous and deadly, but when the serpent is raised up and "fiery," it is healing. We have to go back to the Garden of Eden to fully understand this, because not only did Adam and Eve fall in the Garden, the serpent fell also. Since we know the serpent symbolizes both the life force and consciousness, this energy can be manifested in earthly ways or heavenly ones. In the teachings of Patanjali and Cayce (EC 264-19 Q & A 13; also see 262–87 Q & A 10, and 444-2 Q & A 23 & 24), the life force within the body can lower or raise our vibrations and consciousness. Moses's story teaches that the kundalini energy within us must be raised up in order for us to commune with God, for God's natural condition is a higher vibration and consciousness than we normally experience.

The process of raising the energy begins with an understanding of where the energy is in the body, how it is raised, and the path it follows through the body. According to the Yoga Sutras, the energy is "coiled" like a serpent (kundalini) in the lower part of the torso. It moves up the spinal column (sushumna) through the spiritual centers—chakras (wheels) and padmas (lotuses)—to the base of the brain and over through the brain to the brow. The path of the kundalini through the body is represented by a cobra in the striking position or by a shepherd's crook (a staff with a large hook on the upper end, flared out at the very tip). See illustration 27.

Many books today teach that the kundalini culminates at the crown of the head, but the more ancient images and teachings, as well as Cayce's, always depict it culminating at the forehead. This will cause some confusion to those who have for years studied and practiced using the crown chakra as the highest spiritual center in the body. Cayce insisted that the true path of the kundalini comes over and through the crown chakra, unites with the Infinite, and then flows into the third-eye chakra in the frontal lobe of the human brain. (EC 281-54 Q & A 14 and 15) But let's not allow this difference to become a stumbling block. If you have had much success with the crown chakra as the highest and final awakening, then so be it. If you have not been used to this, then consider the energy pathway that the classics and Cayce teach.

The seven spiritual centers are connected with the seven endocrine glands within the human body: (1) the root chakra and lotus connect with the testes in males, and the ovaries in females, (2) the navel chakra and lotus with the Leydig cells, (3) the solar plexus with the adrenals, (4) the heart with the thymus gland, (5) the throat with the thyroid, (6) the crown with the pineal, and (7) the third eye with the pituitary and the hypothalamus. They are also connected with major nerve ganglia, or plexuses, along the spine: pelvic or lumbar, hypogastric or abdominal, epigastric or solar, cardiac or heart, pharyngeal or throat, and the brain itself. Cayce recommended osteopathic adjustments and massage for improving the flow of the kundalini energy. (EC 281-12 Q & A 15) These days, osteopathy has moved away from physical adjustments, leaving that area to chiropractors and, in some cases, well-trained massage therapists.

14

SPIRITUALIZATION OF THE BODY TEMPLE

CHAPTERS 1-3 OF THE REVELATION
THE 7 SPIRITUAL CENTERS (CHAKRAS)

Let's examine the guidance given by the heavenly messenger that comes to John in his mystical revelation. As with dreams, this vision is highly symbolic. Edgar Cayce explains:

> [T]he visions, the experiences, the names, the churches, the places, the dragons, the cities, all are but *emblems* of those forces that may war within the individual in its journey through the material, or from the entering into the material manifestation [i.e., physical body and world] to the entering into the glory, or the awakening in the spirit.
>
> EC 281-16; italics and brackets mine

The seven "churches" symbolize the seven spiritual centers—chakras and lotuses. A chakra is an energy generator, and a lotus is a point of view or perspective. Both may change as one raises the energy and consciousness. In each case, the heavenly messenger begins by describing a characteristic of each spiritual center; it then acknowledges the center's strengths or virtues, followed by the center's shortcomings or vices. Finally, it gives the center a directive, a command. Interestingly, in Pantanjali's teachings, the forehead center is called *ajna*, which means "a command."

Cayce states that the heavenly messenger in the Revelation is giving a critique, an insight, and a directive that *all* of us may follow to achieve higher vibrations and higher consciousness. In breaking down the massive vision of the Revelation, Cayce explained that the first three chapters relate to spiritualizing the body, the next eight to spiritualizing the mind, the next nine to spiritualizing actions, and the final two chapters to the reward for completing the process.

1-Ephesus-Gonads-Root Chakra/Lotus

The portion of our spiritual selves that holds the seven stars (symbolizing the seven angelic forces overseeing each chakra) and walks among the seven golden lamp stands, or candleholders (symbolizing the actual glands in the body), says that this first center's virtue is that it has toiled and persevered and cannot stand evil or false spirituality. Even so, its weakness is that it has left its first love and must therefore remember whence it has fallen, repent, and do the first deeds. Despite all appearances to the contrary, we are celestial, spiritual beings first. We descended from heaven into egocentric consciousness, into matter and this three-dimensional reality. These outer influences have taken hold on us. They possess us. We feel completely terrestrial and physical, subjects of this world. We are alone with our self in one body. Oneness is lost. God consciousness is lost. This chakra reflects these losses. It must reverse its focus, turning away from self-driven worldly realities, and allow for spiritual realities, remembering how it originally loved the spiritual realms and God.

In many of the ancient texts, reversing the flow of energy in the body is a major technique for spiritualizing the body. In a Taoist text there is a breathing technique in which the mind visualizes energy rising up the back of the body with every inhalation of the breath, uniting with the Great Spirit's Breath, and then descending the front of the body with every exhalation, bathing the body in raised, spiritualized energy. This is described as the "backward flow" of the bodily breath, which brings it into reunion with the breath of the Infinite, originally breathed into us in Genesis.

The sexual glands and root chakra have the life force of the body "coiled" within them. This life force needs to be awakened and drawn upward through the body to the brain and over to the frontal lobe and the forehead. There it can be united with our spiritual ideal, or our image, concept, or consciousness of God and our godly nature. Then, with this first love restored, the body is bathed in the resurrected spirit and higher vibration. Over time, the body is spiritualized through this process.

In the heavenly messenger's final comment to this center, it promises that if this center spiritualizes itself, then it will be allowed to eat again from the Tree of Life in the Paradise of God. (Rev. 2:7) In other words, it will regain the immortality and companionship with God that it lost in its descent into matter, physicality, and selfishness.

2-Smyrna-Leydig Cells-Navel Chakra

As the heavenly messenger turns its attention to the church of Smyrna, it identifies itself as the first self and the last self, which was dead and is now alive again. The heavenly messenger is our higher spiritual self, seeking to gain the attention and support of the lower levels of our whole nature. It acknowledges that this center—the navel, or lower abdomen, chakra—has suffered much tribulation, poverty, and slander from those who say they are true Jews, meaning true spiritual seekers, but are in fact of "the synagogue of Satan."

Cayce identifies the second spiritual center as the "seat of the soul." (EC 294-142) The soul's companion is the subconscious mind, according to Cayce. (EC 3744-3) These two abide in the autonomic nervous system of the body and directly affect the endocrine glands and their powerful hormones.

The heavenly messenger is aware of the soul and subconscious mind's poverty and tribulation in a body that is physically driven, with little or no spiritual nourishment. When we are predominantly in our lower chakras and earthly energies, our higher spiritual centers and energies suffer and starve. Despite this bodily condition, the spirit says that the soul remains rich and it should not fear its trials and imprisonment in the body because, at the death of the body, the spirit will give it "the crown of life" (Revelation 2:10), by virtue of the harmonic link between the second and sixth chakras, the navel and the crown, respectively. Notice how nicely this fits with the emanations and their link between the first and tenth orbs, the Great I AM and the little "I am," respectively.

The heavenly messenger warns that this center lets fear take hold of it, and it must let go of fear. The messenger promises that if this center stops being afraid and doubting the truth, it will not suffer the "second death." Cayce explains that the second death is when those who have gained understanding fall back into self-seeking and self-exaltation, accentuating the ego rather than the soul self, and suffer the death of the truth a second time. If this spiritual center lets go of fear, it will never fall away again and thereby never again suffer death of the truth. Cayce explains it this way: "For there is set before thee good and evil, life and death; choose thou. For the spirit of truth makes [one] alive. Fear, doubt, condemnation, bring doubt, illness, fear, and then dissolution (disillusion?); and the hill to be climbed again." (EC 1261-1) In other readings Cayce says that doing what we know is right despite the challenges will remove fear. We certainly do not want to climb the hill again or experience the death of the truth a second time. We want to wear the Crown of the original emanation and live as we were intended to.

3-Pergamos (Pergamum)-Adrenal Glands- Solar Plexus Chakra

As the heavenly messenger approaches this third center, it describes itself as the one with a two-edged sword, revealing this center's power to wield a weapon that can cut for good or evil. The spirit acknowledges that this center held fast to "my name" and did not deny "my witness, my faithful one," even though this center is "where Satan's throne is" and "where Satan dwells." Over and over in the Cayce volumes, we find the concept that within each of us is both the Holy One and the Evil One, wrestling for power and control over us. A good example can be found in the following reading:

What manner of spirit, then, hast thou directing thy life? Look within. See thyself, [see] that which has motivated thee in thy dealings with thy fellow man; or as to what ye have proclaimed is thy concept, thy thought of thy Creator.

Have ye opened thy heart, thy desires to Him? Are they in keeping with that thou would have meted to thee, to thy fellow man, to thy Maker, to thy Savior?

Does the Spirit of the Master and the Father abide with thee? This is His promise. "If ye love me, I will come and abide with thee." Have ye driven Him from thy home, thy church, thy state, yea, from thine own consciousness?

Have ye not rather entertained the anti-Christ?

Have ye considered as to *who* is the author of thy activities day by day? yea, in thy dealings with those in thy home, in thy neighborhood, in thy city, in thy state? Have ye not preferred one above another?

Is that the spirit of truth? Is that the consciousness with which He that is the author of thy faith ministered to those He met day by day?

Has He changed? Have the circumstances, the environs, the times changed? Are not Time, Space and Patience in thy consciousness a manifestation rather of His love, His patience, His longsuffering, His activities with the children of men?

Art thou wiser in thy own conceit than He?

Do ye day by day, in *every* way, say "*Thy will, not mine, be done*"? Rather do ye not say, "Bless me and my house, my son, my children, my kin-folks; for we are a little better and we do a little better"? Do ye not excuse thyself?

Be these in keeping with Spirit as ye now conceive, as ye now understand?

Then gather together, even as He gave; "Let not your hearts be troubled; ye believe in God, believe also in me. And I go to the Father, and if ye love me ye will keep my commandments. For my command-ments are not grievous, but are *living* and *doing* day by day those things that ye *know* to do!"

Patience, love, gentleness! Not gainsaying, not finding fault!

EC 262-117

Thus, this center is a most dangerous and a most potentially power-ful chakra, given the energy of the powerful solar plexus and the adre-nal gland's "fight or flight" hormones. In many yoga texts, its power is often identified as second only to the crown chakra. According to Cayce, during physical growth and during meditation, if the balance is main-tained, the energy of the life force, the kundalini, crosses the solar plexus each time it passes to another center. (EC 281-53)

But this center is also the place of anger (EC 281-54), impulsive reac-tions, and spirit-killing urges. The spirit identifies its weaknesses and vices as eating things "sacrificed to idols" and committing "acts of immorality." Uncontrolled, the messenger says that this center throws "stumbling blocks" in the way of our spiritual efforts. It must stop this! If it does, then the messenger promises that it will "eat of the hidden manna" and "receive a new name."

Cayce says that "new name" refers to our eternal name that uniquely identifies each of us from the rest of creation. (EC 281-13) Somehow, deep within each of us, the messenger whispers that we have not fully denied this aspect of ourselves. We have not killed the witness to our spiritual nature. If we spiritualize this center, then a new name will be given to us, a name that only we who receive it will know. John receives his new name written upon a white stone, indicating that it will endure as does a stone, or as we would say, It's written in stone.

The manna refers to this center's desires for physical gratifications, often symbolized as bread; yet, as Jesus so wonderfully put it, we do not live by bread alone, but by every word that comes out of the mouth of God. (Matthew 4:4) These words from God's mouth, Cayce says, are the hidden manna. (EC 281-13) As the messenger warned, it will come upon this center "quickly with the sword of my mouth" if it doesn't overcome its negative influences.

4–Thyatira–Thymus Gland–Heart Chakra

Now the messenger moves to the fourth center, identifying itself as the Son of God, with eyes like fire and feet like fine brass. In other words, it has the vision of the spirit and the understanding that only comes from being tested in the furnace of life. It acknowledges that the heart chakra has charity, faith, patience, service, and achievements, the most recent achievements being greater than the first ones. But it also has one major issue with this center: It lives life without love, seeking only gratification and pleasure. This is represented by the false prophet Jezebel, whose motto is to get all you want, no matter how you obtain it, and by acts of fornication, which is sex without love, here representative of living physically without spiritual ideals. Then the spirit warns that unless the heart center changes, it will suffer "great tribulation" in the bed it has made for itself. When Cayce was asked about the great tribulation, he answered:

The great tribulation and periods of tribulation . . . are the experiences of every soul, every entity. They arise from influences created by man . . . Man may become, with the people of the universe, ruler of any of the various spheres through which the soul passes in its experiences. Hence, as the cycles pass, as the cycles are passing, when there *is* come a time, a period of readjusting in the spheres, (as well as in the little earth, the little soul)—seek, then, as known, to present self spotless before that throne; even as *all* are commanded to be circumspect, in thought, in act, to that which is held by self as that necessary for the closer walk with Him. In that manner only may each atom (as man is an atom, or corpuscle, in the body of the Father) become a helpmeet with Him in bringing that to pass that all may be one with Him. EC 281-16

The spirit goes on to promise that if this spiritual center changes, then he "will give him the morning star." Venus is the morning star. In astrological traditions, Venus represents love, harmony, beauty, and the arts.

5-Sardis-Thyroid Gland-Throat Chakra

The speech delivered by the heavenly messenger identifies this center with the throat. The messenger explains that speech comes from "the seven spirits of God and the seven stars," which are the sum total of all seven centers acting in unison with God's will. The messenger acknowledges that this center has good deeds and a name, is alive, and only a few aspects of its activities are "defiled." Even so, it is dead to the real truth and is imperfect. The spirit messenger encourages this center to strengthen itself because it is closer to death than it realizes. If it strengthens itself spiritually, then it will be clothed in white raiment, its name will not be blotted out of the Book of Life, and the messenger will confess its name "before my Father and his angels."

Notice how much of this center is identified with will and speech. Cayce says that one of the major steps to full spiritual consciousness is letting our will become subordinate to God's will. He often recommended an affirmation, such as this one from the *Search for God* Study Group readings:

Thy will, O God, be done in me, through me, as Thou seest; for the desire of my heart is that I may be the channel of blessings to others in the ways and manners Thou seest; not my way, O Lord, but Thy way.

EC 262-64

6–Philadelphia–Pineal Gland–Crown Chakra

In Cayce's system, the kundalini energy runs up the spine to the base of the brain and then, like a cobra in the striking position, runs from the base to the crown of the head, continuing only then to the third eye, in the frontal lobe and the forehead. This is exactly how the serpent on the pharaoh's *nemes* headdress is depicted, and reflects many ancient images of the winged, or raised, serpent, from India to the Mayan lands. The sixth chakra is the Crown; the seventh is the Third Eye, on the forehead.

As the spiritual messenger approaches the sixth center, located deep within the brain, it references that part of itself that is "holy, true, has the key of David, opens and no one can shut, shuts and no one can open," which is to say that only the spiritual part of our being can allow the spiritual process to proceed. This is considered to be one of the most holy centers in the human body. It is the place of "the mount of God," according to Cayce. (EC 2501-7) If we enliven this center with the spirit and spiritual intentions, then we draw all the lower centers up to this high place and unite them with God's Spirit. Moses learned to raise the serpent and then ascended the mount (this chakra) to meet God, face to face.

The heavenly messenger acknowledges the works of this center; it has kept God's word and not denied God's name: "I AM that I am." This center knows the truth of its spiritual nature, and despite how weak it has become from material struggles, it retains the truth of its real nature and the real purpose of incarnate life. This is the only center that the messenger finds no fault with. There is nothing this center has to do except continue to hold onto its truth. Therefore, the messenger promises to draw all the cells of the body before it and make them bow to its truth. It also promises to keep this center from the temptation that has and is coming to the rest of the body as a test of the body's true desires, whether they are spiritual or strictly material and self-centered.

In Patanjali's arrangement, the crown chakra is the highest center in the body; the kundalini, having risen up the spine, moves through the brain to the opening of the crown. In Revelation 3:11, the messenger actually mentions the "crown" in reference to this sixth center. In Cayce's arrangement, the energy flows up the spine through the brain to the pineal gland, opening this crown chakra, which receives the inflowing energy and awareness of heaven but then flows on to the frontal lobe and forehead, filling the "cup that runneth over" (Psalm 23:5), which is the Third Eye and the master glands of the body: the pituitary and hypothalamus.

If we fully awaken this center, then the spiritual messenger promises to make us "a pillar in the temple of My God" and we will "never go out from it again." The spiritual messenger will also write the name of God, God's city, and its new name upon us, and we shall never forget again.

7-Laodicea-Pituitary Gland-Third Eye Chakra

Finally, the heavenly messenger arrives at the highest center in the body. The aspect of the spiritual messenger that is in this center is called "the Amen, the faithful and true witness, the Beginning of the creation of God." This is the master center of the body. But the spirit is upset with this center because it is "neither cold nor hot." Because it is lukewarm about the spiritualization process, the spirit is ready to "spit you out of my mouth." This center says that it is rich and needs nothing, but the heavenly messenger challenges, saying it is actually "wretched and miserable and poor and blind and naked" (harkening back to the original activities in the Garden, when Adam and Eve hid from God).

Amazingly, this center has no redeeming qualities and no virtue to acknowledge. It is stagnant and unenthusiastic, contributing nothing to the overall spiritualization of the body. The messenger therefore warns it to get truth forged in the fires of the spirit, white garments of purity that its nakedness will be clothed, and eye salve to anoint its eyes to see the real truth. However, in a backhanded way, the messenger acknowledges its love for this center, saying: "Those whom I love, I reprove and discipline."

Our spiritualization process must raise bodily energy and vibrations to the level of this most important chakra in order to fire it up, get it hot, for the spiritual awakening.

Redirecting the Energy of the Body Temple
Chapters 4 and 5 of the Revelation

Now we shift from addressing each spiritual center to addressing other parts of the body temple.

The Throne–24 Elders–7 Spirits–Lake of Glass– 4 Beasts
A New Condition Throughout the Body

Now that the heavenly messenger has addressed and awakened all seven centers within the body to the spiritualization process, it takes the body to a new level of vibration. In the vision we see a throne in the midst of heaven, and the godly, spiritual portion of our being is seated upon this throne. John records the imagery this way:

> I looked, and lo, in heaven an open door! And the first voice, which I had heard speaking to me like a trumpet, said, "Come up hither, and I will show you what must take place after this." At once I was in the Spirit, and lo, a throne stood in heaven, with one seated on the throne! And he who sat there appeared like jasper and carnelian and round the throne was a rainbow that looked like an emerald.
>
> Revelation 4:1-3

(Note: A carnelian is a reddish brown, semi–precious stone used to protect a spiritual traveler after death and guard against evil. It was once thought that wearing a carnelian would purify the blood. Emeralds were thought to enhance clairvoyance.)

Around this image of our spirit self and the throne are the twenty-four elders, which Cayce identifies as the twelve paired (24) cranial nerves within our physical brains! Amazing how the imagery depicts physical anatomy—or how physical anatomy reflects spiritual channels and forces.

The throne is before a "sea of glass like crystal," symbolizing the depths beneath outer consciousness and the stillness required to reach this level of consciousness.

Energy is being emitted from the brain in the form of "flashes of lightning and sounds and peals of thunder." Seven "lamps of fire" were before the throne, representing the "seven spirits of God," emblematic of the spiritual forces of our seven chakras and glands. These are the lotus (padma) aspect of each spiritual center, which are awakening as this process continues. Their fragrance begins to subdue earthly desires and energies and to lift body and mind to higher levels, higher vibrations.

Also around the throne are the "four beasts," seen also by Ezekiel and Daniel. Surprisingly, we find these same beasts represented in ancient Egyptian mysticism as the four children of Horus: one with the head of a jackal, one with the head of a man, one with the head of a baboon, and one with the head of a falcon. The heads of these four appear on the canopic jars of mummification. Horus was the messiah of the ancient Egyptians, rescuing the world from his uncle Set's domination (Set, Seti, or Seth was the name for Satan in ancient Egypt). In one of the most famous scenes on ancient Egyptian papyruses, the four children of Horus are wrapped like mummies and standing on an open lotus. They are intoxicated by the fragrance of the holy flower and are submissive before the throne of Osiris, Horus's father and guardian of the way through the Netherworld to the Heavens. This scene reflects how the four lower chakras become intoxicated by the heavenly fragrance of the opening lotuses and turn their attention to higher forces and the higher self.

Here is how each of the prophets described the four beasts:

> And from the midst of it [the throne] came the likeness of four living creatures. And this was their appearance: they had the form of men, but each had four faces, and each of them had four wings. As for the likeness of their faces, each had the face of a man in front; the four had the face of a lion

on the right side, the four had the face of an ox on the left
side, and the four had the face of an eagle at the back.

Ezkeiel 1:10

And four great beasts came up out of the sea, different from
one another. The first was like a lion and had eagles' wings.
And behold, another beast, a second one, like a bear. After
this I looked, and lo, another, like a leopard, with four wings
of a bird on its back; and the beast had four heads; and
dominion was given to it. After this I saw in the night visions, and behold, a fourth beast, terrible and dreadful and
exceedingly strong.   Daniel 7:3-7

And round the throne, on each side of the throne, are four
living creatures, full of eyes in front and behind. The first
living creature like a lion, the second living creature like an
ox, the third living creature with the face of a man, and the
fourth living creature like a flying eagle. And the four living
creatures, each of them with six wings.   Revelation 4:6-8

According to Cayce, these four beasts are "the four destructive influences that make the greater desire for the carnal forces, that arise as the
beasts within self to destroy." (EC 281-16) We have learned what these
destructive influences are from the messenger's comments to the first
four spiritual centers: (1) leaving our first love; (2) fear; (3) anger, impulsive reactions, and spirit-killing urges; and (4) living life without love
and ideals.

All of these destructive influences were personified in Cain. Though
he first sought God's love, he later did not desire it. He killed his brother
impulsively in anger and spitefulness, only to then become so afraid
that he could not go on without God's promise of protection. Finally, he
goes out to live life for himself and his own gratification, without any
spiritual interests or intentions.

In the book of Job, Satan claimed that Job was the same way, having
no interest in God and the spiritual life, and would curse God to His
face if He touched Job's physical life and body. Cayce said that these

destructive influences must be dealt with and subdued (EC 281-16); as God said to Cain, "Sin is crouching at the door [of your consciousness], its desire is for you, but you must master it." (Genesis 4:7)

As has been stated, these four beasts also represent the four lower chakras.

As the Revelation vision continues, these four lower urges and influences are raised to higher consciousness and vibration, turning away from material, earthly pursuits, and are now contributing to the spiritualization of the body, as indicated in this passage: "the four beasts gave glory and honor and thanks to him who sits on the throne." When this is done, the cranial nerves are affected: "the twenty-four elders will fall down before him who sits on the throne," and they in turn begin to contribute to the spiritualization of the body. They "cast their crowns to him who sits on the throne." Now the spiritual self opens the seven seals of the body, which again symbolizes the opening of the seven spiritual centers—both physically and consciously.

Cayce states that the book with the seven seals is the human body. (EC 281-29) We are truly worthy to open the seals only when we have sufficiently subordinated our desire and will to allow God's will to fully guide the higher stages of our awakening, cleansing, and spiritualization for the ultimate communion.

Our worthiness is identified in the Revelation as "the Lion of the tribe of Judah, the root and offspring of David," all terms associated with the Messiah, only this is the little messiah within each of us, our spiritual self reborn! This spiritual-self has so made its will subordinate to God's that it is represented in the vision as the "Lamb of God." Now we may safely open the seals of our spiritual centers and release the powerful life force, moving it from the lower chakras to the higher with God's protection and assistance, guided always by God's all-knowing, all-wise presence.

The Seven Seals and Seven Trumpets
Chapters 6–10 of the Revelation
Cleansing the Seven Centers

Now, with the seven spiritual centers awakened, the higher self and the life force rising, the lower urges subdued, and our spiritual self seated again on the throne of consciousness, we begin a series of cleansings. This begins with John's vision of the famous "Four Horsemen of the Apocalypse," who ride out with specific colors, devices, and missions. Cayce picks up on the colors for each spiritual center and adds musical notes, key words from the Lord's Prayer, the four elements, the endocrine glands, and even planets within our solar system. See illustration 28.

We might ask, How could the planets in the solar system have any relevance to the spiritual centers and endocrine glands in our bodies? Cayce's answer is that we are a microcosm of our Infinite Eternal Creator, thus all that is in the macrocosm has a reflexive presence within us. (EC 2984-1) At first glance, it may seem paradoxical that these outer influences are also within us and that universal "things," such as planets, find a relating point within our being, but as the Ancient Egyptian god Hermes (Thoth) stated: "As within so without, as above so below." The body and the mind are arranged in a manner that reflects the arrangement of the universe.

Each spiritual center in the body has a corresponding relationship with the seven primary colors of the spectrum, the seven basic notes of the Western musical scale, seven key words in the Lord's Prayer, and seven planets within this solar system. Nevertheless, Cayce does hedge his teaching on this in several readings, explaining that such correlations are only relatively correct because of the many variables in human spiritual development that would cause another color, or note, or word, or planet to better represent that center. Cayce's comments on this are throughout so many readings that is impossible for me to reference them all. But for a sense of his position, read 281-29 and 281-30.

Now, as we go through the opening of the seals and the sounding of the trumpets, Cayce says that we are experiencing the purifications that influence spiritual development through the vibrational changes in the body. (EC 281-31) The way these purifications are described in Revelation causes one to believe that they are terrifyingly devastating to the physical self. However, Cayce explains that, as progress is made toward giving birth to the spiritual self (which occurs later in chapter 12 of the vision), the physical self needs to become more humble, meek, longsuffering, and patient. It must decrease while the spiritual self increases. Cayce says that the devastating sufferings represent those influences that cleanse the earthly, egocentric self for the birthing of the heavenly, spiritual self. (EC 281-31) This does not mean that one cannot live in the earth and be spiritual. It means that, rather than an earthly being who entertains spiritual concepts and activities, we have become a spiritual being who is temporarily incarnating in the earth. There is quite a difference in these two states of being.

The two parts of our being will be at war with one another unless these cleansings occur, because they result in a singularity of purpose achieved by subduing earthly desires and accentuating heavenly, spiritual ones. Therefore, the fire is to purify; the hail is to crystallize purposes into a oneness of purpose. Less and less of self's desires and more and more of God's desires are depicted as the destruction of a third of the earth, the sea, and the heavens, followed by the falling of a great star from heaven, representing the coming of heavenly influences upon the earthly self. The outer Sun is darkened so that the inner heavenly Light may be given a greater presence within us. All the terrifying events that occur during the opening and sounding of the seven spiritual centers are symbolic of this great transition, this great preparation for the birth of the new, God-centered self.

The World Unites with the Lord

When the cleansings are completed, loud voices from heaven cry out, "The kingdom of the world has become the kingdom of the Lord, and of His Messiah; and He will reign forever and ever." The twenty-four elders (the twelve paired cranial nerves) worship God, saying, "We give Thee thanks, O Lord God, the Almighty, who is and was, because Thou has taken Thy great power and has begun to reign." Then all cells of the body are judged according to their level of attunement and atonement with this new reign. And then, the temple of God is opened, and the Ark of the Covenant appears in the temple, causing flashes of lightning, peals of thunder, earthquakes, and a great hailstorm. The physical body has now reached a level of cleansing, vibration, and attunement to become the temple of God. Cayce describes it this way:

As the Book of Life then is opened, there is seen the effect of that which now has been attained by the opening of the system, the body, the mind; all of those effects that have been created by the ability of the entity to attune self to the consciousness of being at-one with the Divine within. Now we see those in the material world using these influences for self-exaltation, self-indulgence, and self-glorification; and yet we see those using same for the glory, the understanding, the knowledge, and the wisdom of the Father.   EC 281-33

15

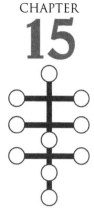

SPIRITUALIZATION OF THE MIND

CHAPTER 11 OF THE REVELATION
THE ROD, TEMPLE, 2 WITNESSES,
AND THE 7TH ANGEL

Spiritualizing the body has reached such a level in this vision that attention now turns to spiritualizing the mind and applying the wisdom in one's life. In this section we awaken our deeper mind and develop a better perspective on the size and nature of heaven and heavenly consciousness. We will meet two witnesses that have helped us know the truth: our conscious mind and our superconscious mind. We will face up to two beasts that have and do challenge us in this spiritualization process: fear and double-mindedness. We will witness the birth of our new selves and face our greatest accuser. We will overcome a flood of emotions and the fall of our egocentric self. Finally, we will unite with the spiritual portion of our minds and be judged according to all we have done with the gifts of free will and life.

This section begins with John receiving a measuring rod with which to measure "the temple of God, and the altar, and them that worship within." Cayce explains that the measuring, which also occurs in Ezekiel's vision, is a sign that each of us is given the freedom and power to set the metes and bounds of our temple, our heaven. Here are Cayce's words on this:

(Q) What is meant by the symbol of the "reed like unto a rod" with which John was told to measure the temple? Rev. 11. Please explain.
(A) How again has it been given by Him? "With what measure ye mete it shall be measured to thee again." Know that he had acceded to the point wherein he is to set the metes and bounds (John as an individual). You, your own souls as individuals, who will you put in your heaven? You of a denomination, you of a certain creed, you of a certain mea-

surement, with what measure you mete it is measured to thee again.

This then is an illustration that to each there is given, what? All power to set that as the metes and bounds of what heaven in itself shall be to those who would gather these, or those, or the self. What would be heaven to a soul that built it for its individual self? Heaven, yes—but alone!

Those that will measure then, those that will set metes and bounds—how has it been given oft? When you name a name, or when you give metes and bounds, you forget that God's force, God's power is *infinite!* and this is beyond the comprehension of the finite mind.

EC 281-32

Cayce identifies this temple in the Revelation not as the body but as the mind. (EC 281-32) He explains that the tabernacle and the holy mount that appear many times in the Scriptures and ancient legends are metaphors, or patterns, for the mind and the mind's connection to God. Throughout history, spiritual seekers met God by entering the tabernacle or going up upon a mount. Measuring the temple indicates that our understanding has now reached a point that we realize the need for a unified activity with the Creative Forces of God. (EC 281-32) Cayce further explains that, as in the ancient physical temple, a veil shields the holy, inner realms of our mind from the worldly thoughts and images of our outer mind. John is now going to spiritualize his mind, uniting the inner and outer mind through a series of cleansings. Ultimately, this process leads us to a new wholeness that is consciously aware of God and God's Mind, just as God was in the temple and with the people of ancient Israel.

The temple is described first in Exodus 25. Moses goes up upon the Mount of God and returns with the word of God, commanding a new temple to be built. The temple is seen again in the book of Ezekiel (see Ezekiel 40-42) when Ezekiel has the same experience as the disciple John, even to being given a reed with which to measure the temple. The temple is also explained in detail by the disciple Paul in his letter to the Hebrews.

Let's begin our study of the temple with God's first words about the subject in Exodus 25: 8 -9: "And let them make me a sanctuary, that I may dwell among them. According to all that I show thee, the pattern of the tabernacle, and the pattern of all the furniture thereof, even so shall you make it."

It is to be a sanctuary that will allow the infinite God to dwell in the finite world with us. Moses physically manifested this temple with poles and curtains, as God revealed to him from the holy mount. Ezekiel and John experience the temple while "in the spirit," both being told to measure it and understand its true nature. Paul remarks how the old, physical temple has now become an inner, heavenly temple, resulting in God dwelling within each of us.

The ancient temple described by God to Moses has a court and a tabernacle. The tabernacle is composed of two separate parts of its own: the "holy place" and the "most holy place," often called the "holy of holies." These three areas (court, holy place, and holy of holies) are separated by three distinct veils, or curtains, symbolic of the three levels of our being (physical, mental, and spiritual) and the three levels of our mind (conscious, subconscious, and superconscious). One large curtain surrounds the whole temple. Through the first curtain, one entered the court, our outer consciousness. Another curtain surrounds the tabernacle. Through the second curtain, one entered the first chamber of the tabernacle, the holy place, our soul mind, which Cayce identifies as the subconscious. Then we come to the third curtain, which shielded the holy of holies and the superconscious level of our mind, which is intimately connected with God's mind. It is in the holy of holies that God has promised to meet us.

The whole temple was portable. It could be disassembled and reassembled as the tribes traveled or camped. Each of the three areas of the temple contained specific items. In the court were the water basin for cleansing and purification, and the altar for sacrificial offerings. Inside the chamber of the holy place, to the south side of the chamber, was the large menorah of seven candles. On a table to the north side of the chamber was the bread of the presence of God (sometimes referred to as the "showbread"), and in the center was an altar of incense. In the next and last inner chamber, the holy of holies, was the Ark of the Covenant, where God had promised to meet the priest directly.

You can see how this arrangement would lend itself to a series of steps that would help the ancient seekers make a transition from outer life to inner attunement with God. First was the process of cleansing and ablution, and the offering up of one's earthly pleasures (prized lambs, goats, grains, and so on). Then, upon entering the first inner chamber, one would light the seven candles, representing the raising of vibrations in the spiritual centers of the body, and light the incense that would rise upward to the heavens. In this same chamber is the bread of the presence of God, which symbolizes the nourishment that will result from contact with God in the next chamber, Finally, one would enter the holy of holies to commune with God. The Ark contained three items: (1) the tablets of the Ten Commandments (which are the covenant: "If you keep these commandments, then I will be your God); (2) the staff that came alive again by budding, belonging to the first high priest, Aaron; and (3) the manna that fell from heaven to feed the people in the desert, forever symbolic of God's ability to care for us no matter what the physical limitations. The Ark was made of acacia wood covered in gold. Two kneeling cherub angels were atop the Ark, wings bent in a submissive, humble manner, and amid them was the "mercy seat," to help those of us who so often feel less than worthy to experience God.

According to Cayce, the greater spiritual forces are met in the holy of holies.

Now the vision moves away from measuring the temple and introduces us to the two witnesses. Most students of the Revelation interpret the two witnesses as Moses and Elijah, the two that appeared with Jesus on the Mount during his transfiguration. (Matthew 17:3) Some identify the witnesses as Enoch and Ezekiel. Paul identifies Enoch as a witness:

> By faith Enoch was translated that he should not see death; and he was not found, because God translated him [see Genesis 5:24]; for he hath had witness borne to him that before his translation he had been well-pleasing unto God.
> Hebrew 11:5

Elijah is often identified as a witness because of this passage in 2 Kings, which is reminiscent of Enoch's earlier experience:

> And it came to pass, as they [Elijah and Elisha] still went on, and talked, that, behold, there appeared a chariot of fire, and horses of fire, which parted them both asunder; and Elijah went up by a whirlwind into heaven. And Elisha saw it, and he cried, "My father, my father, the chariots of Israel and the horsemen thereof!" And he saw him [Elijah] no more.   2 Kings 2:11

But once again, Edgar Cayce, from his deep, meditative state, identifies the two witnesses of the Revelation as parts of our individual minds. (EC 281-32 and 281-33) One witness is the mental–physical mind, and the other is the mental–spiritual mind—one the conscious mind and one the superconscious mind. Cayce explains that the subconscious is the bridge between these two, which unites one's human self with one's divine self. We are microcosmic trinities: our beings physical, mental, and spiritual, and our minds conscious, subconscious, and superconscious, each corresponding, respectively, to three basic realms—earth, netherworld, and heaven. According to Cayce, the superconscious is a witness because of the "innate forces" that come from its contact with the spiritual realms. As Jesus noted to Nicodemus, no one ascends to heaven who did not first come down from heaven. (John 3:13) This heavenly memory, deep within us, causes us to innately feel, or sense, that there is more to life than the physical. We may not know why we sense it, but it is with us and has been with most of humanity throughout the ages. Therefore, it is a witness to the truth. On the other hand, the conscious mind is a witness because of the "emotional effect" of its experiences in material life. Our emotions are a witness that there is more to us than the physical. Where does a tear come from? A smile? A frown? The people and circumstances around us touch places within us that are deeper than the circumstances justify. Two characters on the long–running television series *Star Trek*—Mr. Spock, the Vulcan; and Data, the android—experienced life without emotion. Logic rules for them. However, humans are simply not this way; even the most stoic occasionally weep, smile, and display anger. There is more to us than biological processes and electrical brainwaves. Within us is a depth of being beyond physical life. Therefore, the conscious, emotional part of us is also a witness to the greater truth.

"These then are the two witnesses," says Cayce, "The innate and the emotional; or the spiritual-mental, the physical-mental . . . " (EC 281-33)

The two witnesses—or as the vision later calls them, "the two olive trees and the two candlesticks, standing before the Lord of the earth"— have power and go about prophesying for a set period of time. Then the beast comes out of the abyss to make war against them, overcome them, and kill them. Their dead bodies lie in the street of the great city which is "mystically called Sodom and Egypt, and where also the Lord was crucified." And the "people and tribes and tongues and nations will look at their bodies" for three and one half days, not allowing them to be buried. Those who dwell on the earth will "rejoice over them." But after the three and one half days "the breath of life" comes back into them from God, and they rise again, "causing a great fear to fall upon all who saw." Then the two witnesses are "called up to heaven, and a great earth-quake felled a tenth of the city and seven thousand people died, and the rest were so terrified that they gave glory to the God of heaven." (Revelation 11:3)

Cayce explains these passages:

> The Master gave, "Before the world was, I AM! Now if ye abide in me and I in the Father, then I will bring to thy remembrance *all things* from the foundations of the world!" Yet these are as dead, or the only con-sciousness that arises from same is that which is fanned into life or activity by the application of the laws concerning same. Hence they are as dead, yet become alive again by remembrance, by the application of thought. In what? The light of that which has been attained by the en-tity or soul that has applied the former lessons in its experience.
>
> EC 281-33

And he continues:

> As has been so oft given, all places—as Egypt or Sodom or the Crucifix-ion, or the Lord—are conditions, circumstances, experiences, as well as individual places. Then in the minds of those who would attempt or that would seek knowledge, they represent their own experiences. Thus

these to the people represent—Egypt, the release from bondage; Gomorrah, as a reckoning with sin—as the Lord was crucified there. As has been given, there has never been an experience when His Christmass, His death, His birth, wasn't an experience of the age, the people. Though it may go under many names, as an individual may be under many names, in many environs, there is one—*one* that ever comes as is shown in that later given as to those who have the name in the hand, in the head or in the forehead and the like; that is, what is the intent and purpose. Just as the Savior of the world, as Lord, as Christ—what do these as names indicate? That which is as a help in a time of trouble alone? or that to glory in, in thy joy, thy gladness, thy happiness? How many, O how many have there been that have laughed with God, that have wept with Jesus, that have gloried with the Christ! or rather has it been, "My happiness and my joy is of myself"?

No condemnation; but rather is there the pattern pointed to as was set by Him. He was *all* things to *all* men; rejoiced with those that did rejoice; He wept with those that wept. He was glad, He was happy, He was sorry, He kept the faith.

(Q) What is signified by the revival of these witnesses?

(A) How hath He given? "If ye meditate on these things, I will bring to thy remembrance all things." The reviving, the renewing, by the abilities of the soul to take hold upon the witnesses of the life itself! And what is life? God!   EC 281-33

Once the mind begins its spiritualization process, our actions need to be spiritualized. Cayce's interpretation reveals that we must apply these truths in our lives and come to know directly the influence of these teachings on our lives.

The Mother, Red Dragon, and Child
Chapter 12 of the Revelation

Chapter 12 of the Revelation shows each individual what his or her soul has passed through in creation, in the earth, and in meeting the many challenges along its journey. (EC 281-33)

The chapter begins,

> A great sign appeared in heaven: a woman clothed with the
> sun, and the moon under her feet, and on her head a crown
> of twelve stars; and she was with child; and she cried out,
> being in labor and in pain to deliver the child. And another
> sign appeared in heaven; and behold, a great red dragon
> having seven heads, ten horns, and on his seven heads
> were seven crowns.

Clearly, a serious encounter is setting up. Symbolically, Cayce identifies the woman as the Primeval Mother, the source of all materiality and all that is good and spiritually helpful in materiality. (EC 281-33) Her attire identifies her with the Creation in Genesis—sun, moon, and the stars—and Cayce adds that she is also Mother Earth. She is to deliver "the outgrowth of the application of the Word [the Logos] . . . upon self. For the child . . . is born of applications of the elements in the body (physical, mental, and spiritual) of the individual." (EC 281-34) Those who apply the fruits of the spirit and seek the light through the experiences in materiality gain so much more understanding than even the angels, that someday they will judge the angels. The mother has provided this realm and its opportunities for our spiritual growth. Cayce explains:

> The material plane is a channel, a way and manner through and in which
> each soul, all souls may grow in grace and knowledge and in understanding—thus it behooves all souls that they be oft in prayer, oft in
> those periods when there is an entering into the Holy of Holies as
> within, and the rededicating of self for that of being a channel through
> which the knowledge of God's love for His children may flow to others.
> EC 1751-1

Now the Heavenly Mother wants to deliver us to our glory, that we may reign forevermore. As Cayce states it, "You have reached to that understanding of thy perfection with God" and "how in materiality you may attune the attributes of self." (EC 281-13)

But the red dragon is swooping around, attempting with all its might to stop this from happening, hoping to devour the child as soon as it is born. The dragon is then identified as "the serpent of old," the devil, and Satan, "who deceives the whole world," emblematic of man's rebellious forces and tendencies, even though he has now attained the Book of Life in his body! These must be met, Cayce says. (EC 281-13) In Genesis, we are instructed by God to subdue these influences; master them. (Genesis 4:7) But when the child is born, a war breaks out in heaven between the dragon and the archangel Michael and his angels. Ultimately, the dragon is driven out of heaven, and a loud cry goes up: "Now the salvation, and the power, and the kingdom of our God and the authority of His Christ [Messiah] have come"—and here comes the important part— "for the accuser of our brethren has been thrown down, who accuses them before God day and night." This line is important for each of us to comprehend, because the accuser is in our thoughts! It is the doubter in us that continually causes us to believe that we are not worthy of God's companionship. It is that part of us that cannot allow us, naked and ashamed (as in the Garden), to enter into God's all-seeing, all-knowing presence—which was so much the cause for the trouble in the Garden of Eden. Remember: The name Adam refers to all of humanity.

"Adam, where are you?" asks the Lord God.
"I'm hiding," replies Adam.
"Why are you hiding?" asks the Lord God.
"Because I am naked," answers the man.
"Who told you that you were naked?" asks the Lord God.

God might well have gone on to comment, "You were naked yesterday and you had no problem being in my presence. What makes today so different?" Of course, no person told Adam that he was naked; it was the accuser within his own conscience. He had eaten of the Tree of the Knowledge of Good and Evil, and as a result, he knew some of his actions and thoughts were not compatible with God's—so he hid from God. Of course, there was no way for Adam to get outside of the Whole or beyond the All-Knowing, but God loved him so much that He allowed the illusion, for a time, that he could hide. God made clothes for him, providing a sense of privacy. Ultimately, as souls, we must come to know that God is all-merciful, all-loving, and understands our mistakes with free will. This accuser must be removed form our consciousness, for it keeps each of us from realizing our destiny, our purpose of companionship with God and all His creation.

Another example of God's power to cleanse us is found in the book of Zechariah, when Joshua is presented to the Lord:

> And he let me see Joshua, the high priest, in his place before the angel of the Lord, and Satan at his right hand ready to take up a cause against him. And the Lord said to Satan, "May the Lord's word be sharp against you, O Satan, the word of the Lord who has taken Jerusalem for himself. Is this not a burning branch pulled out of the fire?" Now Joshua was clothed in unclean robes, and he was in his place before the angel. And he made answer and said to those who were there before him, "Take the unclean robes off him, and let him be clothed in clean robes, and let them put a clean headdress on his head." So they put a clean headdress on his head, clothing him with clean robes; and to him he said, "See, I have taken your sin away from you." And the angel of the Lord made a statement to Joshua, and said, "These are the words of the Lord of armies: If you will go in my ways and keep what I have put in your care, then you will be judge over my Temple and have the care of my house, and I will give you the right to come in among those who are there. Give ear now, O Joshua, the high priest, you and your friends who are seated before you, for these are men who are a sign; for see, I will let my servant the Branch be seen. For see, the stone which I have put before Joshua; on one stone are seven eyes; see, the design cut on it will be my work, says the Lord of armies, and I will take away the sin of that land in one day. In that day, says the Lord of armies, you will be one another's guests under the vine and under the fig tree."   Zechariah 3:1-4

We cannot leave this passage without noting the powerful symbolism of the seven eyes that relate to the seven eyes, seven horns, and seven spirits of God in the Revelation (5:6) and, of course, the seven chakras. The new, clean headdress symbolizes new thoughts, cleansed of incompatible memories that would have kept Joshua from standing before God the All-Knowing.

Later, the Lord says, "I will remove the guilt of this land in a single day." (Zechariah 3:9) And a little later, the Lord adds that this is accomplished "not by might, nor by power, *but by my Spirit.*" (Zechariah 4:6; italics mine) The garments of our consciousness are soiled from our self-centered activities and thoughts, and from our separation from the Tree of Life and the presence of our Creator, but the Spirit of God can and will cleanse us in a moment, rebuke the accuser in our minds, and remove the guilt—if we but allow God's Spirit in.

John's vision in Revelation goes on to reveal that the influences that helped throw the accuser out of our consciousness are the "blood of the Lamb," "the word of their testimony," and the fact that they "did not love their life [on earth] even to death."

If we are not careful, some of the passages can leave us with the impression that spiritual growth is made through self-sacrifice alone. Self-sacrifice is important to spiritual development, but it is not the quintessential ingredient. "Go and learn the meaning of this: 'I seek mercy, not sacrifice,'" Jesus instructed. (Matthew 9:13 and 12:7) Mercy rather than sacrifice is the greater expression of love, and after all, "God is love." (1 John 4:8 and 4:16) Nevertheless, we are cleansing and subduing our earthly selves and desires, making room for heavenly desires and spiritual influences. Yet these must be expressed in our daily physical lives as the fruit of the spirit: love, kindness, patience, understanding, gentleness, longsuffering, and forgiveness. Mercy to those around us, who have struggled with free will, and mercy to ourselves lifts us to God's level more than will self-sacrifice.

In this section of the vision, the dragon is persistent and returns to persecute the Mother. "Two wings of the great eagle were given to the woman" to enable her to escape from the dragon by flying away from his presence for "the time and times and half time," quoting directly from Daniel 7:25, concerning a time limit on the power of the beast. Cayce explains that these wings represent "flight from materiality into those influences through which the body may rest within itself; as physical or mental flight, or that to the astral forces . . . " (EC 281–33) As for "the time and times and half time," Cayce offers these two comments:

> As He gave in those days, "the time and times and half times shall pass, and *then* shall man come to know that in the temple, in the tabernacle of his *own* temple will he meet his God face to face!"   EC 257-201

> These changes in the earth will come to pass, for the time and times and half times are at an end, and there begin those periods for the readjustments. For how hath He given? "The righteous shall inherit the earth." Hast thou, my brethren, a heritage in the earth?   EC 294-185

The serpent–dragon makes another attack upon the woman, this time with a river of water out of its mouth, causing her to be swept away by the flood. But the earth helps out by opening up and swallowing the flood, which enrages the dragon! As you might expect, Cayce states that the dragon's "river of water" is a flood of emotions "upon the influences of the body in all of its relationships to the activities in its relationships to others." He warns us that, in the experience of individuals in the earth, "the flood of emotions . . . make for doubt, fears, tribulation, disturbances, anxieties," but "the earth aids in the quieting of the influence." (EC 281–34) This is a wonderful insight from Cayce. So often spiritual teachers can see only the weaknesses and sins of the flesh and earthly aspects of our being. But Cayce knows that the body is as wonderful an instrument for enlightenment as it is for sin and self-seeking. The earth, too, is as grand a place for manifesting the love, kindness, understanding, and patience of God as it is for sinning and self-seeking. Here we see that the earth and the earthly influences help us deal with the flood of emotions and challenges of the negative influences. As helpful as this is, there is more yet to deal with. Two beasts are coming, and we must face up to them and subdue their influence.

The Two Beasts
Chapter 13 of the Revelation

As we explore this chapter in the vision, keep in mind that we are addressing issues of the mind in the process of spiritualization. The mind is now going to face its dark side and the many challenges to a clear, God-centered mind.

We begin this next phase of the enlightenment process by visualizing fear, says Cayce (EC 281–34), in the form of the beast like a leopard with seven heads and ten horns. By our seeking understanding we have also aroused influences that bring fear. The leopard's seven heads symbolize the vices of the seven spiritual centers within us, and these cause us to see aspects of ourselves that we fear. The fear takes ten different forms, as the ten horns on each of the seven heads of the leopard indicate. The leopard rises out of the sea (as did Daniel's beast), symbolic of the depths of emotion and unseen influences that normally lie below the surface of consciousness.

Because we are opening up our body and mind and seeking to shine God's light upon all aspects of our being, we now see the shadows within us. The dragon, symbolic of man's rebellious spirit, gives his power to this beast. The leopard approaches us, speaking blasphemous things aloud, and with a blasphemous name upon its head. It makes war with the spiritual influences that are arising within us, causing fear to take hold of us. Fear is one of the most commonly addressed issues throughout the Scriptures. Jesus addresses it many times. Here's an example from Matthew 10 that fits with our current passage in the Revelation.

> Fear not them [those who confront your spiritual efforts]; for there is nothing covered, that shall not be revealed; and hid, that shall not be known. What I tell you in the darkness, speak ye in the light; and what ye hear in the ear, proclaim upon the house tops. And be not afraid of them that kill the body, but are not able to kill the soul; but rather fear him who is able to destroy both soul and body in hell. Are not two sparrows sold for a penny? And not one of them shall fall on the ground without your Father's leave; but the very hairs of your head are all numbered. Fear not therefore; ye are of more value than many sparrows.

After fear, the thirteenth chapter of Revelation moves to "those whose names are not written in the Book of Life." Cayce explains that these are those who are seeking spiritualization "for impunity's sake or only for momentary conscience's sake." They "acknowledge the way," but they

> follow closely after the things of the flesh, or the indulgences of the emotions of the body alone, without consideration of others, without other than self's own interest—as is shown by the beast that is loosened—these are they whose names are not written, and these are they who are easily led about by every wind that bloweth.   EC 281-34

We must seek with purpose, with direction, putting our belief, faith, trust, and works in God. Cayce explains:

> Having tasted of the Tree of Life, the knowledge of God, make thyself and thy calling and thy election *sure* in that ye faint not when ye see these troubles, these disturbances that are only of the earth-earthy, that only are the emotions of the desires of self's own show coming to pass in thine experience.   281-34

In other words, fear not at the approach of the first beast.

At this point in the vision, the second beast appears. It has two horns, speaks like a dragon, makes signs and miracles, and has the power to deceive. Cayce identifies this two-horned beast as "double-mindedness." It reflects our human tendency to seek mammon *and* God! We want it all: terrestrial and celestial. Misapplication of the truths through double-mindedness is symbolized in this deceptive beast:

> [T]hough ye may have done this or that, though ye may have healed the sick, though ye may have cast out demons in my name, I know ye not; for ye have followed rather as the beast of self-aggrandizement, self-indulgence, self-glorification.   EC 281-34

Of course, the most famous aspect of this second beast is his number—666—"the mark of the beast." The mark must appear on the right hand and the forehead of everyone who wants to buy or sell. Then verse 18 reads: "This calls for wisdom; let him who has understanding

reckon the number of the beast, for it is a human number . . . " Cayce
says that it represents the vows and obligations, the buying and selling
we make to the work of the beast, rather than the work of God. He
exclaims, "One Lord, One faith, one God, one baptism, one way!" (EC
281–34)

Cayce expands on this by explaining that the reason 666 is a "human
number," or sometimes translated as the "number of a man," is that it
represents only the work of man's hands, without consciousness of God
and God directing. This influence, he explains, penetrates individuals,
groups, and organizations, and binds us with vows and obligations to
the beast's work (EC 281–34), again touching on Jesus' guidance that we
cannot serve mammon and God. "No man can serve two masters; for
either he will hate the one, and love the other; or else he will hold to
one, and despise the other. Ye cannot serve God and mammon." (Matthew 6:24; *mammon* is Aramaic for worldly riches.) It is important that
we understand that the reference to mammon is not necessarily about
our jobs. We are talking about including God and God's guidance in our
labor, our efforts, and our lives, not working simply for our own interests and gratifications. The key to overcoming the second beast is seeking God's guidance and including God in our thoughts and lives;
thereby God may be glorified through our labor, thoughts, and fellowship.

Cayce was asked to comment upon the words "Here is wisdom":

That as ye have gained by the analysis or the study of the activity and
influence of the spirit of truth throughout the whole members of thy
body, physical, mental and spiritual, and have come to the knowledge
of that which has first been given, that there is only *one* God, *one* Christ
[the Messiah who will come to the Jews also, as well as others], one
faith, one baptism; or as Christ hath given—this is the whole law; to
love the Lord thy God with all thy mind, thy body, thy soul; thy neighbor
as thyself. This is the whole law. This is wisdom. This is knowledge.
Knowing that those things which have been put on through the activities of the elements within thine own forces of thy body and mind
are but as the stepping-stones to the knowledge that God is in and
through *all* and in Him ye live and move and have thy being. When
this is fully comprehended, fully understood, ye have the working

knowledge of God in the earth.   EC 281-34; brackets mine

In illustration 26 we see a Gnostic depiction of the kundalini of the body going through the various spiritual centers, each corresponding to numbers and meanings from mystical Kabbalah. In this illustration we see how the number 666 corresponds to the highest possible achievement of the lower mind. Without the influence of the Spirit and the submission of the human portion, one cannot break through to the full spiritual awakening. This is why the number is a human one—the number of humankind—and is limited to our lower, earthly nature. One must take the next step, letting go of the lower self in order for the higher self to be born. And, as we find in the illustration, the next step is the way of the cross and the glory of the higher mind, which is the Lamb, and the next stage in this revelation.

The Lamb, The New Song, and the Angels' Calls
Chapter 14 of the Revelation

Cayce comments that we have now reached a place in the vision that begins the "assurances to the individual" who has "put on the whole armor, with the full understanding," assurances of "great help in those periods of temptation and trial."

The Lamb appears with 144,000 whose names are written in the Book of Life, and harpers sing a new song that no one can learn but the 144,000.

Cayce says that the Lamb is our spiritual mindedness that has "so raised the body as to become as a new being." (EC 281-34) The 144,000 are those "sealed in the Spirit," or shielded by the Spirit of God. In the body, they are the "spiritualized cellular structure of the 12 major divisions of the body," which he matches to the twelve tribes of Israel. (EC 281-36; see illustration 29) The harpists play a new song, representing the "new experience that comes to each soul. Let's keep it individual, see? The new experience that comes to each soul, as to the assurance of that help when necessary of the saints of the Father." (EC 281-29)

In verse 13, John hears a voice tell him to write this: "Blessed are the dead who die in the Lord from henceforth; yea, says the Spirit, that they may rest from their labors; for their works follow with them." Cayce explains:

> The changes that have come and the assurance that has come to each individual who has recognized that the Lamb (or the Christ), or the activities of Jesus [a man] becoming the Christ are the assurance of the activity of the Christ in the passage from the material plane to the celestial. For as He preached to those bound even in the shadows of death, loosened that which made it possible for them to become again conscious of the opportunities for reconstructing themselves in the experiences through which error had come, so blessed then are they who die in the Lord—for the body alone is bound.   EC 281-36

Clearly, our mind and our soul is not bound, and as such, they may rise into the heavens and into the presence of the Infinite, Eternal One, and the oneness that comes from reconnecting with our Creator.

Next in the vision, six angels appear and five have messages. The first calls out in a loud voice,

> Fear God, and give him glory; for the hour of his judgment is come; and worship him that made the heaven and the earth and sea and fountains of waters.

The second calls out,

> Fallen, fallen is Babylon the great, that hath made all the nations to drink of the wine of the wrath of her fornication.

The third calls out,

> If any man worships the beast and his image, and receives a mark on his forehead, or upon his hand, he also shall drink of the wine of the wrath of God, which is prepared unmixed in the cup of his anger; and he shall be tormented with fire and brimstone in the presence of the holy angels, and in the presence of the Lamb; and the smoke of their torment goes up for ever and ever; and they have no rest day and night,

> they that worship the beast and his image, and who receives
> the mark of his name.

The fourth angel calls out in a loud voice,

> Send forth thy sickle, and reap; for the hour to reap is come;
> for the harvest of the earth is ripe.

And the fifth angel calls with a loud voice,

> Send forth thy sharp sickle, and gather the clusters of the
> vine of the earth; for her grapes are fully ripe.

Cayce explains that these five angels and their comments are calls to
"those individuals who have and are a part of the active force in a
material world" who are "to work, to give forth, to give out of their
strength, their selves in *active* service and not as those that would rest"
but as "the reapers, as the harvesters—which to the individual mind
means labors for a definite purpose and service." (EC 281-36)

During the angels' callings, a white cloud appears and one seated
upon the cloud is like a Son of man with a golden crown and a sharp
sickle in his hand. He represents the spiritual self, which is now preparing for active service as a channel of God's love and light in this world.
It is this part of us that needs to be up and doing, for at this stage of our
development, the opportunities are great and the harvest is ripe.

The Seven Plagues and the Tabernacle of Testimony
Chapter 15 of the Revelation

Here come the "seven angels with seven plagues which are the last
cleansings, for with them the wrath of God is ended." This is as wonderful an event as it is terrible, because it is the culmination of the spiritualization process. Cayce begins his explanation of this chapter by saying,
"He [God] hath not willed that any soul shall perish but hath with every
ill provided a means, a way." The pouring out of the plagues is the
meeting of self, Cayce explains. It is facing the karma of our prior use of

free will (in previous incarnations as well as in sojourns in other dimensions of life). It is the final cleansing that prepares us for the great work or service that we may render as pure channels of God's light and love in our lives and in this world. (EC 281-36)

The final verse of this chapter reads, "The temple was filled with smoke from the glory of God and from his power, and no one could enter the temple until the seven plagues of the seven angels were ended," which Cayce explains as, "the final steps in the abilities of the individuals for their effective service, or filled with the smoke as the glory of the Father, see? This is the temple of the body, and—as such—where the Lord hath promised to meet those that are faithful and true." (EC 281-36)

The Seven Bowls
Chapter 16 of the Revelation

These bowls, or vials, of God's wrath poured out upon the earth are, according to Cayce, "the fulfillment of the law." This is the carrying forth in the earth of the law (which is the meaning of the term *God's wrath*). Each individual meets itself according to the laws and commandments of God and one's conscience and purification needs, enabling one to enter completely into the tabernacle to meet God, face to face, without condemnation or unworthiness. According to Cayce, all the vials symbolize the same things: "effective activity upon the various conditions that have become a part of the errors in those that have the mark of the beast." In other words, they each represent a specific cleansing required to meet various errors that keep our lower minds from letting go of sin and the guilt of sin, and to allow our higher minds to reach an awareness that allows us to come fully into the presence of God without fear, self-condemnation, or embarrassment. These purifications are necessary and fulfill the final stage of the spiritualization process. They allow us to stop hiding from God and God's all-knowing presence. Once again we can walk together through life.

The Whore of Babylon and the Fall of Babylon
Chapter 17 and 18 of the Revelation

"Babylon symbolizes self," Cayce says. (EC 281-36) And this chapter of

Revelation is the final chapter, the end of selfish, self-centered seeking.

For us to fully understand the concept of the fall of self, we need to explore two key teachings in the Cayce volumes. The first relates to a major goal for each soul:

> Though all are as one, remember it has been given that the purpose of the heart is to know *yourself* to *be* yourself and yet one with God even as Jesus, even as is represented in God the Father, Christ the Son, and the Holy Spirit; each knowing themselves to be themselves yet *one!*
>
> EC 281-37

Let's not confuse this concept as three gods; rather, it is three aspects of the one, infinite God.

In the following reading, Cayce states this all-important goal and then explains how best to realize it:

> In analyzing self and these emotions—know that it is not by chance that the entity enters any given experience, and that the associations or activities with individuals are not by chance. For, in the spiritual you live and move and have your being in your Maker. He has not willed that any soul should perish, but has with every temptation, with every trial, given opportunities, friends, connections, associations in which the choice by self will bring those privileges as well as opportunities for making hardships or temptations into stepping-stones in your experience.
>
> Know that it is not all just to live—not all just to be good, but good *for* something; that ye may fulfill that purpose for which ye have entered this experience.
>
> And that purpose is that you might know yourself to be yourself, and yet one with the Creative Forces, or God.
>
> Then, study to show thyself approved unto thy ideal.
>
> What, then, *is* thy ideal?
>
> You find yourself a body, a mind, a soul; each with its attributes, manifesting in a material world. And you realize that the body, the mind and the soul are one—and that confusion may cause detrimental influences to body, to mind or to soul.
>
> Then, you must have your ideal as to spiritual values, as to spiritual imports in your experience. And know—whatever may be your desire, it

must have its inception in *spiritual* attitudes.

What, then, is your spiritual ideal?

In your mental body you find at times confusion. But what is your mental ideal? One willing to pay the price in study, in application, that you may gain the proper concept not only of your relationships to spiritual forces from within and without, but your relationships with your fellow man in every phase of your experience?

Then, your ideal is not what you may acquire by "Gimmie—Gimmie—Gimmie," but "What may I do, what may I give, in my relationships to others to make that association the *beautiful experience*," for which ye long so always!

Then the ideal is, "What may I do or be to others, that they may be better, may have a greater concept of the purposes of life, by even being acquainted or associated with myself?"

This should be your ideal, in your material life.

It is not that the body is all of meat, nor all of position, nor all of that activity in a social manner, nor all of play or work—but *all* of these enter into the experience. Just as the mental and spiritual body apply, or need, or rely upon the attributes of the phases of the whole, so is it necessary that there be the ideal in the material relationships. And these also must, as in mind, have a spiritual conception—if you would grow in grace, in knowledge, in understanding.

Then, as you find: If you would have friends, show yourself to be a friend to others. If you would have love in your life, it is necessary that you be *lovely* to others. If you would have that in your material experience to supply the physical needs of the body, the gratifying or satisfying or contenting of self in its relationships to material things, *work* in such a manner that others may be *inspired* by that manner in which you conduct yourself.

Not as one afraid—neither as one that is unmindful of the body needs or the body privileges. But abuse *not* your opportunities, if you would be the gainer in this experience.   EC 2030-1

If knowing self is important to the spiritualization process, then why do we have this all-important step of the fall of self? The answer is found in the second teaching that Cayce expounds upon often, the crucifixion of the selfish, self-centered self, so that the true self may arise. We must subdue . . .

> those influences which constantly seek expressions of self rather than of a living, constructive influence of a *crucified* Savior. Then, crucify desire in self; that ye may be awakened to the real abilities of helpfulness that lie within thy grasp.   EC 2474-1

Here's another of his comments about the fall of self:

> What is the purpose of the Revelation: Was it for the purpose of confusing, of being mysterious? . . . . Rather was it not to present that each entity, each soul, might find within itself that which answers to that within, that makes the real answer to that as was before stated, "My Spirit bears witness with thy spirit"? And until the answer is in accord, in attune, [and there is] the consciousness of the prompting of the ability in a manifested material world to make same practical?
>
> Then as the progress is made, as the understanding comes more and more, *never, never* does it make the manifested individual entity other than the more humble, the more meek, the more longsuffering, the more patient. Of this ye may be sure.
>
> Then in all of the experiences of the opening of the centers as are represented, and those vibrations that find expression in the various temperaments of individual souls, these come not as justifications in *self* but justification in the Lamb of God!   EC 281-31

We must come to know ourselves to be our true selves, yet one with God and all of creation. Yet we must do this not to glorify self but to magnify God and God's love in and through us. This includes crucifying self-exalting activities, attitudes, and selfish desires in order for us to fully realize the glory that is ours in a unified life with God and God's creation.

The fall of self is the fall of those aspects of our being that limit us from realizing our true potential and joy. That is why all of heaven shouts with joy when Babylon, the self, is fallen.

CHAPTER

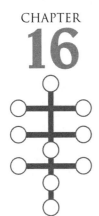

16

SPIRITUAL REUNION

HALLELUJAH!
THE MARRIAGE OF THE LAMB
CHAPTERS 19-22 OF THE REVELATION

As we have seen through the whole vision, the activities, angels, dragons, earthquakes, various beasts, and a whore have all symbolized influences upon and aspects of our body, mind, and spirit. Now we are ready for the marriage of the Lamb. The Lamb represents the spiritual mind, according to Cayce. (EC 281-36) The individual has now been raised to a level of vibration and consciousness that it can realize its association with the spiritual. It has become a new being—a spiritualized being, a God-conscious being—motivated by spiritual purposes. This achievement causes a great multitude in heaven to cry out, "Hallelujah!" An angel tells John to write, "Blessed are those who are invited to the marriage supper of the Lamb."

Then the heavens are opened and a white horse is seen, and "he who sat upon it is called Faithful and True," with a name inscribed which "no one knows but himself," and on his robe and thigh are inscribed "King of kings and Lord of lords." This rider represents our spiritual selves in the microcosmic interpretation of the vision. He wears a robe dipped in blood, symbolizing the sacrifices made along the challenging way to spiritual consciousness. The two beasts and the kings of the earth are defeated by this rider and his armies. The dragon ("the ancient serpent, who is the devil and Satan") is bound for a thousand years and thrown into the bottomless pit. In explaining the meaning of Satan being bound for a thousand years, Cayce widens his normal focus of interpreting Revelation from the individual standpoint to include that of a global view:

In the same manner that the prayer of ten just should save a city, the deeds, the prayers of the faithful will allow that period when the incarnation of those only that are in the Lord shall rule the earth, and the period is as a thousand years.

Thus is Satan bound, thus is Satan banished from the earth. The desire to do evil is only of him. And when there are—as the symbols—those only whose desire and purpose of their heart is to glorify the Father, these will be those periods when this shall come to pass.

Be *ye all determined* within thy minds, thy hearts, thy purposes, to be of that number!"   EC 281-37

There is now a curious passage in chapter 20 that speaks of two resurrections and two deaths, the first and the second. Cayce explains it this way:

The first [resurrection] is of those who have not tasted death in the sense of the dread of same. The second [resurrection] is of those who have *gained* the understanding that in Him there *is* no death. EC 281-37

Here Cayce distinguishes between two groups of people: those who have lost their fear of death because they believe and have faith in the promise of an afterlife, and those whose transition with the Lord is akin to falling asleep to this world and awakening within the heavens. These two groups are also distinguished in the Revelation when the angel instructs, "He who is righteous, let him do righteousness still. He who is holy, let him be holy still." (Rev 22:11) The difference is that the holy ones have the presence of God awakened within the temple of their bodies and minds, while the righteous do good for goodness' sake. The true Kabblists sought to fully experience God's presence and contain this holiness in the orbs of their being—not simply to believe in God.

In another of his readings, Cayce expands on this, saying:

How is the way shown by the Master? What is the promise in Him? The last to be overcome is death. Death of what? The *soul* cannot die; for it is of God. The body may be revivified, rejuvenated. And it is to that end it may, the body, *transcend* the earth and its influence.   EC 262-85

Immortality returns. Actually, it was never gone—we only thought it was—and as one thinks, so is it. In Cayce's comments just quoted, he reveals that, at a high level of spiritualization, even our physical body can become a portion of our immortal being, allowing us, as it was with Enoch, to walk with God and not physically die, simply absorbing the material body into our immortal being. The Hopi people have a legend that once, a long time ago, souls came and went in this dimension, manifesting a physical body when they were here and having it disappear within them as they left for higher realms of existence. Cayce foresees those days coming again.

Cayce and the Revelation also see another period of struggle coming after this golden age of Satan bound—a time of no evil, no temptation.

After the thousand–year period, the Revelation states that Satan and his followers are loosed again for a little while. They march up against the saints and the holy city but are ultimately destroyed in a fire from heaven. Now "a great white throne comes down from heaven," and "he who sits upon it opens the Book of Life" and judges all "by what was written in the Book, by what they had done." This represents one's spiritual mind reviewing all aspects of one's being, determining what is and has been good and constructive, and what has been evil and destructive. This brings great knowledge to one's consciousness. Here are some valuable words from Cayce on gaining knowledge:

> As has been said, man must overcome through the knowledge and association of that knowledge with God's word made manifest in the flesh. The last to be overcome is death, and the knowledge of life is the knowledge of death. See? Any who may seek knowledge is seeking the greatest gifts of the gods of the universe, and in using such knowledge to worship God renders a service to his fellow man. For, as given, the greatest service to God is service to his creatures; for, as shown in the Holy One, without spot or blemish, yet gave Himself that others through Him might have the advocate to the approach to the Father without fear; in that He had passed through the flesh and the rules of the earthly, fleshly existence, taking on all the weaknesses of the flesh, yet never abusing, never misusing, never misconstruing, never giving to others a wrong impression of the knowledge of the universe; never giving any

save loving brotherhood; the desire to stand in the place of him that would receive condemnation for wrong committed by or in the body; never relying on any who would bring reproach for knowledge, or place such conditions in the hands of him who disregards such understanding of God's laws.

Then, in asking for such knowledge through any of the means of communication of the universal forces (that only take of a small portion of the great storehouse), beware that such knowledge is directed in the channel that give succor and aid, and stands in that way and manner as was given by Him who was given to the world as an ensample and made Himself of no estate that He might give, give, give to all peoples, no matter what clime, what race, what color. They that would seek Him earlier will find Him and, in time, have life and have life more abundantly.   EC 254-17

This is beyond any specific religion or any religion at all. It is spiritual, not religious. The Logos, the Adam Kadmon, has manifested in our lives many times as an example to us of how we may realize our full potential with God and God's creation. It is not that the Logos, or Messiah, is between us and our Creator but that it is, rather, the way to our Creator.

The Vision Ends with Gifts
Chapters 21 and 22 of the Revelation

And I saw a new heaven and a new earth; for the first heaven and the first earth were passed away; and there was no more sea. And I John saw the holy city, New Jerusalem, coming down from God out of heaven, prepared as a bride adorned for her husband. And I heard a great voice out of heaven saying, "Behold, the tabernacle of God is with men, and he will dwell with them, and they shall be his people, and God himself shall be with them, and be their God. And God shall wipe away all tears from their eyes; and there shall be no more death, neither sorrow, nor crying, neither shall there be any more pain, for the former things are passed away." And he that sat upon the throne said, "Behold, I make all things new." And he said unto me: "Write. For these words are true and faithful." And he said unto me, "It is done. I am Alpha and Omega, the beginning and the end. I will give unto him that is athirst of the fountain of the water of life freely. He that overcomes shall inherit all things; and I will be his God, and he shall be my son [my daughter].   Revelation 21:1-7

And he showed me a pure river of water of life, clear as crystal, proceeding out of the throne of God and of the Lamb. In the midst of the street of it, and on either side of the river, was the tree of life, which bare twelve manner of fruits, and yielded her fruit every month. And the leaves of the tree were for the healing of the nations. And there shall be no more curse; but the throne of God and of the Lamb shall be in it; and his servants shall serve him. And they shall see his face; and his name shall be in their foreheads. And there shall be no night there; and they need no candle, neither light of the sun; for the Lord God gives them light; and they shall reign forever and ever. And he said unto me, "These sayings are faithful and true. And the Lord God of the holy prophets sent his angel to show unto his servants the things which must shortly be done." Revelation 22:1-6

What a wonderful way to end this vision about spiritualizing body and mind and birthing our spiritual self. The curse upon us as we left the Garden of Eden is removed. The Tree of Life, which was guarded against us, is now available to our eating, symbolizing our regaining immortality. The water of life flows through us, and we may take of it freely. God is with us again. The Light of God is our light. There will no longer be any night or darkness, no sorrow or pain, no loneliness or confusion. We shall live together with one another and our Creator forever.

Bibliography

Abelson, J. *Jewish Mysticism: An Introduction to the Kabbalah*. Mineola, NY: Dover Publishing, 1913.

Afilalo, Rabbi Raphael, trans. and com. *The Kabbalah of the Ari Z'al according to the Ramhal Rabbi Moshe Hayim Luzzatto*. Montreal, Canada: Kabbalah Editions, 2004.

Cooper, David. *God Is a Verb: Kabbalah and the Practice of Mystical Judaism*. New York, NY: Penguin Group, 1998.

Coudert, Allison. *The Impact of the Kabbalah in the Seventeenth Century*. Boston, MA: Brill, 1999.

Davidson, Gustav. *A Dictionary of Angels—Including the Fallen Angels*. New York, NY: The Free Press, 1967.

Freehof, Lillian. *Bible Legends: An Introduction to Midrash*. 1906. http://books.google.com/.

Friedlander, Gerald. *Pirke de Rabbi Eliezer: (The chapters of Rabbi Eliezer the Great)*. New York, NY: 2002.

Godwin, Malcolm. *Angels: An Endangered Species*. New York, NY: Simon & Schuster, 1990.

Green, Arthur. *A Guide to the Zohar*. Stanford, CA: Stanford University Press, 2004.

Joseph, Rabbi. *Midrash of Shemhazai and Azazel*. http://www.scribd.com.

Kaplan, Rabbi Aryeh, trans. *The Seven Beggars & Other Kabbalistic Tales of Rebbe Nachman of Breslov*. Woodstock, VT: Jewish Lights Publishing, 2005.

_____. *The Lost Princess & Other Kabbalistic Tales of Rebbe Nachman of Breslov*. Woodstock, VT: Jewish Lights Publishing, 2005.

Klein, E., trans. and com. *Kabbalah of Creation: The Mysticism of Isaac Luria, Founder of Modern Kabbalah*. Berkeley, CA: North Atlantic Books, 2000.

Kurzweil, Arthur. *Kabbalah for Dummies*. Hoboken, NJ: Wiley Publishing, 2007.

Mathers, S. L. MacGregor, trans. *The Kabbalah Unveiled: Containing the following books of the Zohar: The Book of Concealed Mystery, The Greater Holy*

Assembly, the Lesser Holy Assembly. New York, NY: Samuel Weiser, 1968.

Matt, Daniel. *The Essential Kabbalah: The Heart of Jewish Mysticism.* New York City, NY: HarperCollins, 1996.

Michaelson, Jay. *God in Your Body: Kabbalah, Mindfulness, and Embodied Spiritual Practice.* Woodstock, VT: Jewish Lights Publishing, 2007.

Morray-Jones, Christopher. *A Transparent Illusion: The Dangerous Vision of Water in Hekhalot Mysticism: A Source-Critical and Tradition-Historical Inquiry* (Supplements to the *Journal for the Study of Judaism*). Boston, MA: Brill, 2002. http://books.google.com/.

Ponce, Charles. *Kabbalah: An Introduction with Illumination for the World Today.* San Francisco, CA: Straight Arrow Books, 1973.

Schafer, Peter. *The Hidden and Manifest God: Some Major Themes in Early Jewish Mysticism.* Translated by Aubrey Pomerance. Albany, NY: State University of New York Press, 1992.

Schneersohn of Lubavitch, Rabbi Shalom. *The Tree of Life (Kuntres Etz HaChayim), a Chassidic treatise.* circa 1700s. http://www.sichosinenglish.org/books/the-tree-of-life-kuntres-etz-hachayim/.

Scholem, Gershom. Alchemy and Kabbalah. Spring Publications, 2006. http://books.google.com/.

_____. *On the Kabbalah and Its Symbolism.* New York, NY: Pantheon Books, 1996.

_____. *Origins of the Kabbalah.* Translated by the Jewish Publication Society. Princeton, NJ: Princeton University Press, 1962.

Spoer, Hans. *The Origin and Interpretation of the Tetragrammaton, 1901.* http://www.jstor.org/pss/528023.

Weiner, Herbert. *9 1/2 Mystics: The Kabbalah Today.* Foreword by Elie Wiesel. New York, NY: Touchstone, 1969.

Index

A.R.E. PRESS

The A.R.E. Press publishes books, videos, audiotapes, CDs, and DVDs meant to improve the quality of our readers' lives—personally, professionally, and spiritually. We hope our products support your endeavors to realize your career potential, to enhance your relationships, to improve your health, and to encourage you to make the changes necessary to live a loving, joyful, and fulfilling life.

For more information or to receive a free catalog, call:

800–333–4499

Or write:

A.R.E. Press
215 67th Street
Virginia Beach, VA 23451-2061

ARE PRESS.COM

EDGAR CAYCE'S A.R.E.

What Is A.R.E.?

The Association for Research and Enlightenment, Inc., (A.R.E.®) was founded in 1931 to research and make available information on psychic development, dreams, holistic health, meditation, and life after death. As an open-membership research organization, the A.R.E. continues to study and publish such information, to initiate research, and to promote conferences, distance learning, and regional events. Edgar Cayce, the most documented psychic of our time, was the moving force in the establishment of A.R.E.

Who Was Edgar Cayce?

Edgar Cayce (1877–1945) was born on a farm near Hopkinsville, Ky. He was an average individual in most respects. Yet, throughout his life, he manifested one of the most remarkable psychic talents of all time. As a young man, he found that he was able to enter into a self-induced trance state, which enabled him to place his mind in contact with an unlimited source of information. While asleep, he could answer questions or give accurate discourses on any topic. These discourses, more than 14,000 in number, were transcribed as he spoke and are called "readings."

Given the name and location of an individual anywhere in the world, he could correctly describe a person's condition and outline a regimen of treatment. The consistent accuracy of his diagnoses and the effectiveness of the treatments he prescribed made him a medical phenomenon, and he came to be called the "father of holistic medicine."

Eventually, the scope of Cayce's readings expanded to include such subjects as world religions, philosophy, psychology, parapsychology, dreams, history, the missing years of Jesus, ancient civilizations, soul growth, psychic development, prophecy, and reincarnation.

A.R.E. Membership

People from all walks of life have discovered meaningful and life-transforming insights through membership in A.R.E. To learn more about Edgar Cayce's A.R.E. and how membership in the A.R.E. can enhance your life, visit our Web site at EdgarCayce.org, or call us toll-free at 800-333-4499.

Edgar Cayce's A.R.E.
215 67th Street
Virginia Beach, VA 23451–2061

EDGARCAYCE.ORG